ON BEHALF OF THE FAMILY FARM

IOWA AND THE MIDWEST EXPERIENCE

SERIES EDITOR
William B. Friedricks
Iowa History Center at Simpson College

*The University of Iowa Press gratefully acknowledges
Humanities Iowa for its generous support of the
Iowa and the Midwest Experience series.*

On Behalf of the Family Farm

Iowa Farm Women's Activism since 1945

JENNY BARKER DEVINE

UNIVERSITY OF IOWA PRESS
Iowa City

University of Iowa Press, Iowa City 52242

COPYRIGHT © 2013 BY THE UNIVERSITY OF IOWA PRESS

www.uiowapress.org
Printed in the United States of America
Design by Teresa W. Wingfield

The University of Iowa Press is a member of Green Press Initiative and is committed to preserving natural resources.

Printed on acid-free paper

LCCN: 2012950295
ISBN-13: 978-1-60938-149-3
ISBN-10: 1-60938-149-1

For
T. J., Liz, and Danny

THIS BOOK PROJECT STARTED more than a decade ago when my college roommate suggested I interview her grandmother, a farm woman, for my senior honor's thesis. As I ventured into the history of rural women, there seemed to be more questions than answers at every turn, and I am thankful for all those people who have helped me explore those questions along the way. Pamela Riney-Kehrberg at Iowa State University provided incredible guidance as my mentor and teacher. Amy Bix, Cornelia Flora, Charles Dobbs, and David Hollander also provided constructive critiques of my work, as well as support. Dorothy Schwieder and Deborah Fink always made themselves available for discussion and offered valuable insights and suggestions, as well as a real belief that research on the history of rural women matters.

No writer is complete without a good editor, and I am fortunate to have several. Marvin Bergman at the State Historical Society of Iowa supplied indispensable advice through the years that helped me better frame my arguments and understand the complexities of historical analysis. Two chapters in this book are based on earlier articles that Marv guided through the editorial process: chapter 1 is based on "'Quite a Ripple But No Revolution': The Changing Roles of Women in the Iowa Farm Bureau Federation," *Annals of Iowa* 64, no. 1 (Winter 2005), 1–36, and chapter 2 draws from "'The Secret to a Successful Farm Organization': Township Farm Bureau Women's Clubs in Iowa, 1945–1970," *Annals of Iowa* 69, no. 4 (Fall 2010), 41–73. Claire Strom at *Agricultural History* saw real potential in the Porkettes, providing guidance and suggestions that led to the article behind chapter 5: "'Hop to the Top with the Iowa Chop': The Iowa Porkettes and Cultivating Feminism in the Midwest, 1964–1992," *Agricultural History* 83, no. 4 (Fall 2009), 477–502. Editors Gayle Gullett and Susan E. Gray, as well as the anonymous referees who reviewed my work, offered practical advice that helped move my theoretical framework forward in the article, "The Answer to the Auxiliary Syndrome: Women Involved in Farm Economics (WIFE) and New Organizing Strategies for Farm Women, 1976–1985," *Frontiers: A Journal of Women's Studies* 30, no. 3 (2009), 117–41. Bill Fredericks saw promise in earlier versions of this manuscript, and even when I had doubts, he encouraged me to envision an extremely unruly dissertation as a polished book manuscript. Without his belief in this project, it might still be gathering dust on a shelf. Finally, Catherine Cocks and Charlotte Wright at the University of Iowa Press patiently and expertly guided the manuscript through its final revisions.

I am indebted to the staff at the Iowa State University Special Collections Department: Tanya Zanish-Belcher, Michele Christian, Laura Sullivan, Melissa Gottwald, Becky Jordan, and Brad Kuennen, who were not only resourceful and helpful in this research but also kind enough to provide employment and support throughout my years in graduate school. Karen Mason and Janet Weaver always provided a warm welcome at the Iowa Women's Archives in Iowa City, along with indispensable advice, resources, and service that went above and beyond. Doris Malkmus, who interviewed numerous rural women for the oral history collection, Voices from the Land, provided a wealth of information for this study, as well as guidance during the early days of this project. I truly appreciated the helpfulness of the staff at the University of Iowa Special Collections Department, the Western Historical Manuscript Collection in Columbia, Missouri, as well as the Special Collections Department at the University of Nebraska–Lincoln. Finally, thank you to the staff at the Women's History Resource Center, located at the national headquarters of the General Federation of Women's Clubs in Washington, D.C.

I am especially grateful for the institutions and organizations that expressed their belief in this project by way of financial assistance. The State Historical Society of Iowa provided funding for two chapters in this book, with additional funds coming from the Missouri State Historical Society, Phi Alpha Theta, the General Federation of Women's Clubs, the Carrie Chapman Catt Center for Women in Politics, Sigma Xi, and the Agricultural History Society. The family of Ernest G. Hildner provided an endowment for the Ernest G. Hildner Faculty Enrichment Fund at Illinois College that paid for the chapter about the Iowa Farmers Union, and I am thankful for their generosity. All of this support allowed me to make endless photocopies, pay for gas and lodging, and indulge in countless hours of writing and research. I also owe a world of thanks to Karen Dean, my department chair, and Elizabeth Tobin, the dean of academic affairs at Illinois College, for a course release that gave me the time to work on this manuscript.

Members of the Rural Women's Studies Association and the Agricultural History Society listened to drafts and presentations at conferences over the years and offered their encouragement and words of advice. Joe Anderson, Sara Egge, Steve Hochstadt, Jennifer Rivera, Joe Genetin-Pilawa, and Mitch Whightsil all pitched in to read, proof, and offer extremely valuable suggestions on various rough drafts, as did fellow graduate students at Iowa State University over the course of several seminars. For their friendship and willingness to help out, I am extremely grateful.

My interest in agriculture, especially women in agriculture, began at a very early age when my great-grandma Penisten told me how she raised and sold chickens so she could attend high school in town. Barely literate, her father believed so strongly in the value of an education that he said nothing when my great-grandma drowned her sister's cat for attacking those chickens. Her experience motivated me to look deeper into the lives of farm women, who often encountered difficult choices as they sought to make better lives for themselves. This book is written with the deepest respect for those whose stories are presented here, and I hope I have accurately portrayed their lives. Any mistakes or omissions are entirely my own.

My parents have always been kind enough to indulge their historian daughter, as we spent our summers traveling and seeing America. Thank you for your endless support of my education and interest in history.

My sister, Karen Crowley, created the very thorough index for this volume and I am glad to have such a talented writer and editor in the family.

T. J. Devine, my husband, never doubted for a second that I could see this project through. His patience and encouragement are the stuff of legend. He and our children, Liz and Danny, inspire me in countless ways every day.

ON BEHALF OF THE FAMILY FARM

Introduction

For it is a grim but bracing truth that we must constantly re-vitalize and re-create our cherished ideals.

THELMA JOHNSON, CHAIRWOMAN OF THE IOWA FARM BUREAU
FEDERATION WOMEN'S COMMITTEE, 1969

IN APRIL 1970 FARM WOMAN Helen Karnes posed the following question to readers of the *Farm Journal*: Has anyone ever noticed the treatment women get from farm organizations? Women rarely served on boards or took on leadership roles. At meetings, men assumed that women wanted to watch fashion shows or engage in "girl talk," rather than "listen in on meetings intended to improve our farming." Because most of the women Karnes knew saw themselves as partners on the farm with their husbands, she wanted to know why more women were not present at meetings. The problem, she decided, was a dismissive attitude on the part of men. "There's no law that says we can't walk in," she concluded, "but it would be nice to feel welcome." In response, the editors of *Farm Journal* attempted to ignite a debate among the readership, asking, "Are women themselves in part responsible? Or are farmers more conservative in giving women their due than men in other organizations?" The editors even offered to pay for any letters they published, but not one letter on the topic appeared in the *Farm Journal* over the following year.[1]

That readers failed to respond, or that editors did not publish responses, is at first surprising given the provocative nature of the questions. Throughout the twentieth century, Midwestern farm women claimed to have reciprocal relationships with men and to have shaped their communities through civic, religious, and agricultural organizations. Karnes made a significant departure from the rhetoric of mutuality between farm men and women when she identified sexism as a problem. She questioned long-standing gendered divisions of labor, the certainty of gendered spaces in the countryside, and men's dominance over public spaces. This posed a risk to a farm woman who likely depended on men, both within her family and in the community, for access to land, financial resources, and community institutions. The readers' silence on the issue may not be an indication of apathy then but perhaps a hesitancy to grapple directly with loaded questions that could potentially disrupt vulnerable rural neighborhoods and communities in the midst of rapid social and economic change. In the Midwest after 1945, incorporating women more fully into the public discussions of agricultural policy and production required a disruption of time-honored gendered divisions of labor and the development of entirely new, complex strategies, not only in organizations but in rural communities, on family farms, and between married couples.

Karnes's experience, like those of women in a variety of farm organizations, offers a glimpse into the diverse strategies that women employed after 1945 to assert their identities as producers in communities dependent on the rhythms and customs of agricultural production. Confronting the realities of modern agriculture required considerable adjustment on multiple fronts. For agricultural organizations leaders and members wondered who should speak for agriculture, to whom they should speak, and how. Throughout the twentieth century, this remained a male responsibility as women worked primarily in supportive capacities. By the early 1970s, however, small groups of women began to assert that organizing could and should become women's work as their husbands became consumed with the demands of modern agricultural production. Those who wanted to be effective advocates argued that they wasted their talents by limiting their activities to domestic, maternal, and community issues. They needed access to public spaces and funding for their work. They needed to speak on behalf of farming as a whole, and their voices needed to influence policy. Drawing on notions of romantic agrarianism, whiteness, and middle-class privilege, farm women developed home-grown agrarian feminisms that moved them into these public spaces. They practiced a "politics of dependence" that allowed them to challenge male authority in state and federal politics, agribusinesses, and farm organizations by emphasizing their experiences as farm laborers in addition to their dependent roles as wives and mothers in heterosexual marriages. Arriving at this point was part of an evolutionary process wherein women presented new interpretations of time-honored agrarian ideals that identified women as public leaders.

The purpose of this book is to explore how women navigated gendered dynamics and sexism in the countryside as they dealt with the power and the limitations of social feminisms and transformative leadership experi-

ences in all-female settings. The stories of women who actively participated in the Iowa Farm Bureau Federation, the Iowa Farmers Union, the
National Farmers Organization, and the Iowa Porkettes present examples
of the ways in which women adapted their rhetoric and politicized aspects
of their daily work, responded to female leadership at the state level, related to male leaders, coped with limited resources, and claimed a presence
in male-dominated spaces in order to work toward favorable agricultural
policies. Creating new spaces for women and fostering agrarian feminisms
meant negotiating "competing loyalties" created by strict delineations of
gender and social class. Women's efforts, therefore, were not entirely a response to sexism or gendered marginalization but rather part of a larger process wherein women imagined new forms of community and redefined their
proper roles in ways that conformed to understandings of gendered work in
rural society.[2]

Midwestern farm women began organizing auxiliaries and clubs on a
large scale during the Progressive era, when women's activism was largely
informed by social feminisms that emphasized the political applications of
women's supposedly innate abilities as mothers and caregivers. Social feminisms allowed women to create safe, separate spaces where they could engage in activism on specific issues, such as public health, maternal and infant
care, education, or industrial safety, without challenging male-dominated
political systems. This framework appealed to farm women, who could
easily gather in feminized spaces such as homes and schoolhouses to discuss how their homemaking skills might be used to better the countryside.
After 1945, however, the motivating rhetoric behind farm activism gradually
shifted from simply improving farms and local communities to saving them
from a debilitating decline. Agrarian feminisms and a politics of dependence
emerged from this shift, allowing women entrance into public spaces where
they could act and speak with authority on behalf of agriculture. Women
active in organizations continued to stress their dependence on men, but
agrarian feminisms emphasized working partnerships between husbands
and wives, women's work in agricultural production, and women's unique
ways of understanding large-scale, conventional farming.

All of this unfolded in the decades following the Second World War, when
corn-belt agriculture required greater capital and investments in technology.
At midcentury Iowa was predominantly rural, with a relatively stable agricultural system characterized by diversified, family-owned farming operations.
Within a generation, however, farmers had discarded their parents' production methods, moved toward specialization, or left farming altogether. Ac-

cording to historian J. L. Anderson, the postwar countryside featured larger farms, fewer people, and higher standards of living that created an entirely "new physical and social landscape." Such changes in Iowa were representative of corn- and grain-producing areas of the Midwest, with the most dramatic transformations in the scale and cost of doing business. Confining this study to organizations within Iowa's boundaries, therefore, sheds light on the varied responses to agricultural problems among farm families with similar production methods, goals, and expectations over a vast geographic area.[3]

Like farm families across the Midwest, Iowans were enthusiastic joiners who sought memberships in local churches, service clubs, fraternal groups, and a variety of agricultural organizations as a means to strengthen and support their communities. The organizations in this study are representative — both in their ideology and their purpose — of the major agricultural groups active across the region. Iowa provides especially fertile ground for the study of grassroots farm politics, however, because the state played a pivotal role in federal farm politics. Between the 1920s and the 1960s Iowa remained a leader in the farm bloc, a bipartisan congressional coalition that worked for favorable agricultural policies and situated itself in opposition to urban industrialism. The grassroots strategies that succeeded or failed with Iowa farmers, then, had the potential to shape strategy and policy at the federal level. The Iowa Farm Bureau Federation was the largest state subsidiary of the American Farm Bureau Federation, which held considerable sway in Washington, D.C. Similarly, the National Farmers Organization and the National Pork Producers (with which the Iowa Porkettes were affiliated) were founded and headquartered in Iowa, providing Iowa's members with closer access to national leadership and legislative liaisons. The only group without a considerable presence was the Farmers Union, which tended to hold more sway with the grain growers of the Great Plains. Yet that group's tireless efforts to build, maintain, and control membership in Iowa is indicative of the state's importance in the union's overall plan to expand membership nationally. Many rural families enjoyed memberships in multiple organizations and moved with ease between them, but in the decades after 1945, the national and state leaders of these groups vied for the energy and resources of farm families, often demanding complete loyalty.

For women navigating these emerging landscapes and competing interests meant altering the ways in which they and their families related to financial institutions, state and federal government, and a host of growing agribusinesses. As women and their farmer husbands sought to understand these entities that were physically and conceptually distant from their rural communities, new technologies dramatically altered the home place. Appliances and packaged foods eased the physical burden of housework while more sophisticated machinery allowed fewer farmers to cultivate more acres. Young people migrated to the cities, local businesses lost clientele, and small towns seemed less viable. Home gardens and poultry operations became obsolete, but farm women continued to work as field workers, livestock handlers, bookkeepers, farm managers, errand runners, wage earners off the farm, and even political activists. Women's work often became a matter of personal preference, losing the general homogeneity that had been shared across time and space for more than a century. Regardless of the roles and types of work they chose, most women remained closely connected to the farm and vested in its success. And in order to be successful women had to interact with agribusinesses, organizations, government personnel, and financial agents, all of whom operated in the public spaces that had largely excluded women.

Because of deeply engrained beliefs about gender-appropriate behaviors, Midwestern farm women at midcentury would not have identified sexism as the root cause of their marginalization. In fact, women and men considered the fulfillment of appropriate gender roles as the cornerstone of a romantic agrarian ideology. Espoused in the writings of Thomas Jefferson and applied by generations of reformers and politicians, agrarian ideology identified men as active citizens, agricultural producers, and heads of households. Romantic agrarianism upheld independent farmers as an enterprising "chosen" people who served as the backbone of a democratic republic. Farming demanded the commitment and labor of entire families, so rather than encouraging women to question male authority, Jeffersonian agrarianism required that women "seek fulfillment in lives that matched the agrarian prescription." For the most part, throughout much of the twentieth century Midwestern farm women still believed that the term "farmer" implied a male head of household and that they were "farm wives" devoted to "establishing the rightful supremacy of the male farmer."[4]

Each of the farm organizations in this study promoted agrarian ideals that made several basic assumptions about the demographics and attitudes of its membership. Leaders took for granted that their constituents were married, heterosexual couples who identified as white and who harbored middle-class aspirations to own land that could be passed down through several generations. And for the most part the women in this study fit these assumptions. They expected to work hard throughout their lives, but they also expected that their work would lead to the material comforts and financial independence promised within the tenets of agrarianism, whiteness, and middle-class privilege. After 1945 a consensus produced by the Cold War led white Midwesterners to abandon ethnic identities, languages other than English, and ties to their European roots, subjugating their heritage to community celebrations or the occasional festival. As historians Andrew R. L. Cayton and Susan E. Gray note, white ethnicity became "superfluous" in the postwar period as white, rural residents collectively rebuffed a developing urban landscape inhabited by racial minorities. White Iowans took very seriously popular depictions of Midwesterners' common sense, faith in democracy, humility, unfailing work ethic, and stoicism. Farm leaders capitalized on these reflections of hope, juxtaposed them with daily realities, and promised members opportunities to protect their families from the economic and technological changes that compromised the stability of rural life in the corn belt.[5]

This collective identity and associated promises fueled by agrarian ideals resonated with Iowa's farm women, who were especially vulnerable in periods of economic uncertainty. Limited employment prospects, domestic responsibilities, and physical isolation left them with few options for self-support. For some, engaging in the political process with other women alleviated these fears and made up for the disappearance of women's familial and social neighborhood networks that had long characterized rural life. Anthropologist Deborah Fink observes that by the early 1980s Midwestern farm women joined clubs and groups in order to find new "sisters" and rebuild support systems lost through depopulation. Biological sisters, female relatives, and longtime family friends had migrated to urban areas and could no longer relate to daily life on the farm. Forced to look elsewhere for social and emotional support, farm women joined groups that brought them together to address mutual interests in politics, marketing, and commodities.[6]

Turning to organizations made sense to farm women because they had eagerly participated in educational, social, and political activities since the late nineteenth century. They joined the Farmers' Alliance, the Grange, state farm bureau federations, and the Farmers Union, which identified as family organizations with reciprocal roles for men and women that reflected the gendered divisions of labor on the farm. Male leaders of these organizations typically supported the involvement of women in supportive capacities, banking on the idea that active, interested wives would encourage husbands to renew their memberships year after year. Historians of rural American women have generally favored the term "mutuality" to describe these interdependent interactions between men and women in households, commu-

nities, and organizations because even though women were legally and socially subordinate to men, women's productive labor and cooperative efforts
to operate family farms permitted considerable flexibility, autonomy, and
decision-making power. Historian Mary Neth found that mutuality offered
both men and women a "positive valuation of labor," with "communal, not
hierarchical definitions of worth." Farm women defended the value of their
work because it not only supported men's activities in the sense that it freed
men to pursue their occupations, but it actually provided the services and
capital necessary for economic survival.[7]

In farm organizations women utilized this rhetoric of mutuality to justify their participation in women's auxiliaries, committees, and supportive
roles. Beginning in the 1910s, female leaders working through the Cooperative Extension Service and major organizations promoted social feminisms,
or the idea that women's activities in home economics, youth, education,
and organizational support were an essential part of mutual efforts with men
to improve conditions in the countryside. Historian Nancy K. Berlage observes that the Farm Bureau, founded in 1919 as one of the largest and most
politically influential national groups, offered women "access to new forms
of cultural and political authority," wherein they "stressed their identity as
rural citizens with a stake in agriculture and rural life as a whole, rather than
emphasizing gender."[8]

The social feminisms and strategies of mutuality that emerged in the early
twentieth century allowed women to use readily available resources, such as
existing neighborhood networks, to add a political dimension to their daily
work. Organizing required little financial investment on the part of female
members or male leaders, and women could easily rationalize making room
for club activities in their busy work schedules. Because notions of appropriate gendered behavior shaped women's lives more than any other factor, this model that was developed during the early twentieth century became the standard for future generations, influencing women's choices as
they attempted to create new strategies and to renegotiate gendered spaces
in a variety of organizations. Between 1910 and 1945 Iowa's largest general
farm organizations, the Iowa Farm Bureau Federation (IFBF) and the Iowa
Farmers Union (IFU), espoused very different political ideologies but utilized remarkably similar top-down models for female leadership. The first
chapter in this book, therefore, considers how female leaders utilized social
feminisms to feminize specific tasks, such as membership drives, education,
and youth activities. In order to justify their organizational work, female
leaders utilized a rhetoric similar to that of Progressive-era reformers, who

defined farm women's activism as an extension of their work in the home and their maternal responsibilities.

These early organizing efforts were immensely successful, reaching thousands of women across the state. By 1945 local leaders at the county and township levels had taken lessons on leadership to heart. They believed themselves capable of selecting and leading activities without the guidance of state leaders. National and state leaders associated with the Farm Bureau were also increasingly anxious to grant local chapters greater control over their programming because financial and logistical limitations hindered centralized leadership systems. As the second chapter illustrates, women who joined township clubs took membership and leadership roles seriously but favored recreation and leisure over the political, agricultural, and social-reform issues promoted by state leaders. Local clubs chose activities that fostered neighborhood unity, allowing them to cope with a quickly modernizing countryside, express a middle-class consciousness, and enjoy a burgeoning consumerism that implied higher standards of living. In many ways club members of the 1950s fulfilled the visions of modern living purported by clubwomen of the 1920s and 1930s. Their primary public activities included philanthropy, annual neighborhood picnics, community-service projects, and booths for county fairs. Members expressed loyalty to their clubs and a sense of empowerment, but by the early 1960s membership began to waver as depopulation took women out of rural areas and those with a greater interest in agricultural policy decided to apply their efforts elsewhere. As political scientist Louise I. Carbert points out, strategies of mutuality "justified women's political activity outside of private households in terms of their familial responsibilities" but held "no pervasiveness with policy analysts, administrators, or agronomists."[9]

A woman's ability to obtain power within a family, join a club, or seek leadership positions within an organization depended entirely on men's notions of proper gender roles and not on the actual economic, social, or political value of her work. As husbands, fathers, agricultural professionals, political actors, and community leaders, men maintained control over transportation, resources, work schedules, and information dissemination. This required women to define their activism and evolving work roles as part of their normal, supportive labor on the farm. Generations of farm women had expressed their deference to male authority by describing their masculine work in the fields, with livestock, in farm organizations, or as wage earners, as "helping" their husbands. Historian Katherine Jellison found that women's deference intensified in the years after the Second World War because identifying women as helpers assured men of their masculinity as they adjusted to the relative ease of mechanized farm work. It also allowed women to "deflect criticism that they were abandoning their household duties" and deviating from prescribed gender roles if they engaged in farm labor or work for wages.[10]

The same was true of women working in farm organizations and, as the third chapter demonstrates, the development of agrarian feminisms and entry into public spaces required more than a new consciousness among women. Men also needed to recognize the strategic and financial value of women's work outside the private, domestic arena. Choosing a very different path from that of the IFBF, the postwar years saw the women of the IFU actually vote to dissolve the women's auxiliary in favor of integrative policies promising women full membership. Yet a crisis, fueled by Cold War fears of communist infiltration and the threat of charter revocation by national leaders, proved to be a more significant catalyst in prompting male leaders to ask for women's help. In this case, male leaders utilized female leadership and capitalized on their skills as local organizers and educators in the hopes of securing the support of members at the grass roots. Once the crisis had passed, however, it became clear that women's contributions resulted in no permanent changes or dramatically new perceptions of appropriate gender roles. The IFU continued to espouse a rhetoric of gender equality, but this did little to propel women into leadership roles on par with those held by men. In fact, the restoration of gendered work proved an important indicator of organizational, and thereby societal, stability.

Entry into public arenas required farm women to employ careful phrasing and subtle strategies that remained in keeping with local customs. Patriarchy remained firmly entrenched in the countryside, and few women offered direct challenges to male privilege because doing so undermined the social networks vital to small communities. Yet these women confronted a drastically different world than their mothers had known, and they understood that established organizations could not, or would not, address the issues they deemed significant. As a result, they co-opted strategies and rhetoric from the burgeoning social movements of the postwar period, including feminism. Standard interpretations of feminisms in the United States after 1945, especially those of the Second Wave, typically emphasize developments in major metropolitan areas, with an implicit assumption that feminisms slowly spread from elite urban centers to rural peripheries, where socially conservative farm women rejected notions of "women's lib." Midwestern farm women certainly rejected the feminist label associated with a movement for radical or wage-earning women because feminism, as portrayed in the media and popular discourse, was incompatible with their goals of maintaining a family farm. Their main objections during the 1970s were not based on threats to the nuclear family but rather on the inference that women lacked work experience. Many farm women asserted that they had always been liberated by their participation on family farms. As Louise Carbert points out, even mundane farm tasks, like milking, were tremendously significant in women's identification with feminism, demonstrating that "the route that women take to becoming feminist is more complex and more profoundly grounded in everyday life than has been anticipated."[11]

In understanding how women drew from feminism and shaped feminist ideologies into their own agrarian feminisms, it is helpful to apply what legal scholar Lisa R. Pruitt terms "spaces of dependence" when delineating the reasons for the lack of mobility among rural American women. Pruitt argues that, unlike urban women, those living in rural areas face narrow choices when seeking economic and social resources. They depend more on informal social and kinship networks for emotional, material, and social support. I argue, then, that after 1945 women active in farm organizations gradually abandoned strategies of mutuality that had defined farm women's activism since the nineteenth century and pursued a "politics of dependence." By publicly recognizing and even embracing their dependence on men and the interdependence of the family, women could move into public spaces and speak with authority on agricultural issues without upsetting their traditional female roles in rural communities.[12]

Like social feminisms and strategies of mutuality, the politics of dependence also stemmed from common divisions of labor within farm households, but it differed in that it justified women's entry into clearly defined male spaces: retail establishments, businesses, commodity sales, financial institutions, wage labor, and elective politics. Women pursuing strategies of mutuality emphasized maternalism and domesticity, wherein their inherent roles as wives, mothers, and workers within a private home entitled them to dominion over issues related to family, education, and the local community. The politics of dependence, on the other hand, tended to place a greater emphasis on women's roles as valued partners in heterosexual marriages, as agricultural producers, and as political actors moving into public spaces on behalf of their husbands.

Given these characteristics and contradictions, the use of the term "agrarian feminism" to describe farm women's movements is problematic. In popular discourse and even in the historiography, farm women embody self-realization, ingenuity, and strength, but few farm women actually identified as feminist, and the oppressive influence of patriarchy is unavoidable. The term "agrarian feminism" depends on careful periodization after 1945 and refers not to a singular movement but a shift in consciousness and political activity for a minority of farm women that coincided with broader social and political movements in the late twentieth century. This was more than mere entry into public life and social reform but the emergence of new strategies for dealing with the consequences of the second agricultural revolution that specifically addressed women's roles as public actors. Use of the term "feminism" here also builds on historian Estelle B. Freedman's suggestion that feminism may be a flexible, malleable framework for historical inquiry that allows for a greater understanding of cultural expressions and expectations. Even if women refuse to identify as feminist, they are "living and breathing [feminist] politics whenever they stand up for themselves, their families and their rights." Recognizing this as a viable framework allows us to understand the development of women's strategies across time and space, especially in rural environments.[13]

Early manifestations of agrarian feminisms can be discerned in the policies and rhetoric of new organizations founded in the 1950s and 1960s, which identified the technological and economic changes in agriculture as indicators of larger, impending social, political, and economic emergencies in the American countryside. Groups like the National Farm Organization (NFO), founded in Iowa in 1955 as a collective bargaining association, employed militaristic language that identified the NFO as engaged in a battle with corporations and an unsympathetic government. Farm women became "Rosie the Riveter" figures, who made personal sacrifices, worked hard, and devoted themselves entirely to a just cause only "for the duration." At the same time there was no auxiliary system, youth program, or educational component to delineate as female space. Just as women enjoyed broader work options at the homeplace, the NFO needed all available volunteers at the grass roots and offered women some flexibility in choosing how they could best contribute.

The fourth chapter focuses on the personal stories of NFO women, who dealt with the consequences of this new rhetoric and organizational structure. Women recognized the NFO as an entirely new organization, in which they learned from one another and emphasized personal strengths. Their politicization of the family as a working unit represents an early expression of a politics of dependence that validates women's entry into public spaces, including meetings, offices, and sales barns, in times of economic urgency.

Women were also recognized, even revered, for tending homes and farms while their husbands worked as organizers. As a result the NFO simultaneously recognized women's ability to perform farm work while envisioning a point in time when prosperity in the countryside would allow women to take on the role of full-time homemaker.

The NFO struggled to establish its legitimacy throughout the 1960s and 1970s, and over time members expressed disillusionment with the founders' ideals. For women in the NFO and more broadly, it became clear that their labor was still very much needed on the farm. Ideals of leisure and consumption were unrealistic and for many farm women impractical. A small but vocal cohort of farm women began to point out that organizational rhetoric purporting female empowerment, integrative strategies, and equal opportunities for men and women was mere public expression that conveyed idealized gender roles but did not reflect daily realities. Agrarian ideals obscured the fact that women were never truly equal partners with their husbands. They remained in the margins due to the fact that women rarely held joint ownership of the land, signed for loans, registered vehicles or equipment in their names, or left any legal records attesting to their economic contributions. Their prosperity was based entirely on a trust that the men in their families would value and care for them. By the late 1960s, agriculture gave way to agribusiness, land values skyrocketed, taxes and revenue became a matter for federal records, and accurate bookkeeping became a necessity. Many women realized they needed to renegotiate the strategies of mutual labor valuation, not only with their husbands but with the larger public world.

The second agricultural revolution, rife with subsidies, tax codes, and quantifiable values for individuals' labor, provided fertile soil for women to more fully develop agrarian feminisms and express a politics of dependence. By the mid-1960s, women in agricultural organizations began to question the extent to which sexism had limited their activities with established groups. They began transforming their time-honored auxiliaries and clubs into new channels for effecting changes in agriculture. Creating secure spaces for women in independent, female-led organizations that did not depend on men for financial support or leadership became a priority. The Iowa Porkettes, whose story is the focus of the fifth chapter, exemplified this process. Initially formed as the auxiliary to the Iowa Pork Producers Association, the Iowa Porkettes were themselves the product of new trends in hog production that led to dramatic increases in the number of hogs raised in the state. The Porkettes hoped to make their operations profitable by promoting pork products to urban consumers. By the early 1970s they recognized that by charging minimal dues and failing to assert their presence in the pork industry, they had undermined their central mission. As a result empowering women from pork-producing families became a primary focus, and the members worked throughout the 1970s to establish themselves as professional spokespersons in a burgeoning industry by drawing on strategies from established farm organizations, modern agribusiness, and even Second Wave feminisms. They joined a vocal movement of farm women who demanded attention from policy makers and asserted that, as women, they shared a unique perspective on agricultural production.[14]

The subtleties of gendered relationships in rural communities have long puzzled scholars, especially when confronted with farm women who imparted a rhetoric of power in a patriarchal society that clearly limited their choices. Katherine Jellison, for example, maintains that women's motivations for maintaining an identity rooted in agriculture, with connotations of hard work and sacrifice, "were complex and had nothing to do with the development of a feminist ideology or any type of organized challenge to patriarchy." Historians Mark Friedberger and William Pratt have also asserted that farm women's activism remained invisible, politically insignificant, and entirely unaffected by feminism until the 1980s. At that time high interest rates on farm loans, coupled with low commodity prices, resulted in the farm crisis. Thousands of families across the country had borrowed money to expand their farming operations but could not repay the interest and ended up losing their farms in foreclosure. Friedberger argues that these conditions forced women, whose husbands were unable to cope with the economic downturn, into the political arena where they had formerly had no voice.[15]

The women who joined and created farm organizations after 1945 tell a very different story. This study attempts to meet farm women at various moments in time and to understand subtle shifts in gendered dynamics, changing attitudes, and women's motivations for organizing in the context of their familial and community responsibilities. By carefully selecting issues and identifying external threats to the agrarian way of life, women could safely empower one another to enter public spaces, while adhering to gendered expectations. Their efforts have not been counted as part of the women's movement, however, because these women identified more with movements of earlier farm women and those involved in the production of food and fiber. Over the past century farm women have consistently placed agricultural issues such as land and commodity prices, government policy, and farm safety well before issues of gender equality. In order to address these problems productively, however, women also confronted gendered marginalization in ways that made sense in their rural environments.[16]

This study considers only a small number of farm women, who typically enjoyed positive experiences interacting with other men and women acting on behalf of agriculture. This study does not portray the experiences of countless families displaced by economic and technological changes throughout the twentieth century or those who chose to leave farming for more stable urban occupations. It does not consider those women who did not take action or who did not join organizations because of marginal farming conditions, oppressive circumstances in the home, isolated living conditions, or work demands both on and off the farm. Women who joined agricultural groups, especially those who became active members or leaders, were often those who came from relatively stable economic circumstances, those who had the support of their families and their husbands, and those who simply believed they had something to contribute through their organizational activity. This study begs the question, then, as to how an understanding of women's organizations can contribute to our understanding of rural America when these organizations represented only a handful of farm women.

Even in the early twenty-first century, Iowa's farm women continue to seek out opportunities and set forth a vision for agriculture based on the needs of family and community. Understanding the roots of this vision and the ways in which women have articulated it can help move activists forward. The main objective of this study is to introduce agrarian feminisms and the politics of dependence as conceptual models for considering the intersections of agriculture, gender, regional identity, and modernization. Even in the midst of dramatic social, cultural, political, and economic change after 1945, farm women still shared strong connections to agriculture, even if they only enjoyed conceptual ownership of their farms and relied entirely on family and husbands for support. Farm women understood their dependence, and they desired familial stability and middle-class standards of living that seemed increasingly elusive more than they desired a public voice. Their desires could only be met by balancing their gendered expectations with their entry into the public arenas of agribusiness, wage work, and political activism. As they refined their messages, these activists emphasized that they—and farmers in general—possessed special knowledge and skills rarely valued by urban Americans. They were stewards of the land, of resources, of food, and ultimately of democracy. As women, they worked not for individual achievement or notoriety but for one simple goal—to save the family farm and thereby ensure the preservation of a fundamental American institution.

CHAPTER ONE

This Rich Gift of Voluntary Leadership

Rural Women's Activism in Iowa

AT THE 1921 IOWA STATE FAIR, Sarah Elizabeth Richardson, a farm woman from Mahaska County, Iowa, made an appeal for the inclusion of women in the Iowa Farm Bureau Federation (IFBF). She asserted that "the Federation machine, great and glorious though it is, will never be able to function 100 percent efficiently until the women have climbed into the bandwagon." In order to guarantee success for the entire organization, she urged IFBF leaders to "get the women, if you want to hold the men." This speech prompted the organization's male leaders to act, and in April 1922 the IFBF secretary, E. H. Cunningham, convened a group of eleven women to discuss how women might contribute to the organization on the state level. This meeting led to the creation of an interim Women's Committee, which became permanent in 1923.[1]

In 1937, after serving fifteen years as the chairwoman of the Iowa Farm Bureau Federation's Women's Committee (IFBFWC), Richardson still eagerly promoted mutuality and the importance of women within the organization. That year she wrote that both men and women must be "interested and active" members so that the goal of "a happy, contented, prosperous family on every farm" might be achieved. Richardson concluded, "The women's committee in state, county, and township and school district is not a division, but rather a commission to carry out the program."[2]

Richardson's insistence that women not only be involved but fully recognized as advocates for farm families is representative of the rhetoric developed by Midwestern farm women's organizations during the first half of the twentieth century. Between the 1920s and 1950s the Iowa Farm Bureau Federation's women's committee expanded female membership, consolidated statewide control, and established a permanent, legitimate base for farm women's activism. Organizing strategies that utilized social feminisms, identified outside threats to farming as a way of life, and justified activism as an extension of their duties at home mirrored similar efforts within other organizations, including the Iowa Farmers Union. Richardson's careful selection of labels that placed value on women's work did not necessarily convince male leaders and policy makers, but it empowered women to politicize everyday tasks and assert that their nonpartisan programs on membership, education, patriotism, and the home were an indispensable part of bettering the lives of all farm people. In keeping with Progressive-era clubwomen's movements, they embarked on efforts to clearly define feminine issues and delineate separate female spaces in the IFBF. Education, refinement, and leisure were key components of defining female spaces, and even if prosperity proved elusive, structured meetings and organized leisure offered brief opportunities to engage in affluent behavior. The story of the Women's Committee of the IFBF demonstrates how Iowa's farm women adapted social feminisms to rural realities and laid the groundwork for a politics of dependence that emerged in rural women's organizations after 1945.

Founded in 1919, the IFBF consolidated existing county organizations under statewide leadership and became a social and political partner, as well as a financial contributor, with the government-sponsored extension service. This relationship generated plentiful resources and rampant misconceptions that allowed the Farm Bureau to build a membership base nearly ten times larger than the second largest organization in the state, the Iowa Farmers Union (IFU). This complex and interdependent relationship began in the early twentieth century, when the extension service relied on federal dollars as well as donations from local and private donors to carry out its activities. To ensure greater statewide consistency in extension activities, the Iowa General Assembly passed legislation in 1913 to create county farm aid associations, or farm bureaus, that would apply membership dues toward extension service agents' salaries, office space, and educational materials. In 1924 Extension Director R. K. Bliss estimated that farm bureau memberships provided approximately $330,000 for extension service activities, more than three times the federal contribution. In some areas extension service agents and farm bureau leaders worked together so closely that many rural residents falsely believed that they needed to be farm bureau members in order to take advantage of extension service activities.[3]

If its connection to the extension service enhanced the ability of the IFBF to reach farm families so too did its connection to the American Farm Bureau Federation (AFBF), the national organization that provided oversight to the state affiliates and coordinated lobbying efforts in Washington, D.C. By 1921 Iowa had contributed 95,926 members, the largest number of members from any one state, to an overall national membership of nearly half a million. That same year Iowa's Republican senator, William S. Kenyon, teamed with Gray Silver, the chief lobbyist for the AFBF in Washington, D.C., to form a congressional farm bloc. A coalition of Midwestern Republicans from the corn belt and Democrats from the cotton South, the farm bloc succeeded during the 1920s in passing several significant pieces of legislation aimed at protecting American agricultural goods, including the Capper-Volstead Act, which exempted agricultural cooperatives from antitrust laws. The Iowa Farm Bureau's emphasis on education and electoral politics, therefore, played an important role in securing popular support for state and federal policies over the course of several decades. The IFBF lost no time in reminding its female members that they were now voters who could use their ballots to prevail on politicians for change.[4]

In Iowa women had been active in the county farm bureaus as leaders and members since the 1910s, but in January 1919 only one woman, a home demonstration agent, was present at the inaugural meeting of the IFBF. In 1920 the all-male IFBF executive committee adopted a resolution recognizing the lack of interest on the part of "the farmer's wife in the Farm Bureau organization, due no doubt to the lack of knowledge as to the status of the farmer's wife in the ranks of the organization." Yet the committee's object of increasing women's participation was not based on a desire to promote gender equity. Because the Farm Bureau advertised itself as a family organization, many leaders deduced that more men would attend meetings if their wives and children were also invited.[5]

The programs of the IFBFWC, which was founded in 1922, proved extremely popular. By 1924 the women's committee had organized over 1,100 townships. In 1925 their programs reached an estimated 158,000 women in the state. Within just a few years of its formation, then, the women's committee had established itself as an integral and indispensable part of the IFBF, responsible for social activities, membership drives, youth activities, and community service.[6]

In general male leaders throughout the 1920s recognized the presence of women with ample praise for their leadership abilities and at least publicly put forth no resistance to the development of new programs. In a speech at the 1923 state Farm Bureau Convention, IFBF Secretary E. H. Cunningham told members that the organization should give women's work serious consideration since it was "unquestionably the most stabilizing influence in the organization." He favored the idea of mutual cooperation, with men working for the "farm problems" and women for the "home problems," and he hoped to create the "most harmonious co-operation within the ranks of a farm organization."[7]

A reporter writing about the 1923 convention noted the increased numbers of women in attendance. The reporter described how the women's note-books and pencils were in "constant use" and lightheartedly warned, "If the 'lords of creation' don't look alive one of these days the lady workers will be reaching for the steering wheel." Then, three years later, in 1926, when more than 300 women attended the annual convention, an observer noted the different perceptions of work and involvement between rural and urban women when he wrote, "I have listened all over the place and haven't heard a single man show any resentment or antagonism toward the women. Can't say as much for some conventions of city folks." It is possible that this reporter expected to hear discriminatory language like that used by antisuffragists, that political activity would harm women's feminine sensibilities. Such rhetoric is entirely absent from early farm women's clubs because members, both male and female, considered club work to be gender-appropriate for women.[8]

Women established county programs without arousing much, if any, heated debate among male leaders about whether women should partake in organizational activities. More often, county leaders and extension agents complimented the women's work and made efforts to ensure that women's programs received equal attention. This was significant in Iowa because in most counties the chair of the Farm Bureau women's committee also served as the vice president of the entire county organization, and women often served on budget and leadership committees. In an address to the IFBF in January 1924, R. K. Bliss, the director of the Cooperative Extension Service, called the establishment of the IFBFWC "one of the most constructive acts" of the Farm Bureau. He reminded the audience that "the women have been one of the most important factors in developing township and community meetings. What would our township and community meetings amount to if it were not for the women?"[9]

Bliss and extension leaders put this idea into practice by requiring that the county and township chairs of the women's committees also serve as the vice presidents of the entire county or township organization. They also suggested to county and township organizers that women could take on leadership roles by serving on a variety of committees. The 1922 extension organizers in Clay County complained that local people were "indifferent" and unwilling to serve in leadership positions. By strengthening the county's forty-three women's clubs and mobilizing their eight hundred female members to provide refreshments, entertainment, and social activities, organizers hoped to increase overall attendance at general meetings. Although women served as vice-chairs, extension organizers in Clay County reported that women's work carried enough importance so that "in reality, there are two township chairmen in each township, one man and one woman."[10]

The main obstacles for women during these early years were not vocal male opponents or reluctant female leaders but rather the shortage of active male supporters who would work to establish specific programs, appoint leaders, and allocate financial resources. Even in 1924, when women's activities had become firmly established and when only two counties remained unorganized, Richardson reported at the annual convention that the women's programs were "handicapped by total lack of working funds." Limited funds and resources was a common problem for women's organizations. The IFBFWC adopted a unified state plan in 1923, but its provisions were vague and focused on local improvements, rather than the consolidation of local organizations under state leadership. The committee's local emphasis should not be surprising: this was the most economic and efficient way to develop leadership. Because the extension service and county dues funded these local programs, they required no financial assistance from the state federation.[11]

The day after Richardson's speech at the 1924 convention, the executive committee, convinced by "a very insistent demand for increased service and wider activities," appropriated $4,000 for women's activities. According to a notice in the *Iowa Farm Bureau Messenger*, IFBFWC leaders had been "looking forward to the time when the women's work in the Farm Bureau could be given something more tangible than just words of praise." With their budget secure the IFBFWC adopted a new five-point program: to consolidate and solidify the general policies of the women's committee, to cooperate with other women's organizations, to develop a system of diplomas for work done by farm bureau women, to support a special study of marketing, and to adopt a standardized report form to be used by women statewide. Funding allowed the women's committee to act more effectively on its state plan and to create uniform programs across the state — activities that would define the IFBFWC throughout the 1930s and 1940s. During the mid- to late 1920s, however, the committee continued to focus on developing county leaders.[12]

In order to build county organizations and develop local leadership, Iowa Farm Bureau women relied on a highly developed system of training schools created by the IFBFWC and the extension service. This system set the IFBFWC apart from other farm women's organizations in Iowa because it could offer practical instruction and adult education in addition to its social and political benefits. County farm bureau leaders, in conjunction with home demonstration agents, formed educational and organizational networks with representatives from the state, townships, and school districts. Courses lasted for five months and usually consisted of a single one-day meeting each month. During the rest of the month, then, township leaders trained school district cooperators and gathered feedback before the next lesson. This provided local women with a means of voicing their opinion about the lesson and developing their own curriculum.

The development of the training-school system depended on the active participation of the extension service. Although the extension service claimed to work with various organizations, including the Grange and the Iowa Farmer's Union, the Farm Bureau enjoyed a close administrative partnership with, and made significant financial contributions to, extension service activities. The training-school system grew out of this partnership and benefited both parties in their efforts to reach rural families. Neale S. Knowles, the head of the home economics division of the Iowa State Cooperative Extension Service from 1908 to 1935, initially developed this method of filtering information through local instructors because it allowed agents and county leaders to reach fifteen to twenty times the number of households they could reach on their own. Farm Bureau leaders likewise used this method to recruit new members, and they relied on the practical extension activities to attract individuals who might not otherwise be interested in a social and political organization.[13]

The training-school system met with immediate success and expanded rapidly during the 1920s. The first training school in Iowa took place in Monroe County in April 1921. That year, 2,050 women attended training schools in eighteen different counties. Projects included clothing, sewing, home management and furnishing, nutrition, and poultry. In 1922 and 1923, Knowles noticed an "unusual awakening of interest in the counties without agents," as 40,985 women attended 2,566 training schools just on clothing; nutrition training schools attracted 12,906 women that year; 4,862 were present for home furnishings; and 2,916 attended schools on strengthening the Farm Bureau. Training schools were also established to instruct women on efficient home management, the construction of fireless cookers, the use of pressure cookers, kitchen arrangement, the marketing of eggs and poultry, and the management of farm and home accounts. The sudden surge in popularity may be attributed to several factors, including better communication, automobile ownership, and improved roads, but it may also be due to a rising awareness of inequality between urban and rural standards of living.[14]

By attending home demonstration programs, women could not only

Women demonstrating a fireless cooker, 1925. Freedom Township Women's Club
Records, Iowa Women's Archives, University of Iowa Libraries.

learn how to quickly and cheaply modernize their homes and their methods, but they could also learn about leadership and community involvement. They used the meetings as an opportunity to build associations with
other farm women and farm families for a deeper sense of community pride
and solidarity. In 1922 Kossuth County chair Evelyn Graham reported that
the monthly Farm Bureau meetings filled a "long felt want" and provided
women with a chance to develop "community spirit and a desire to help each
other." Home demonstration programs that encouraged women to be "well
dressed" and "well fed" provided a much needed boost to a woman's confidence that she too could "enjoy the world outside the four walls of her own
home as much as her city sisters do."[15]

Although most women participated in programs geared toward the
home, instructors and participants often politicized their activities, justifying home demonstration programs as essential to overall community improvement. Women of the Mahaska County Farm Bureau believed that the
training-school system developed "a spirit of service and the opportunity to
assist in the building of the county and township Farm Bureau." This spirit of
service came out of projects focusing on foods and nutrition, home nursing,
the making of braided rugs, the washing and carding of wool, cheese making,

the use of sewing machine attachments, and the making of dress forms. At the IFBF's annual convention in 1926, Richardson told members that because women made consumer choices about spending for the home, they should be "good businessmen," not only as homemakers but also as partners in the farming enterprise. By efficiently managing the farm and getting involved in the farm bureau, women could work to ensure greater profits for farmers through reduced freight rates, equalized taxation, and "legislation that takes notice of the farmer's needs." At the same convention farm bureau member Minnie Friedley of Black Hawk County spoke to the women about the importance of nutrition in rearing healthy, responsible children. After she pointed out that the state often intervened on behalf of poorly fed children, one woman in the audience remarked, "Well, it never occurred to me before that I was saving taxes when I made the baby take his vegetables!"[16]

By the end of the 1920s, local women's groups demanded more training schools on cultivating good citizenship, voting, the nature of good government, democracy, and parliamentary law. In 1925 the first statewide citizenship course for women surveyed the organization of governments and the levying of taxes at the township, county, state, and federal levels. The course also discussed how farm bureau members could become involved at each level and strongly encouraged women to take "seriously the privileges of citizenship recently granted" to them.[17]

One key advantage of the training-school system was the fact that it offered guidance on practical matters at minimal cost and for a brief time. Because the knowledge they gained would be readily applied in their homes, women could easily justify participation to husbands concerned about cost, time away from home, and political affiliations. Furthermore, women could attend training schools and join homemakers clubs on their own without relying on their husbands' memberships in the IFBF. Organizations like the Iowa Farmers Union (IFU) welcomed women as voting members and had an active women's auxiliary, but because their meetings were set up to accommodate entire families, a woman's participation typically depended upon a mutual interest with her husband. On the other hand, training schools that dealt with topics related to the family and home were safe, familiar places just for women, where they could politicize their everyday activities without arousing the suspicions of husbands and neighbors and without fully committing themselves to a major farm organization. Ultimately, many women found participation to be a transformative experience as their input shaped the curriculum and gave voice to the values they placed on their work. For those women who were especially inspired to act on the politics of homemaking, training schools also offered an introduction to the IFBF, an organization that claimed to welcome their energies and efforts.

For the IFBFWC training schools that offered potential members a sampling of their services proved to be an important recruiting tool. Securing new members through canvassing was rarely successful. In 1922, when Ruth Buxton Sayre became the women's chairperson of Virginia Township in Warren County, it took her several weeks to secure the five local leaders and nine school district cooperators necessary to organize the township. Sayre drove along dusty township roads in her Model T Ford, with her young daughters in the back seat, only to meet women who claimed to be too busy for farm bureau activities. Others refused because their husbands would not want them to do "anything like that." For some families, their membership in the farm bureau may have been a matter of economics. At five dollars per annual membership, participation may have been too expensive for farmers struggling to repay debts and mortgages. Training schools, on the other hand, allowed women a low-cost, nonthreatening introduction, allowing them to decide over time whether farm bureau membership was right for them.[18]

Instructors did not suggest that the farm women attending training schools should challenge existing political systems but rather that they understand and use the system to secure funding for rural education and health and to advocate farm policies that ensured stable commodity prices. Leaders strongly encouraged women to exercise their voting rights, especially for the good of the farm. In an address at the 1926 annual convention, Addie Wood of Moville asserted that women should vote responsibly and have a "unified purpose and an active program." Wood believed that if farm women organized around community issues such as health, education, and agriculture, each could "do her share toward placing the American farm home in a proper position to aid in the demand for agricultural equity." And women in local clubs took advantage of federal and state resources available to them. In 1925 the women of the Freedom Township Women's Club, a farm bureau club in Palo Alto County, attended a training school about the Sheppard-Towner Maternity and Infancy Protection Act, which provided federal funds for maternal and infant heath care. They then sponsored two clinics for mothers and children at members' homes, hosting a nurse and a doctor from the State University of Iowa who conducted examinations of fifteen children and consulted with mothers about malnutrition.[19]

Farm bureau programs also encouraged women to become more involved in community affairs by seeking leadership positions at the local level. To that end female township leaders and school district cooperators also joined their male counterparts in attending county leadership training schools. There, with state leaders at the helm, they discussed the development of local meetings, the duties of leaders and committees, the nature of community ideals, agricultural issues, and leadership within rural organizations. Leadership schools provided practical experience in conducting meetings and contact with state leaders and prominent members of the community. Although they shared these meetings with men, in many instances women dominated the proceedings. Photographs from training schools in Mahaska, Fremont, and Monona counties between 1922 and 1928 reveal the strong and active presence of women. This trend continued through the following decade, with 144 women and 125 men attending leadership training schools in 17 counties during the winter of 1932 and 1933. Although the extension service sponsored many of these activities, leadership training was clearly geared toward building farm bureau membership.[20]

As thousands of women participated in training schools, in which the farm bureau was ever present, it is easy to understand why members of competing organizations like the IFU harbored resentment against the relationship between the farm bureau and the extension service. The Farmers Union at the national and state levels framed agricultural politics within a liberal discussion of farmers as a distinct socioeconomic class, disadvantaged in the capitalist system and at risk for economic displacement. The IFU focused its efforts on securing prices and profits for farmers through cooperative marketing while criticizing the farm bureau and the extension service for encouraging farmers to simply increase production without paying attention to market conditions. Labeling extension programs as a "farmers circus," one 1926 editorial in a monthly newspaper, the *Iowa Union Farmer*, claimed that lessons "demonstrating to the farmers['] wives how to wash the baby," were inherently irresponsible because they did not address the fundamental problem in the countryside: a lack of income. The IFU also attacked corporate interests and headlines attacking "Wall Street manipulators" were common in the *Iowa Union Farmer*. Yet, like the IFBF, the IFU also advocated education and working through the political process to promote change. For women this meant working in feminized spaces on gender-specific projects, demonstrating that gender, rather than ideology, determined "appropriate" behavior for women within organizations. The establishment of the IFU women's auxiliary in 1924 mirrored the creation of the IFBFWC and shows how resources and funding, rather than the mere determination of female leaders, were the real factors in the growth and development of women's groups.[21]

A 1928 meeting in Mahaska County. Special Collections Department, Iowa State University Library.

Founded in 1917, the IFU also set out to consolidate existing county unions under state and national leadership. The National Farmers Union (NFU) organized units into numbered local unions committed to cooperative marketing and purchasing. The divergent political ideologies of the IFBF and the IFU have captured the attention of scholars, but the two organizations were remarkably similar in their organizing strategies and recruitment methods. Both offered competing products — such as insurance, cooperative marketing and purchasing agreements, and educational opportunities. The success of each organization really depended on the willingness of members to buy into the products and services that would in turn finance the social and political activities. The National Farmers Union offered oversight and occasionally sent in full-time organizers, but it did not have the resources or personnel to institute a centralized recruiting effort like the training-school system. As a result, the IFU considered extension service personnel as field agents for the IFBF, selling products and complacent politics.

Most local groups came together through the efforts of county volunteers who were typically full-time farmers themselves. Canvassing often required more time and resources than most farmers could spare, making recruiting primarily a family and neighborhood effort that depended on personal connections to other members. For this reason some historians have identified the Farmers Union as more representative of farmers' grass-roots interests, since local unions were formed without the influence of an extension agent. Membership in county cooperatives included entire families, with voting privileges extended to anyone, male or female, over sixteen years of age. For women, whose activities often depended on family and marital dynamics, joining the IFU was often a joint decision with their husbands. Membership rolls recorded only men's names, and membership cards were typically issued to entire families, rather than individuals. Women were usually present at local gatherings and occasionally took on leadership roles. In 1923 Mary E. Osborn of Taylor County garnered attention as the energetic president of Local No. 462, where she was credited for its growing dues-paying membership, the "regularity of their meetings and the splendid attendance and interest." She was the exception, however, as most women who attended meetings took charge of entertainment, refreshments, and educational activities for children. At the March 1923 meeting of the Flat Rock Local No. 634 in Van Buren County, members decided to switch roles, with the men acting as "waiters" and serving an evening meal to the women present. Described by the members as "fun," this was clearly an unusual reversal.[22]

In 1924 male leaders of the IFU asked Mary Dunn, a farm woman from Marshalltown, Iowa, to organize a statewide auxiliary. Dunn spoke at meetings throughout Iowa and urged women to think beyond their farmsteads and "pressing needs" at home. Using rhetoric similar to Richardson's, Dunn wrote that if women wished to remain on their farms, then "it is for us who are now living on the farms to give to the farm family and farming business a social, economic, and political value more important than they have ever before enjoyed." Club work, she asserted, was a "patriotic duty." Interestingly, this rhetoric did not resonate as well with IFU women, and Dunn encountered some resistance from women who feared exclusion from the IFU. During the summer of 1925, she made an appeal for the benefits of an exclusively female organization when she assured women that they would not lose the "rights and privileges [they] enjoy in the FE&CU." Dunn was glad that women sought to "safeguard" their standing in the main organization, but she stated that women could (and should) maintain their membership and voting rights in the IFU while participating in the auxiliary. Yet these dissenting voices were part of a vocal minority that did little to convince the whole. By 1925 the first IFU ladies' auxiliaries were flourishing, with activities identical to those of the IFBFWC. Local women's auxiliaries ran meetings using roll calls and Robert's Rules of Order. They kept careful minutes and focused on membership drives and fundraising. They also engaged in leisure activities, including luncheons, poetry readings, and music, as well as shared work such as sewing, quilting, and baking.[23]

Unlike the IFBFWC, which utilized expert advice, the IFU women's auxiliary emphasized homegrown women's leadership and intentionally declared its independence from any outside influences, such as the extension service. Their women's auxiliary, they claimed, was better aligned with farm women's interests because members designed and carried out most of the curriculum. One of their official purposes as an auxiliary was to "counteract the influence of [urban] Women's Clubs and other reactionary groups who are working for themselves and not for farmers." In May 1931 Lillie Blumgren, a member of the women's auxiliary, wrote that the extension service workers were the product of "eastern capitalists and politicians" who passed rural legislation at the suggestion of city clubwomen. She demanded that ladies of the IFU "develop a class consciousness" and a "real farm women's organization" that would truly fight for agriculture. Their claims of authenticity remained strong throughout the decade, and in 1934 the president, Hattie VerSteegh, of New Sharon, Iowa, reminded members to take pride in the fact that "our organization stands on its own. No outside interests are ever going to support it." But declarations of independence like this did not necessarily affect their activities or their ability as women to develop unique community-service activities, address political issues, or move into public spaces. Like the IFBFWC the IFU ladies' auxiliaries successfully delineated and legitimated female spaces within a major organization and politicized women's work with messages of mutual valuation of labor. Their experience, placed in comparison to the IFBF, shows that women from varied backgrounds found separate organizing strategies to be useful and successful in empowering women, even if these strategies did not promote gender equality or create new opportunities for women to work within the larger, male-led organization. Resources were key to building membership numbers, however, and the IFU struggled to secure meager financial resources and utilized recruiting systems that limited women's ability to act independently of their husbands and families.[24]

As the agricultural depression of the 1920s and 1930s took its toll on Iowa farm families, women's activities became even more important to farm organizations. At the onset of the Great Depression, between 1930 and 1933, IFBF membership slipped from 63,968 to 18,016 paid family memberships, reaching the lowest point in the history of the organization. Similarly, by 1933 the IFU had dropped to just 4,964 members, even as their ideas about cooperative marketing and price supports gained popularity with federal policy makers.

For those who were able to stay on the farm, women's activities with poultry, produce, and homespun goods were often an integral part of keeping the family farm solvent. Women's work not only reduced cash expenses but often provided a regular cash income. In some cases living conditions and social status actually improved for many rural women. Owing to their unique skills and ability to "make-do," they no longer believed themselves inferior to urban women. At the same time improved roads and rural electrification meant greater mobility and less time spent on daily chores, which in turn provided more frequent opportunities to participate in social activities.[25, 26]

Just as many women sustained the family farm, so too did they sustain farm organizations. Although IFBF membership numbers dropped sharply during the Great Depression, women still participated in extension programs and carried on with organization work for the farm bureau. For example, in 1929 Cherokee County agent Clarence Turner proposed that the farm bureau try to develop more female leaders since the women's programs "no doubt played an important part in keeping the membership at its present figure." Even in 1935, when the Cherokee County Farm Bureau had a membership of only 506 families, less than half of the average between 1921 and 1929, there were 116 female school district cooperators in 15 townships, 147 local leaders, and 1,286 women who attended demonstration meetings. Across the state in 1930, 187,737 people attended home-economics demonstration meetings, and in 1931, 10,169 women still served as local leaders to help filter the lessons to the local levels.[27]

By the mid-1930s it was this sustaining influence that gave women greater leverage in the state organization. Falling membership in the early 1930s meant fewer membership dues and less revenue from farm bureau commercial services, cooperatives, and insurance. By the middle of the decade, the IFBF was in a precarious financial position. In 1935 IFBF secretary-treasurer V. B. Hamilton began to reorganize the financial and administrative structures of the farm bureau. First, he created a resolutions committee, made up of ten men and one woman, to formulate policies. Second, the IFBF established an administrative board to manage the budget and business aspects of the organization. Of primary concern was uniform record keeping for the commercial services at the county level in order to prevent instances of "misappropriation" by trusted employees. Hamilton was also concerned about the future of the women's committee, and he found ready leadership in Ruth Sayre, who assumed leadership of the IFBFWC in 1937. For farm bureau women, centralization allowed for greater communication and would encourage growth over the next ten years.[28]

Sayre, a farmwoman from Ackworth, Iowa, and the mother of four children had married into agriculture in 1918; she had long been interested in reshaping the women's programs. In 1933, perhaps due to the dismal membership numbers, she persuaded Charles E. Hearst, president of the IFBF, to grant the chairperson of the women's committee a voting seat, rather than an ex-officio position, on the executive board. Rather than describing it as a significant event, however, Sayre believed it was inevitable. She later said, "In the pioneer tradition of Iowa, women were always partners on the farm. . . . Why shouldn't they be partners in the Farm Bureau? I was pleased when women were released from their water-tight compartment and allowed to become involved in the whole Farm Bureau program, because that was the Iowa way." By means of a voting seat, women gained an official voice on organizational matters and could begin to increase their influence at the state level.[29]

In her first year as IFBFWC chair, Sayre set out to centralize women's activities by developing township farm bureaus and improving the women's bureaucracy. She wanted to see the establishment of a farm bureau, along with a strong program for women, in every township in Iowa. Sayre admitted that she had "no training in business administration and learned it the hard way," but she was strongly influenced by civic-minded female relatives and a lifetime of involvement with female-led civic and religious groups. She encouraged women to look beyond their farmsteads; in 1937 she declared that it was "not enough today for a woman to cook and bake and sew." If women organized as community housekeepers who worked for the betterment of agriculture and rural life, they would "radiate a power and a strength that stretches far beyond our individual horizons." To this end Sayre called for greater systematic organization. Her policies required women to record the minutes of their meetings, receive training from extension agents and IFBF staff members, and follow broader trends in women's clubs across the country, in both rural and urban areas, to inject more political and social issues into their regular agendas.[30]

She worked toward these goals by fostering direct communication with members and providing readily available forms and reading materials specifically for women. During the late 1930s Roger Fleming, head of the IFBF's newly created research department, worked with Sayre to create six pamphlets for county leaders on the subjects of health, libraries, taxes, international trade, and rural roads. Through these booklets, which also provided questionnaires by which leaders might gauge their success, the women's committee could more evenly disseminate its programs. The approach appeared to work, at least in generating interest in women's clubs. In 1937, 726 townships reported active women's committees participating in state-led programs; after two years, the number grew to 1,010 (of 1,016 township farm bureaus). This period also saw growth in the main organization. Figures from January 1937 show a 44 percent increase in membership, from 30,830 in 1935 to nearly 45,000 individuals in 1936. Not only did the IFBF have the largest membership gain in the country, but the organization seemed to have recovered from the slipping numbers caused by hard economic times.[31]

Communication was the most essential element in consolidating the overall authority of the IFBF and introducing social and political issues into women's clubs. In 1937 the organization introduced an information department, which was responsible for producing a monthly magazine, the *Iowa Bureau Farmer*. The IFBF had been without a central publication since 1926, when it had discontinued its four-page monthly newspaper, the *Farm Bureau Messenger*. Between 1926 and 1937, the official publication of the American Farm Bureau Federation inserted state news pages to be circulated in specific areas. Yet by the end of the 1930s, members of the IFBF wanted a more local, sophisticated means of communication. Each month the new *Iowa Bureau Farmer* featured a column by the president, Francis Johnson, photographs, features on various leaders, and articles on the political and social activities of the IFBF. Since each family membership included a subscription, the magazine enjoyed a large circulation. In 1939 the *Iowa Bureau Farmer* had a circulation of 35,000. By 1942 circulation stood at 53,442, and in 1943 it had increased to nearly 64,000.[32]

The IFBFWC readily used this medium. Its main spokesperson was Bess Newcomer, a Moulton, Iowa, farm woman, who published a total of ninety-seven columns between 1937 and 1950, writing on a near-monthly basis after 1941. Her columns are especially useful in understanding how the IFBFWC attempted to inject a deeper political consciousness into women's activities. Newcomer was involved with the IFBF throughout those years, and her writings reflect women's attitudes at that time. Born on a farm west of Moulton, Iowa, in 1893, Newcomer was raised by her mother, a widow, who supported the family through the sale of milk products and eggs to a hotel in Moulton and managed the farm with the help of family and neighbors. In 1913 Newcomer graduated from Drake University in Des Moines, Iowa; she taught school for several years before returning to the farm in 1922 with her husband, Ralph Newcomer. Shortly thereafter, she became involved with the county farm bureau women's organization, and in 1937 Newcomer was elected as the Eighth District committee woman by the women of that district. She served in that capacity until 1948.[33]

During the 1930s and 1940s, Newcomer was not the only woman writer featured in the *Iowa Bureau Farmer*, but she was the first woman to be a regular columnist. She always chose her own content and pictures, and she claimed that the editors did not restrict content or length. Furthermore, Newcomer declared that her column was "not a column for women, as editors' surveys showed men [readers] in equal numbers." The majority of her columns were on the topic of membership and included commentary on the organization, leadership, and the obligations of members.

Newcomer's writings clearly illustrate that the IFBFWC had evolved during these years from a women's organization devoted to the home, family, and local issues into an organization concerned with major social, political, and agricultural issues. Early columns tended to focus on building membership, using tax dollars to create rural libraries, supporting the war effort, and advocating good citizenship, soil conservation, and responsible farming practices. In the immediate postwar years she devoted more attention to consolidating rural schools, promoting fair tax policies for farmers, sustaining the idea of the family farm, and maintaining leadership within the organization. The issues changed in their relevance, especially as technology and the modernization of the rural home affected how women functioned within the IFBF. Like Sayre, Newcomer advocated organization and centralization as keys to achieving the goals of the women's committee. She always supported Sayre as a leader with a natural ability to "gauge the processes of our growing or for our failure to grow."[34]

In addition to printed materials, Sayre and IFBFWC leaders promoted communication within the organization by creating opportunities for women to interact personally. During the summer of 1941, the committee established a state camp for farm women in order to bring county leaders together at a time other than the annual IFBF convention. The 173 women who attended the first camp slept in bunks at the Iowa state fairgrounds. During the weekend they spoke with IFBF leaders, toured the state offices, and selected programs on nutrition and libraries for the coming year. Newcomer overwhelmingly approved of the camp's proceedings and described how the women's visit to the state office gave them a new respect for the work of male leaders. Though the accommodations were rustic, members of the women's committee found it beneficial to hold a women's meeting entirely removed from IFBF conventions, and the summer conference became an annual event.[35]

In 1942, however, the IFBFWC introduced dramatic changes to enhance the summer conference to promote professionalism and comfort. They abandoned the bunk beds at the fairgrounds and moved the "camp" to the Hotel Kirkwood in Des Moines, where women "enjoyed meals they didn't plan and dishes they didn't wash." The hotel staff also welcomed the farm women because they were the only guests to make their own beds and leave the rooms spotless. In addition to training activists, then, the summer conferences would offer women an opportunity to enjoy affluent, urban living and remove themselves from their daily responsibilities.[36]

When the United States entered the war in December 1941, the IFBFWC capitalized on popular opinion that emphasized women's working roles in American society to further highlight their seriousness of purpose. Making good use of wartime rhetoric, in 1943 the women's committee handbook was titled "VICTORY in the Hands of Women," although it still addressed the standard programs on health, libraries, music, and organization, rather than mobilization on the home front. Promoting the new handbook in her column, Newcomer wrote that the title did not imply that women should dictate the course of war. Rather, farm women could ensure a speedy resolution if they spent "every energy to help produce more food and fiber and, at the same time, keep home and community on an even keel." The following year, at the 1944 summer conference, more than two hundred women from ninety counties met with IFBF leaders to ask how they could best contribute to the overall organization. They concluded that women's place in the organization was "anywhere" because they had "stepped in the shoes still warm from the feet of their war-bound men."[37]

In 1944 Newcomer also observed that many state, county, and township leaders had left the organization to join the armed forces, while others stopped participating due to labor shortages on their farms. Regular IFBF meetings had been "curtailed and formal leadership training shelved for the duration." Now armed with information about economic and social policy, only the IFBFWC could fill the leadership void. Daunting as they were, Newcomer's ideas found a ready audience in women in township clubs who were eager to discuss urgent wartime concerns about production, inflation, rationing, and long-term economic planning. With mechanisms for communication and organization in place, the IFBFWC readily fostered this interest and encouraged women to take action on agricultural and economic issues out of patriotic duty.[38]

Newcomer's columns framed wartime problems as everyday problems that women encountered on their own farms, most notably rationing of canning sugar, shortages of vital supplies, fears for their young sons in the military, and labor shortages. Although farm workers received draft exemptions, young people still left the countryside in droves for military service and high-paying defense jobs. In January 1943 Newcomer criticized federal policies that set production goals but did little to encourage laborers to stay on the farm. She cited examples from across the country where crops had withered in the fields and animals suffered because there were not enough hands to do the work. Newcomer believed that part of the problem could be alleviated if "farm boys" were given greater recognition for their service in the form of an emblem to wear for serving in an "essential war capacity." Yet such recognition was little consolation in a wartime system where "free enterprise is destroyed because the government determines the storage, distribution, and the price of our products." In March 1943 she echoed those sentiments. "We know too well," she wrote, "no amount of prodding (or subsidies either) is going to get the job done if farmers are deprived of the very means of increased production—enough help, enough machinery, fair prices, decent health, and education."[39]

By connecting labor shortages with poor standards of living on the farm, Newcomer successfully linked women's concerns with the home to federal agricultural policy, further encouraging women to pursue such topics in their regular meetings. She also offered practical advice on how they could personally influence business decisions on their farms. Newcomer believed that, while farmers were willing to do their share in the war effort, they should be wary of increased production goals that could lead to economic disaster during peacetime. As early as 1942, she asked farm families to plan ahead carefully and, through the IFBF, lobby for an effective postwar farm policy in order to avoid an economic depression like the one that followed World War I. In July 1944 she called on farm bureau members to "lead out in after-war planning" and work for a clearly defined postwar plan from the government. She asked, "Why does our government expect us to yearly invest in heavy capital and much labor in food production yet have so little to say in sketching the blueprints of the program?" Then, in October 1944, Newcomer warned that if history should repeat itself and the war should end without a favorable agricultural policy in place, farm families would suffer. To avoid calamity, farm families needed to organize and bring greater attention to their problems. "It is a kind of agricultural suicide," she wrote, "to ignore or underestimate the securing of prestige that should be accorded farmers and their contribution to America in war or peace."[40]

In 1945 the IFBFWC canceled the summer conference in light of wartime shortages and opted instead to hold a series of nine smaller conferences in each district, attended by district committee women and extension leaders who "rode the circuit." A total of 450 farm women attended the nine conferences, where women's committee leaders found strong opinions about women's place not only in the IFBF but also in the postwar world. At one conference in Chariton, Iowa, the women concluded that they had "more to say than they used to have" on issues related to agriculture, legislation, and conservation. They declared that "women are partly to blame for low standards in farm homes of Iowa, with their silly martyr-complex making them feel self-righteous using 'Gay 90's' equipment when the farm is highly mechanized." To this Newcomer added that "*thinking* does not have gender or age," and women's activism was essential in maintaining price structure and high incomes.[41]

Iowa Farm Bureau women acted with new vigor in the immediate postwar years. In November 1945 Newcomer wrote that this was the time for increased action and that no farm family could afford to "sit sunning itself in the false glow of a wartime prosperity." She challenged the leadership to reach out to farm families and to plan programs with enough depth that they "become part of [farm families] and their bright future." Their energy may be attributed to their wartime experiences combined with a tighter organization under Sayre's leadership. By 1945 the summer conference had become a regular event, as had separate meetings for women at the IFBF annual conferences in Des Moines. At the IFBF annual conference in 1945, the women's committee chose to focus on programs concerning leadership, world relations, public relations, 4-H clubs, health, and education. Such programs were hardly new to the IFBFWC, but the prosperity of the war years, combined with fears of a postwar depression, prompted them to step up demands for improved standards of living in rural areas.[42]

The IFBFWC was not unique in its use of wartime concerns to enhance its mission and purpose. The women's auxiliary of the IFU also strengthened its central leadership and justified women's further participation in politics and policy as a wartime necessity. By the late 1930s, it had also begun issuing official "year books," to highlight the accomplishments of state leaders and to dispense advice for administering local programs. After the war auxiliary leaders strongly encouraged members to learn more about international relations, with particular attention to agriculture and famine in war-torn countries. In some areas women's commitments to social and political issues allowed them to transcend long-standing boundaries in their local areas. In 1946 the women's auxiliary of the Clinton County Farmers Union announced the formation of a new coalition with the Clinton County Farm Bureau, the Parent-Teachers Association, the Labor Congress, the Federation of Women's Clubs, and several other civic and educational groups. The new coalition, the Federation of Clinton County, represented an attempt to "conserve human resources," coordinate efforts, and enhance public services. Claiming to be the first coalition of its kind in the state, and optimistic that other auxiliaries would follow suit, IFU Auxiliary President Pearl Green hoped "a lot of good would be a result."[43]

Building and maintaining an active membership consumed the IFBF and the IFBFWC between 1945 and 1950. This was the essential element to achieving the women's goals, as civic improvement usually required local consensus and large numbers of volunteers. Membership grew considerably during the war, rising from 40,590 in 1940 to 90,051 in 1945. In 1946 the IFBF set a state quota at 100,000 families, which it achieved by April of that year. In 1947, when membership reached nearly 122,000, the IFBF experienced the largest annual increase in membership since its founding. Radio broadcasts, as well as better roads and automobiles, allowed farm bureau women to initiate more extensive membership drives. They found families ready and willing to join. Fears of a postwar depression may have prompted many farm families to become politically active, but membership growth was more likely a matter of economics. Farm income grew nearly 400 percent during the war, coming closer than ever to meeting the average U.S. income. More farm families could afford to indulge in leisure activities — as well as farm bureau products, like insurance (a product that included IFBF membership).[44]

Newcomer asserted that the time had come for women to step out of their homes and apply what they had learned in more public spaces. Rapid growth did not necessarily translate into action, and in April 1946 she wrote, "We should be concerned that our organization be fine-textured as well as big." Local women's clubs that failed to develop an action plan in keeping with the designs of state leaders were merely social clubs of little use to the IFBF, according to Newcomer. She warned, "We cannot afford to let this rich gift of voluntary leadership gather dust on the shelf." Although acknowledging that women faced limitations within the IFBF, Newcomer declared, "In short, WE BELONG." She called for increasing women's involvement and influence within the greater organization. Interestingly, though, she did not frame her argument in terms of gendered discrimination. Political and economic instability—outside forces set upon men and women on the farm—were the primary culprits. Farm women shared in the work of their husbands and therefore in the business of farming. Improved conditions for farm families did not entail challenging husbands' authority or male authority within an organization but joining forces to change the social, political, and economic systems that depressed commodity prices.[45]

Historian Susan Lynn has suggested that within women's organizations more generally, the maternalistic rhetoric of social feminisms changed dramatically after 1945. During the 1920s women emphasized social welfare, protective legislation, and other "municipal housekeeping" measures. After 1945 as the U.S. confronted Cold War realities and engaged with questions of international relations, women increasingly turned to justice, governance, and civil liberties. The IFBFWC and the women's auxiliary of the IFU certainly reflected this trend, as state leaders of both groups developed new organizing strategies that empowered women to politicize their daily labors and relate social, political, and economic issues to their own experiences. By bringing women together in female spaces to talk, share work, and engage in various projects, farm women's organizations offered opportunities for personal transformations, the development of women's leadership, and a rhetoric that justified women's involvement to indifferent male leaders and hesitant husbands. After 1945 as the Midwest entered a period of transition and depopulation, female spaces within organizations often provided women with a means of sustaining social networks.[46]

Organizations like the IFBFWC and the IFU women's auxiliary set important precedents for farm women's activism that continued to shape women's perceptions after 1945. It was a widely shared belief that women were best organized separately or, if integrated into a major organization, given charge of educational and social activities. Both men and women placed significant emphasis on the supportive roles of women, especially inducing men's participation. Typical of the rhetoric designed to encourage women, in the March 1942 issue of the *Iowa Union Farmer*, IFU member Vera McCrea wrote:

> *Back of practically every man who speaks up in a meeting stands a woman who has encouraged him to take an active part in the affairs of his organization. . . . Back of practically every member who does not attend meetings, or who, if he does, do so perfunctorily and without interest, stands a woman who says: "Oh, what's the use? Why bother?"*

This often promoted idea suggests that women were only supposed to apply the knowledge they gained to enhance their roles as helpmeets and dependent wives. They bettered farm families not through direct interaction with policy makers but by encouraging their husbands to do so.[47]

The social feminisms that shaped these strategies were rife with limitations that inhibited women from taking on even more vocal roles in broader organizations, but it is important to note that the transformative leadership strategies that politicized everyday work roles proved useful for women who lived in a period of rapid social and economic change. The rhetoric of women's organizations was intended to elevate women's self-worth, and they truly believed that the information gained through meetings allowed them to be more effective wives and mothers. Most importantly, clubs provided women with spaces to preserve neighborhoods and social networks. As agriculture became a more specialized profession, however, new organizations in the postwar period followed suit. Women with specific interests sought new outlets after 1945 and often struggled to renegotiate and redefine their roles within the gendered boundaries firmly established in the first half of the century. Subsequent chapters explore how the varied political, social, and economic circumstances of farm women, as well as the nature of their interactions with men, broader historical forces, and sweeping changes in agricultural production fostered the development of new strategies for entry into the public arena of agricultural politics and activism.

CHAPTER TWO

As Natural a Process

Women's Leadership in Township Farm Bureau Clubs

IN 1945 NELL M. FORSYTH of Muscatine County, Iowa, penned the twenty-five-year history of the Cedar Valley Community Club, a township homemaker's club affiliated with the Iowa Farm Bureau Federation and the Iowa State Cooperative Extension Service. Forsyth, a founding member of the local club, lauded the efforts of state IFBF leaders and county home economists but noted that after more than two decades seasoned club members had tired of uninspired extension projects that produced "cheese that soon molded, hats that were never worn, and concocted meals that the hired help would never eat." By 1945 club members saw themselves as community leaders who could "help solve some of the most perplexing questions, both local and national." The women of Cedar Valley "needed no outside speaker to construct an interesting meeting" and no longer required direct guidance from state leaders. Forsyth concluded, "'Growing up' is as natural a process for a Club as well as an individual."[1]

The story of the Cedar Valley Community Club would have been familiar to farm women across Iowa since those who joined home demonstration clubs in the 1920s as young homemakers had matured into veteran clubwomen. Their experiences demonstrate how the social feminisms discussed in the previous chapter played out in the everyday lives of women involved with club activities, highlighting a pivotal time when women were required to take on more leadership duties. During and immediately after the Second World War, farm families enjoyed unprecedented economic prosperity, farm bureau membership reached record numbers, and women's clubs thrived. Nationally, the AFBF reached more than 1.5 million families, but more than half of its membership was concentrated in the upper Midwest. In 1955 Iowa still led the nation in the number of farm bureau memberships, with 142,819 families, who continued to serve as a testing ground for strategies and policies. The AFBF maintained its influence in Washington, D.C., and by the mid-1950s it was said to represent "one-third of the farmers who produce 80 percent of the total value of farm commodities sold." In the interests of well-established farmers, the organization worked toward policies to decentralize agencies such as the USDA, the Soil Conservation Service, and the Farm Credit Administration, and it put more emphasis on agricultural policy at the state and local levels.[2]

The same was true with the grass roots, and after nearly three decades of strong state-centered programming through the nine-member Iowa Farm Bureau women's committee (IFBFWC), club activities in the postwar period were characterized by a greater focus on local leadership. The IFBFWC supported this trend as shifting rural demographics required new, more flexible programs to address the evolving needs of farm families and the farm bureau ended its official association with the extension service. Nonetheless, state leaders maintained high standards and advised local clubwomen to engage in activities related to politics, agricultural policy, safety, rural health, law and order, international relations, and the preservation of democracy. By 1958 the IFBFWC declared that women's clubs had moved beyond simple home demonstration activities, graduating from "'chief cook and bottle washer' status into full fledged study and action groups which tackle problems ranging from world trade to school finance."[3]

Members of township farm bureau clubs incorporated these messages into their local strategies by taking on more responsibility for leadership and township programming. They became increasingly selective, setting aside lofty political goals in favor of activities centered on their neighborhoods, social events, and new trends in homemaking. As they encountered unprecedented levels of affluence, they translated a conscious approach to consumerism, femininity, and leisure into political action. Club membership no longer helped women to learn to "make do" with less; rather it was an indicator of one's place in the new affluent society, a role that required a new skill set and responsible decision making. Member rejection of IFBFWC directives was not an indicator of resistance to IFBFWC programs but rather illustrated the manifestation of social feminisms in the countryside. Local women's choices clearly demonstrated that they readily bought into lofty rhetoric but tailored social feminisms to their practical limitations and unique situations.

For active female farm bureau members with years of experience, membership not only provided an indicator of social status and power within a community, it also allowed some degree of personal empowerment and independence. Members believed themselves qualified to identify appropriate activities, even if their programs deviated significantly from those carefully designed by state and county leaders. Members of township clubs readily adopted the rhetoric of the IFBFWC that identified women as sophisticated activists whose clubs were essential to the overall mission of the farm bureau—although they typically viewed club meetings as opportunities for leisure and respite from their daily labors. Membership and leadership roles in local clubs were often fluid and flexible, reflecting gendered divisions of labor, shared work, and women's idealized roles as homemakers. In the immediate postwar period, when technology drastically changed the nature of agricultural production and rural depopulation reduced their overall numbers, township clubs connected women to larger county, state, and national networks and offered women spaces in which to cope with changes in agriculture and rural life.

The roots of social feminisms can be traced to the women's movements of the late nineteenth and early twentieth century, but such rhetoric maintained its power well after the Second World War and appeared in both urban and rural settings. In her study of the National Federation of Republican Women, for example, historian Catherine Rymph found that after 1945 women increasingly focused on the "day-to-day work that received little glory but was critical to sustaining and building the party." Rather than questioning male leaders, who often disregarded female participation, Republican women made themselves indispensable by feminizing such tasks as canvassing, voter registration, and organizing of small-scale political events. By emphasizing domesticity, "hospitality and neighborliness," Republican women connected "partisan politics to the everyday lives of citizens in their communities." This is similar to farm bureau women's clubs, whose members asserted that activism could take place while carrying out one's daily activities. In 1954, when organizing a membership drive in Palo Alto County, county publicity chairperson Olga Rouse informed members that they did not need to go door to door or talk with unknown persons but rather should "create interest in the organization by personal contact with their neighbors. We can invite our neighbor women to meetings and Farm Bureau activities. We can talk to them about the advantages of belonging."[4]

The empowering nature of social feminism can be difficult to detect, especially in the rural context, because women celebrated feminine ideals and rarely challenged men's authority. The strength and persistence of farm women's clubs, however, clearly demonstrate the pervasiveness of social feminisms and their appeal to local club members. The conception of women as activists and vital farm bureau members was not limited to state leaders, and by the late 1940s social feminisms clearly informed members of farm bureau township women's clubs who desired greater local control over club activities. In 1948, when the women of Freedom Township in Palo Alto

County celebrated the club's twenty-fifth anniversary, they wrote and performed a play that not only recounted key developments but concluded by looking forward to a bright future in which each woman of Freedom Township would find "new paths of usefulness, not only in her community, but in her county, her country, and her world." The club's future development depended not on challenging patriarchy or seeking the integration of women into the IFBF but in continuing to develop leadership in an all-female club.[5]

Social feminisms provided the language and context for women to assert their preferences at the local level, but changing rural demographics after 1945, as well as new policies within the IFBF and the extension service, also necessitated alternative strategies in rural women's activism. Maintaining rural communities in which women shared work, friendship, and common ideals became especially important in the postwar period, as more families moved away from the farm and informal neighborhood networks became less stable. Between 1950 and 1970 the average farm size in Iowa increased from 160 acres to nearly 250 acres, while the number of farms declined from 107,183 to 72,257. In 1950, 29.9 percent of Iowans lived on farms, but by 1960 this number had dropped to 24 percent, and in 1970 it fell again to 18.1 percent. By 1980 just 13.4 percent of Iowans lived on farms. Although rural depopulation was a nationwide trend, these changes were especially unsettling in states known for their agricultural productivity.[6]

Further complicating the situation was the fact that by 1950 farm women lived in a vastly different world from their predecessors of the 1920s. In 1950, 90.1 percent of Iowa farms had electricity, compared to just 21 percent in 1930. Electricity allowed farm families to invest in household equipment, and by 1960, 87.4 percent of Iowa farm homes had piped water, 96.3 percent had a washing machine, 64.3 had a freezer, 91.3 had a telephone, and 90.6 had a television. Moreover, declining prices for food and consumer goods made it more cost effective for women to purchase, rather than to make, what they needed for their families. Modern conveniences and the consumption of consumer goods required women to learn new homemaking techniques and to learn about agribusiness or to earn a cash income. More women took over the business aspects of their family farming operations, while in 1960 nearly 20 percent of farm women over fourteen years of age held jobs off the farm, compared to just 13 percent in 1950. As their labor evolved, fewer younger women chose to become involved in homemakers clubs, often citing a lack of time or an interest in other activities. By 1957 one national survey of extension service clubwomen found that only 11 percent of the 11,500 women surveyed were under the age of thirty. The majority of extension service clubwomen across the nation, 51 percent, were between thirty and forty-nine, while the remaining 38 percent were over the age of fifty.[7]

Unfortunately income level and social class cannot be easily measured as contributing factors to the shift toward local leadership. Although some scholars have alluded to the fact that farm bureau members tended to come from more prosperous farms, and perhaps preferred exclusive membership, sufficient data has not been compiled to draw broad, definitive conclusions. In her study of the American Farm Bureau Federation, historian Nancy K. Berlage also hesitated to make "reductionist assumptions" about the economic backgrounds of farm bureau members, citing the fact that "county membership lists are often incomplete or non-existent." Some evidence suggests that women involved in the farm bureau and the extension programs in the postwar period aspired to standards of living akin to urban and suburban middle-class families. In 1955 Marshall County home economist Greta W. Bowers reported a rapid growth in the number of families with conveniences such as freezers, televisions, decorative fireplaces, and musical instruments. As rural homes became "increasingly more modern," Bowers found more women demanding lessons in contemporary interior design and the selection of "accessories that add beauty." She predicted that as farm families enjoyed more material comforts, the rural woman, like her urban counterpart, would have "more time to devote to her church and other civic affairs." Middle-class aspirations are further reflected in the photographs pasted into the scrapbooks of the Freedom Township Women's Club, in Palo Alto County: these photographs reveal that by the late 1940s women attended meetings with professionally styled hair, in fashionable dresses, and with newly remodeled homes as their backdrop. Their meetings were clearly opportunities to engage in leisure activities and to exhibit their tastes as consumers, and they may have inadvertently limited membership to those with the means to participate.[8]

The records of the IFBFWC, as well as those of township clubs, are silent on the issue of social class and economic difference. Instead, age was their primary concern. Although township clubs celebrated founding members and possible second- or even third-generation members, the overall increasing age of club members was a more frequent factor than any other when discussing programming changes, the recruitment of new members, and by the late 1960s, reasons for declining membership. The extension service and the IFBFWC began to recognize the varied needs of individuals at various life stages, and they struggled to define the evolving needs of modern farm families. As they adapted programs to help rural residents adjust to depopu-

lation, mechanization, electrification, and the rising costs of agricultural production, these organizations also acknowledged that women often worked
as farm laborers and bookkeepers. The extension service began offering instruction through the Farm and Home Development program, designed to
assist married couples with making decisions about production, implements,
and marketing. Beginning in the 1940s, the IFBF also began offering programs for "young marrieds," in which couples under thirty addressed such
issues as landownership versus tenancy, buying and leasing machinery, organizational participation, the importance of rural communities, and off-farm
work. The IFBFWC strongly supported women's participation in groups for
"young marrieds," hoping that the younger women would later become involved in women's clubs, although by the late 1960s this expectation had not
materialized and membership numbers experienced a rapid decline.[9]

In addition to the evolving needs of farm families, the major organizational change that led the IFBFWC to focus on local developments occurred
in 1954, when state and federal policy ordered the extension service to end
its relationship with the farm bureau. By 1951 the IFBF provided more than
34 percent of the annual budget for the extension service, which seemed
to many politicians and policy makers a conflict of interest, given the farm
bureau's strong political presence. As a result of the separation, county
and township clubwomen could no longer rely on the assistance of extension home economists for planning activities. For example, the women of
Freedom Township in Palo Alto County depended on their county home
economist, Signora McFadden, to occasionally attend meetings and give
lessons, bring members up to date about farm bureau and extension programs, and provide informational materials for the next year's work. Each
month, McFadden also sent postcards to remind members about upcoming
meetings and provided announcements to local newspapers. McFadden
ended this practice in 1955, requiring the township club to assume responsibility for planning, for procuring farm bureau materials from the state and
county offices, and for publicity. County farm bureaus throughout the state
continued informal relationships with extension personnel, but in a speech
at the 1955 state conference, IFBFWC chairperson Christine Inman urged
county and township clubs to cultivate new farm bureau leaders. In light
of the separation, she said, "we have a tremendous responsibility to make
policy and to carry it out. We need leadership. We must develop people dedicated to carrying out our plans."[10]

Over the next several years, the *Iowa Farm Bureau Spokesman* featured
articles that lauded the efforts of county and township women's clubs to

carry on despite the absence of county home economists. Intended to inspire members of women's clubs, one 1957 article told the story of Buchanan County, which lost its county home economist in August 1956. As the most experienced female leaders in the county, farm bureau women instituted their own programs under the guidance of Mrs. Raymond Kirsch, the county women's committee chairperson. Working with women in twelve townships, farm bureau women oversaw the completion of more than 300 projects, including copper embossing, Swedish embroidery, home landscaping, and even a survey of rural mail delivery routes. The IFBFWC clearly expected women to assess the needs of families in the county and to organize activities accordingly, although such expectations could prove frustrating in counties that maintained extension home economists. In her 1959 annual report, Linn County home economist Grace B. Drenkhahn chronicled her efforts to organize "cooperative organizational teas" for women on the extension service's Family Living Committee and the county farm bureau women's committee. But Drenkhahn found that the farm bureau women simply assumed responsibility for planning the program, often subordinating the desires of the Family Living Committee.[11]

State leaders on the IFBFWC and local leaders at the county and township level agreed on the necessity for strong local leadership, but their visions of how this would take shape differed significantly. Concerned about the declining numbers of young farm women in their clubs, county and township leaders asked for more programs "directed to helping families acquire mental rather than physical or manual skills." Younger farm women were better educated, more likely to have urban backgrounds, and more likely to have had formal training in home economics. Similarly, seasoned members with honed domestic skills whose children were either in school or out of the home sought activities that offered intellectual and social respite from the constant demands of farming. In response, the IFBFWC encouraged women to develop new interests outside of agricultural production and home economics and to see their township meetings as forums for discussion about politics and social policy. At the 1952 IFBFWC summer conference, Marie Garnjobst, the third district committee person from Clay County, spoke about the need to alter existing programs and told county leaders, "We must evaluate activities and determine whether or not the program helps our women to become more intelligent, more effective, and more responsible as citizens." Good leaders who "sought progress" at the county level, Garnjobst stated, were those who encouraged women to adopt the state plans and asked women to think beyond the farm and home.[12]

The IFBFWC continued to utilize the strategies set in motion during the 1930s under the leadership of Ruth Sayre and sought to ensure that serious discussion of social and political issues took place in local meetings by producing handbooks for local leaders, designing informational courses to be taught at the county level, and encouraging women to use roll calls with political themes such as "freedoms I would not want to lose." The IFBFWC enjoyed tremendous resources rarely seen by farm women's organizations. In 1953 the women's committee operated on a budget of nearly $30,000, more than twice what the farm bureau allocated to the legislative, research, or youth departments. This budget allowed the state to distribute materials at no cost to members, and as a result state leaders required local clubs to appoint chairpersons to study specific issues and then report back to the other members at their monthly meetings. For example, in September 1956, at the first meeting of the Franklin Township Women's Club in O'Brien County, members elected chairpersons to study "freedom in the United States," "the promotion of agricultural commodities," "safety on the farm," "rural mail delivery," "conservation," "schools," and "rural health." During their one-year term, these women read extension and farm bureau materials on their assigned topics, and they clipped articles from newspapers or magazines to share at meetings. They typically provided enough information for women to become aware of various issues but not necessarily enough to explore problems in great detail. Studying "international issues," for example, might include brief lessons about geography, instruction on starting a correspondence with an international pen pal, or a presentation by a local student recently returned from a study-abroad experience. For many of the members, though, meetings were their primary source for news and discussion of these issues. Occasionally, members also developed community improvement projects based on what they learned. In 1948 the women of the Freedom Township Women's Club in Palo Alto County studied public health, then cooperated with other civic and political groups to form the Palo Alto County Health Council. With a member of the women's club at its head, the new health council sought a tax levy to support a county health nurse.[13]

In order to measure the success of IFBFWC programs and ensure that women effectively utilized materials distributed by state leaders, townships clubs submitted annual reports and "score sheets." Beginning in the 1950s, the IFBFWC collected township "score sheets" at county leadership workshops. Township clubs could earn points in a variety of areas: for members of township clubs who attended county meetings, for the number of meetings held, for providing evidence that "a Farm Bureau lesson or emphasis was presented at each township meeting," for having their photographs published in the *Iowa Farm Bureau Spokesman*, for donating to the farm bureau teacher scholarship fund, for having chairmen to cover various issues, and for their unique township and county activities. The club's total scores were pitted against those of other townships, and townships with high scores were recognized at the annual conferences. County leaders were also required to host annual events, such as Rural Women's Day or Family Night, where township clubs showcased their work through displays, skits, and presentations.[14]

In addition to publications, forms, and events, state leaders also provided constant encouragement and support for local leaders. They believed themselves to be effective leaders and role models for Iowa's farm women simply by offering themselves as examples of effective activists. They often wrote reflections on their own experiences in the columns of the *Iowa Bureau Farmer*. For example, each year small numbers of women with resources and supportive husbands were able to participate in trips to Washington, D.C., where they met with politicians and policy makers. In 1958, when the IFBFWC sent sixty-seven farm women to meet with Congressional representatives, they told Congressman Fred Schwengel:

> *Most of the tractors on our farms are "lady broke." We know what is being planted in the northeast "40" this spring and we know whether or not the new alfalfa seeding came through the winter. We know what it is to be tired and discouraged and the next thing to broke, but we also know the thrill of being close to nature; of working with animals; of producing with our own hands.*

These women identified as farmers with extensive work experience, justifying their presence in the nation's capital by explaining how they were the not ordinary, leisured women celebrated in popular culture. Their testimony was as much a message to Congressman Schwengel as it was to Iowa's farm bureau women that their work had definite political and economic dimensions.[15]

These women also offered more concrete advice to county and township clubs on how they could better fulfill the IFBFWC's vision. At the 1952 IFBFWC summer conference, when state leaders selected annual programs, the ninth district committeeperson, Mrs. Glynn Warren, urged county leaders to raise standards for "Rural Women's Day" by focusing more on the quality of the projects and presentations and less on the social aspects of the event. She said, "Rural Women's Day is a time to show appreciation for the leaders and workers who have contributed to this program through-out the year—but, we should not spend all day pinning on corsages." War-ren stated that "Rural Women's Day" needed to provide "a clear picture of the year's work in Extension Education and Farm Bureau programs" so that state leaders could evaluate the effectiveness of their efforts.[16]

IFBFWC leaders balanced this concrete advice with more abstract prom-ises of personal and intellectual fulfillment. By engaging in their programs, township women could become "modern" farm women who not only worked to better agriculture but who also embraced the urban ideals of consum-erism, femininity, and leisure. Club membership no longer helped women learn to "make do" with less; rather, it was an indicator of leisure time and of one's place in the new affluent society. As the desire for leisure activities and modern conveniences grew, comments about personal appearance, clothing, and style appeared regularly on the women's page of the *Spokesman*, with ad-vice on how to follow the latest trends. Whereas former IFBFWC chairper-son Ruth Sayre, who served during the 1930s and 1940s, had been revered for her economical clothing and worn winter coat, in 1961 IFBFWC chairperson Alice Van Wert declared, "The American farm wife today is as hat-conscious and familiar with the latest in hair-dos and clothes as any woman in the city." In other words, farm women could move away from iconic images of farmer's wives as provincial drudges and instead present themselves as sophisticated, worldly women.[17]

Generally, women in county and township clubs responded to the IFBFWC's rhetoric and attempted to integrate more discussions about agri-cultural activism, politics, and social policy into their programs. Letters from women to the editor of the *Iowa Farm Bureau Spokesman* demonstrate that they were very aware of the political and social issues facing rural America, and they wanted to be part of the solution. Throughout the 1950s and 1960s, however, the IFBFWC provided little financial or logistical support for town-ship clubs to actually apply information as community activists. For ex-ample, the IFBFWC encouraged women to study commodity promotion in order to understand agricultural markets. Yet rather than studying or orga-nizing promotional activities in urban areas to educate consumers, town-ship clubs primarily promoted commodities to themselves and other farm families. In 1958, for example, the Freedom Township Women's Club in Palo Alto County translated commodity promotion into the distribution to club members of paper napkins from the local Mallard Creamery that "pictured and encouraged the use of meat, milk, butter, and eggs in the home." They also studied pamphlets printed by the Iowa State Dairy Commission and used these to write an article in the *Iowa Farm Bureau Spokesman* to point out "the highly beneficial qualities of animal proteins in the daily consumption of these products." Likewise, in March 1960 the Highland Do-Better Club in O'Brien County participated with a local pork producers association in a Lard Promotion Day. The women sponsored a "Bake It With Lard" contest, hoping to raise some money from the sale of winning entries. But the contestants, judges, and spectators were all from the local farming community and likely understood the importance of this aspect of marketing.[18]

Women in township clubs preferred community activities that offered tangible results and that did not require them to challenge the established conventions in their rural communities pertaining to politics and gender. In the fall of 1952, when confronted with rural school consolidation, the women of Freedom Township in Palo Alto County became concerned that when the township school closed, residents would be left without a central meeting area or a place to vote in local elections. They established a committee to look into the issue, but rather than pursuing the matter through official political channels, they began informal discussions with neighborhood landowners and members of the school board to secure use of the facility. In April 1953 they purchased the building and declared the school to be "ours." They began budgeting for property taxes and physical improvements. Throughout the summer they painted the walls, sewed curtains, and installed an electric stove, using volunteer labor and donated materials. Over the next decade they held their monthly meetings, as well as special events, pancake suppers, and 4-H recognition days, at their Freedom Township Hall. They fulfilled a need in the community by preserving a local meeting place and did so by utilizing social networks, employing the assistance of familiar residents, and tapping local resources.[19]

When planning monthly meetings, most township clubs preferred inexpensive activities that required minimal planning and combined practical advice with opportunities for social interaction. This allowed club members to express personal preferences and desires to maintain a strong club, since women would only attend meetings that seemed relevant to their daily lives. Historian Mary Neth argues that farm bureaus in Midwestern states tended to have "less active participation, less social attachment, and less commitment from farmers than other groups" and that membership did not necessarily imply a "full acceptance of [the farm bureau's] agricultural policies. Attendance records from the late 1950s and early 1960s support this conclusion and reveal that most women did not attend meetings on a regular basis. For example, between October 1959 and June 1960 of the twenty-one mem-

Painting a ceiling in the 1950s. Freedom Township Women's Club Records, Iowa Women's Archives, University of Iowa Libraries.

bers listed on the roll for the Franklin Township Women's Club in O'Brien County, only one had perfect attendance. Ten missed between three and five meetings, while seven missed more than six meetings. The women who tended to miss meetings, however, participated in major events such as pot-luck suppers, achievement days, and community events. Franklin Township was not unique, and similar patterns appeared consistently in membership rolls for several townships, suggesting that women's membership allowed them to remain connected to the local community and to friends, rather than serving as an expression of loyalty to the IFBF.[20]

IFBFWC leaders understood that local planning was essential in securing and keeping members, but even with score sheets and clearly written hand-books they could not control the activities and projects selected by town-ship clubs. Deviations from state—and even county—plans were common and are evident in the 1959 state, county, and township handbooks utilized by the women of Freedom Township in Palo Alto County. The 1959 IFBFWC handbook outlined discussion subjects such as legislation, conservation and water rights, commodities, world trade, and marketing and included an introduction from the state chairpersons that advised, "The finest program of work and the most comprehensive reference book are of no value unless they are used." In contrast, the Palo Alto County Farm Bureau women's committee provided handbooks to each township that only required clubs to hold meetings with informational sessions on nutrition, cooking methods, and first aid. Handwritten notes in the county handbook, however, reveal that when the Freedom Township Women's Club held the meeting devoted to first aid, it entailed only a brief presentation. The meeting was actually an all-day event featuring a covered-dish luncheon, with a plan to "do fancy work during the day." Other meetings that year allowed for short presentations by the chairpersons elected to study various issues, but they typically focused on more social activities. The members shared book reviews, remodeled their Township Hall, planned a township family picnic, hosted a Mother's Day tea, held "achievement days" for boys' and girls' 4-H clubs, organized a family Christmas party, and studied such topics as table settings, gift wrapping, and "Iowa."[21]

The women of Freedom Township demonstrated an awareness of the programs designed by the IFBFWC but deliberately chose not to follow them. In 1960, when the IFBFWC asked county and township women to study civil defense, the cover of the Palo Alto county handbooks featured a pencil sketch of a mushroom cloud, and the Freedom Township Women's Club organized a special civil-defense committee. The committee could easily have followed the twelve monthly programs designed by the IFBFWC for local clubs, which included "What is civil defense mobilization?" and "What is radioactive fallout and how can we protect ourselves?" The IFBFWC also suggested that members take a Red Cross first-aid training course, learn about home fallout shelters, watch films on civil defense, learn about atomic science, and construct home first-aid kits. The IFBFWC handbook provided lists of films and materials that women needed only to send for if they wanted to use them: participating in the program would not have incurred a major expense for any club. Yet, other than a short presentation by the club civil-defense chairperson at one meeting, the women of Freedom Township had no programs that aligned with the goals of the IFBFWC. In addition to their annual social events, such as the family picnic, 4-H achievement day, and the Christmas party, the members elected to study lessons titled, "Ways with Cheese," "Understanding Our Children and Grandchildren," "How to Save Time in the Kitchen," "Laundry Problems," and "Landscaping your Home."[22]

The remote location of Palo Alto County, in the north-central region of the state, far from urban centers, might explain why the women of Freedom Township neglected to study civil defense, but this also occurred in Scott County. There, farm families lived in close proximity to the cities of Davenport, Iowa, and Rock Island, Illinois, home to a major military hub, the Rock Island Arsenal. The members of the Cleona Township Women's Club in Scott County selected programs such as "Know your retail stores," "Better grooming," "Figure flattery," and "Research on food nutrients." They also sewed carpet squares for disabled children, hosted an organizational tea, and in December, rather than taking a quiz on civil defense as suggested by state leaders, they hosted a township Christmas party. Only twice did they comply with the state programs: in May 1960 they took a tour of the nearby Rock Island Arsenal to view a mobile hospital, and in October they assembled home first-aid kits. Otherwise, the women of Cleona Township appeared to have few reservations about selecting programs that differed significantly from those recommended by the IFBFWC, and their program selection was typical of women's clubs across the state.[23]

Although women in township clubs neglected state programs, their choices were not necessarily expressions of resistance to farm bureau policies or a rejection of the IFBFWC. For example, the members of Freedom Township Women's Club demonstrated loyalty to the IFBF in 1948, when they sponsored a year-long membership drive, more than doubled their membership, from 44 to 119, and sold new members on the benefits of farm bureau membership. Throughout the late 1940s and 1950s they also participated in the annual Rural Women's Day events by providing refreshments, music, entertainment, and informative displays. For several years, even when they did not follow state programs, Freedom Township won awards for its activities at Rural Women's Day, usually for its record of sending women to county leadership training workshops and for the number of members elected to county leadership positions.[24]

Had it disagreed with IFBF policies or simply found its association to be of little value, any women's club could have ended its relationship with the farm bureau and the extension service and transformed its group into one of the many informal women's clubs that existed in rural areas. The Cedar Valley Women's Club did just that in 1946, only one year after it had celebrated its twenty-fifth anniversary, declaring that it needed no outside help in planning programs. Although they did not explain their exact reasoning, the women of Cedar Valley dropped all political discussions from their meetings and withdrew from county farm bureau activities. Instead, they dis-

Silly hats, 1950s. Freedom Township Women's Club Records, Iowa
Women's Archives, University of Iowa Libraries.

cussed books, held contests, sang songs, played games, finished handiwork,
and helped the hostess with household chores. The Cedar Valley Community Club continued these activities well into the 1990s, demonstrating that
the members not only found value in their group but also had the leadership
and organizational skills to maintain an effective club.[25]

Women with no interest in farm bureau programs had a variety of options for community participation, including church groups, garden clubs,
and other informal clubs. Typical of these informal clubs was the Friendly
Neighbors Club, formed in September 1952 by thirteen farm women near
Deep River, Iowa. They elected officers, drew up bylaws, and decided on
geographical boundaries to limit membership to local residents. Like clubs
associated with the IFBFWC, the Friendly Neighbors Club held monthly
meetings, followed parliamentary procedure, and collected twenty-five-cent
dues. They provided service and support to members, particularly at times of
birth, illness, or death. At their monthly, all-day meetings, the women often
helped the hostess with housework. They also held neighborhood events for
entire families, with large Thanksgiving celebrations, welcome parties for
new families, and going-away parties for those moving out of the area. The

Friendly Neighbors club performed some service projects, but operated primarily as a social group. It was not until January 1957 that members included an educational component in their meetings. They wrote to the federal government for information pertaining to civil defense and then used those materials to study to the topic throughout the spring of that year. But educational activities were limited to the desires of the members, and the meeting minutes did not indicate that any members made education or politics the focus of the club. Although the Friendly Neighbors Club and others like it served essentially the same social purpose as did those associated with the IFBFWC, there were clear distinctions. Informal clubs did not provide the same opportunities for community service, nor did they provide members with the rhetoric of leaders who desired women to take a more public role in civic activities.[26]

That women in township farm bureau clubs selected different activities from those prescribed by state leaders was less a product of resistance than it was the result of club members applying notions of social feminism in their own lives. Articles in the *Iowa Farm Bureau Spokesman*, speakers at Rural Women's Day, and materials produced through IFBF and IFBFWC continually affirmed this belief. Township clubs thrived throughout the 1950s and enjoyed growing or at least steady membership numbers. As local leaders took greater control over selecting and carrying out programs, they fulfilled the mission of the IFBFWC to empower farm women and to provide a setting in which adult education and women's activism could occur. By selecting activities applicable to their daily responsibilities and valued within their communities, local members believed that their clubs advanced standards of living in the countryside and made important contributions to the overall mission of the IFBF. In the immediate postwar period, between 1945 and the early 1960s, the decision by the IFBFWC to focus on developing local leadership proved an effective strategy in addressing the changing needs of farm women.

Over a longer term, however, developing local leadership could not entirely hedge social and demographic changes that altered rural life and women's expectations. Throughout the 1960s and 1970s membership in township women's clubs experienced a sharp decline due to women's changing roles and rural depopulation. The rhetoric of social feminisms utilized by the IFBFWC and township clubwomen was pervasive but restrictive. By the mid-1960s social feminisms continued to inform IFBFWC leaders, but they began to lose their resonance with farm women, who enjoyed broader options for social, political, and wage-earning activities. For women with interests in agricultural production and policy, then, by the mid-1960s activism meant becoming involved in the IFBF alongside men, either as "young marrieds" or on IFBF committees. Throughout the 1960s the Mahaska County Farm Bureau women's committee strongly encouraged women to take on leadership roles within the county farm bureau. Far from serving in token positions, by 1969 sixty-two women served on nearly every Mahaska County Farm Bureau committee, including those that handled the budget, resolutions that helped formulate policy for the state organization, and local affairs. Women also served on the committees for young members, legislative action, farm agreements, and health care.[27]

This is not to say that women abandoned county and township clubs in favor of the IFBF, only that they were no longer compelled to confine their political activities to separate, all-female groups. As they found new outlets for activism and relied less on social feminisms to justify their participation, township women's clubs focused even more on home economics and social events. In 1971 Anita Crawford, a longtime member of the Westburg Township Women's Club and chair of the Buchanan County Farm Bureau women's committee, was selected to serve on the Buchanan County Farm Bureau legislative committee. She had served as legislative chairperson for her township club since 1965, and having been a farm bureau member since the 1930s, she brought considerable experience to the position. At the time of her appointment, she received a letter from county farm bureau chairperson Wayne L. Natvig regarding her new responsibilities in formulating county and state resolutions and making no reference to her gender. She was expected to read a significant amount of materials pertaining to agricultural policy and to travel to district meetings. Throughout her tenure on the legislative committee, however, Crawford remained active in women's activities that were typical of township and county women's clubs. As chairperson of the Buchanan County Farm Bureau women's committee, she asked township leaders to hold programs about agricultural commodities and environmental hazards, including pesticides, nitrates, and clean-up methods. Crawford read widely, often wrote to legislators, and collected large amounts of information on marketing, property taxes, and pending legislation. She attended annual IFBFWC conferences and was very familiar with IFBFWC programs, but she still spent much of her time as county chairperson planning social events such as Rural Women's Day and a rural-urban women's tea.[28]

Membership rolls of clubs that remained intact through this period, including the Highland Do-Better Club in O'Brien County and the Sharon Township Women's Club in Johnson County, illustrate that as older members left the club, younger women interested in homemaking, crafts, and learning the home-production skills of the previous generation often replaced them. Yet the number of young women was not large enough to replace the number of older members who had left, and like township club-women of the immediate postwar period, few of these younger women sought outlets in which to become agricultural activists. Many worked off the farm or were involved on other IFBF committees or other farm organizations. Those who joined women's clubs sought a group where they could develop and celebrate their identities as farm wives. Overall, clubs affiliated with general farm organizations, such as the farm bureau, remained popular among rural residents across the United States. A 1980 survey of American farm women revealed that 41 percent of women involved with agricultural organizations were involved with a women's auxiliary to a general farm organization like the farm bureau. Interestingly, the survey revealed that age, farm employment, and political affiliation proved negligible in identifying those who participated in farm organizations; the extent of an individual woman's involvement depended primarily on her connection to the family farm, whether she shared ownership in the farming operation, her level of education, and the availability of economic resources. For younger women, then, participating in a farm bureau women's club was more likely an indicator of social status and leisure time than it had been for the previous generation. Quite often these women cited a desire to connect with the older generation and preserve skills typically identified as traditional women's work, such as sewing, crafting, and cooking.[29]

More so than changing ideologies, depopulation proved to be a central factor in the decline of township women's clubs. Political scientist Louise Carbert found that by the late 1960s declining memberships in Canadian farm women's organizations were "attributable to the depopulation of farming and rural communities," rather than the continued use of social feminisms or outdated agendas. The IFBFWC attempted to keep farm bureau women in step with changing times by addressing issues such as women's health and by providing materials on economic change, marketing, and agriculture that encouraged women to become more involved with the business of farming. As the rural population aged and lost numbers, recruiting new members became difficult because there were simply fewer women who could join. In sparsely populated Palo Alto County between 1950 and 1970, the total population fell from 15,891 to 13,289, while the number of farms declined from 1,808 to 1,186. Much of the depopulation occurred after 1960, and those who remained tended to be older, established farmers. Citing these conditions, the growing age of its members, and their inability to attract new members, the Freedom Township Women's Club decreased its involvement with the county farm bureau and after 1962 no longer participated in Rural Women's Day. It remained active in maintaining the Freedom Township Hall, purchased by the club in 1953, and by inviting speakers from the local area, completing craft projects, and even assembling "ditty bags" for servicemen in Vietnam. The meetings lost much of the formality that had characterized club functions prior to 1960, and by the early 1970s they more closely resembled gatherings of old friends. The women of Freedom Township were not alone as other clubs across the state made similar decisions over the next three decades.[30]

After 1945 members of both the IFBFWC and township farm bureau women's clubs sought to refine the roles of women as farm wives and as members of a greater organization.

In order to cope with changes in the countryside, such as depopulation, the introduction of agricultural and household technologies, and the separation of the IFBF and the extension service, the IFBFWC and members of township clubs agreed that greater local control allowed women to develop leadership skills and educational programs that best suited their needs and interests. Since the 1920s the IFBFWC had politicized farm women's work and encouraged Iowa farm women to work for higher standards of living by participating in local clubs. State leaders continually identified township clubs as the foundation of the state organization, and by the 1950s seasoned clubwomen demonstrated that they had received this message. At the township and county level they easily conducted meetings and carried out projects they believed to be within the mission of the IFBF, without direct assistance from home demonstration agents or IFBFWC leaders.

In the immediate postwar period the IFBFWC insisted that Iowa farm women devote meetings to political and agricultural issues at the national and international levels, but the great majority of members in local clubs did not share that enthusiasm. Township clubwomen's preferences for social and practical activities reveal that they critically interpreted the rhetoric and plans of state leaders and practiced selectivity when creating unique projects and annual programs. Social feminisms, shaped by domestic and maternal discourses, resonated with farm women in the postwar period. They understood the vital nature of their work to their families, their farms, and their communities, but farm women also lived with the reality that women's voices carried little authority in predominately male agricultural organizations and political circles. And although the IFBFWC assured them that political and international concerns could exist within the domestic realm, most women did not find these issues to be particularly relevant to their daily lives.

State leaders and local members may have disagreed on appropriate programming for club meetings, but for just over a decade, between 1945 and the early 1960s, the development of local leadership appeared to foster the growth of county and township women's clubs. Offering township clubs greater freedom to operate independently enabled the IFBFWC to successfully weather the loss of the extension service, which had been so instrumental in supporting women's activities, and to develop new programs for women of varied ages. Ultimately, this growth proved unsustainable, and membership numbers declined throughout the 1960s and 1970s. This was not due to the programs selected by township clubs, nor did it occur as part of a greater rebellion against the IFBF, the IFBFWC, or the social feminisms that these organizations espoused. Rather, it occurred as a result of depopulation and the emergence of new political outlets for women. The immediate postwar period was a pivotal moment in rural women's activism in Iowa, as women took greater ownership of their clubs and selected activities that they believed would attract the most members. In farm bureau clubs they did not necessarily find political outlets, but they found support, information, and friendships that enabled them to embrace higher standards of living and new technologies, while keeping some semblance of the neighborhoods and informal networks that were quickly disappearing in an era of modernization.

CHAPTER THREE

Does Your Man Belong to the Farmers Union?

Women and Cold War Politics in the Iowa Farmers Union

IN MARCH 1950 EDNA UNTIEDT of Dixon, Iowa, penned a letter to Fred Stover, the president of the Iowa Farmers Union (IFU), in which she lamented farm women's declining interest in the organization. She found that, just as the women of the Iowa Farm Bureau had shifted their focus to leisure activities, few women attended local meetings. Instead, they formed social clubs devoted to handicrafts, gift exchanges, or simply "playing cards." This was problematic because after 1945 the National Farmers Union (NFU) hoped to see its inclusive rhetoric carried out in practice, with women working alongside men in the main organization. At the behest of the national leadership, the IFU ladies auxiliary actually voted to dissolve the state organization in 1948. The following year, in keeping with directives from national leaders to foster and integrate women's leadership, Untiedt became the lone female member of the state board of directors. Still, women's attendance at regular meetings was dismal. Untiedt, a twenty-six-year member of the IFU, complained that farm wives "don't believe in women getting ahead. They say that's a man's job." Were it not for the demands of farm work, she would make more personal visits to women's groups and "do more for the Farmers Union."[1]

Drawing on decades of experience as a leader in the women's auxiliary, Untiedt understood that managing the limitations of social feminisms and devising alternative strategies for women's activism was a complicated process. Orders from the top down contained few specific recommendations and did little to erode prevailing social norms or justify women's activity in traditionally male spaces. The story of women in the IFU during the 1950s illustrates the variable trajectories of social feminisms, how integrative strategies were often conditional and how, even as full members, women were still directed toward specific roles that limited their activities. As historian Roy Wortman has noted, a distinct woman's voice in the NFU could only be attained if people were "willing to both listen and act on her counsel." In other words the concept of inclusivity was not a sufficient motivator. Even modest attempts at integrating women could only be undertaken by a motivated membership with active male leaders who intentionally cultivated women's voices.[2]

In the case of the IFU, the very survival of the organization was at stake. Untiedt hinted at some of the internal tensions in her letter of March 1950, when she jokingly counted herself among a number of "suspicious characters" in the IFU. She related the story of how, when she attended a state board meeting in Grinnell, Iowa, she had called home to her husband, Albert. A neighbor on the party line overheard the conversation and, upon her return home, asked Untiedt endless questions as to her whereabouts. Untiedt assured Stover that the inquisitive neighbor overheard nothing of significance and was "very likely still wondering" what had occurred at the meeting.[3]

After 1945 the liberalism that defined the IFU became inflammatory and dangerous in the context of the Cold War. The Farmers Union stood in stark contrast to the American Farm Bureau Federation by favoring centralized federal control over conservation and subsidy programs, the extension of wartime price supports, economic assistance for low-income and middling farmers, and policies that kept corporate agriculture at bay. They asserted that federal regulation was vital in helping farmers compete and thrive within a free-market economy. Yet these ideas, which were once popular under the New Deal during the 1930s, had lost their appeal as anticommunist fervor guided national politics in the postwar era. Political conservatives cast subsidy and parity programs as thinly veiled, centralized economic planning schemes similar to those in the Soviet Union. Agricultural exports, as well as images of productive, mechanized family farms, were central to Truman's doctrine of containing communism through economic development. In an era when *Washington Post* columnist Drew Pearson asserted "crop shortages can cause Communism," fostering friendly trade and enabling production abroad seemed an obvious answer to the hunger and poverty that spurred revolution. From the perspective of conservative policy makers, then, limiting agricultural production through cash payments and subsidy programs and defending farmers who subsisted on the margins amounted to subversion of American democracy.[4]

By 1950, when the NFU had fewer than 300,000 members nationwide, president James Patton set out to recast the organization's liberal ideology by expressing support for American efforts to subvert communism overseas and at home. He denounced Stover for his support of Henry Wallace as a Progressive Party candidate in the 1948 presidential election and for refusing to endorse President Harry Truman's anticommunist intervention abroad. Stover's disobedience, and his outspoken opposition to the Korean

War, prompted Patton to campaign for Stover's removal and the retraction of Iowa's charter. For nearly a decade, as the two men fought legal and ideological battles, a small handful of IFU women attempted to maintain stability in a volatile organization, working surreptitiously on Stover's behalf and acting primarily on their personal commitment to Stover and his interpretation of IFU principles. Untiedt understood that she could not afford to have local chapters focus on leisure activities when a declining membership and a distressed leadership needed every available worker.[5]

Because Patton inaccurately portrayed Stover as an ineffective and unstable leader in the public media, Stover actively sought the support of local IFU chapters. His corrective strategy depended on building personal relationships with members and reaching out to those responsible for educating the membership: local secretaries, educational leaders, and junior leaders. These were all posts typically occupied by women. Local secretaries in particular corresponded regularly and on very familiar terms with Stover and workers at the state office. He clearly understood that women were vital in building membership and running meetings. Although women continued to work in tandem with their husbands and as actors behind the scenes, when working with Stover they rarely justified their participation with a rhetoric of gendered mutuality. This was not necessarily because the IFU promoted liberal ideologies or practiced gender equality. Women created new roles for themselves based on established social feminisms as they moved from the familiar spaces of women's auxiliaries into the main organization. Their power was confined to the organization and was ultimately ineffective in helping Stover retain his position, but their story shows how men's attitudes and their understanding of gendered divisions of labor shaped women's experiences as activists.

Founded in Texas in 1902 as a cooperative marketing association, the NFU quickly spread through the grain belt and took on a liberal agrarian political ideology that was said to be the "spiritual descendent" of the Populist movement. It developed a rhetoric of class struggle and protest, asserting that fair competition for farmers in the marketplace required government intervention in regulating trade and upholding individual property rights. NFU leaders of the early twentieth century intentionally worked to instill a strong grassroots leadership structure, and in creating women's auxiliaries and a junior division, they infused a vital social dimension that transformed their business into an ideologically driven, general-purpose family organization. By keeping dues low and emphasizing social justice, they focused on policies that would help struggling farmers meet the costs of production.

The organization did not enjoy the same political clout in Washington, D.C. as did the American Farm Bureau Federation, but members attempted to bolster their political presence through alliances with organized labor. Policy makers were most attentive to the NFU during the Great Depression and the Second World War, as the government grappled with the problems of regulating production and environmental conservation.[6]

The NFU arrived in Iowa in 1917, recruiting more than 21,000 enthusiastic farm families in its first year. Unable to compete with the Farm Bureau, however, by 1919 membership had fallen to 10,625 and continued to decline over the next four decades. With only a few thousand members at any given time, many of those who joined did so to ally themselves with others who shared liberal ideologies, to take advantage of the educational and recreational activities, to purchase goods and services, or simply because they strongly disliked the farm bureau's connections to the extension service and the agricultural scientists at Iowa State College. Members often praised the IFU as a grassroots organization that was free from the influence of prescriptive experts or government agents and truer to the actual needs of farm families.[7]

When Stover took the helm of the IFU in 1945, he was part of a new generation of leaders, like Patton, who followed a progressive line that stemmed from their experiences during the lean years of the 1920s and 1930s. Born in Iowa, Stover first came to political activism through the Cerro Gordo County Farm Bureau and gained extensive experience with the federal government, including several years with the Agricultural Adjustment Administration (AAA). As a New Dealer, like Patton and other NFU leaders, Stover advocated for government intervention, price supports, and industrial regulations, rather than voluntary action or cooperatives, as the answer to income inequality for small, family farmers. Stover consistently described himself as a liberal, as someone who believed that the free market required some regulation to help the most vulnerable citizens. One of socialism's defining features is government or cooperative ownership of property and control over the modes of production, something that neither Stover nor the NFU ever endorsed. In fact, both believed their ideas would bolster and improve the prospects for the private ownership of land by allowing smaller-scale farmers to remain in business. An ideological leader, Stover proved popular with the membership because he sold IFU principles before its products and services. In correspondence he often referred to the Farm Bureau as the "keep them dumb and happy organization," implying that IFBF members embraced complacent politics. He insisted that members keep "some resemblance and relationship between what one believes and what one does."[8]

It was not his commitment to New Deal–era programs that troubled Patton but his pacifism. Stover was an eager proponent of democracy, but he detested nationalism and imperialism. He never wavered in his insistence that only peace could bring prosperity, and he was sharply critical of atomic warfare and American military involvement overseas. The best use of the nation's young men, he argued, was as industrial and agricultural laborers, not soldiers. In the hostile political climate of the McCarthy era, Stover found himself at odds with NFU leadership because he refused to justify any war, even when the United States was at war against communism. Stover blamed Wall Street for the growth of American militarism, a fact that greatly troubled critics who believed Stover's position to be an all-out assault on capitalism. From Stover's perspective compulsory military service actually curtailed free markets and individual freedom. He viewed the draft as a "part and parcel of Wall Street's plot to wipe out 3,800,000 family farms." Without young men to work these farms and hold on to privately owned land, corporations could more easily expand their agricultural operations. During the late 1940s and early 1950s these distinctions hardly mattered to Americans, who were consumed with recognizing the signs and symptoms of an impending communist takeover. In this context any criticism of capitalism or refusal to fight communism implied sympathy. Popular culture generally defined liberalism not as a feasible political philosophy within a democracy but rather as a philosophy promoting rapid, unchecked social and political change—in other words, a revolution.[9]

Stover fell under the intense scrutiny of government leaders and ordinary Iowans. The IFU found itself on the defensive alongside groups devoted to organized labor and civil rights, all of which had to deflect criticism that they were socialists or somehow sympathetic to Soviet Communists. Women's voices in all of these groups were particularly vulnerable since self-supporting, outspoken women and feminists became symbols of subversion. In this period many women's groups from across the country and from a broad political spectrum adopted strategies to prove their patriotism and preserve their organizations. The women of the IFU, like many in organized labor and more radical civil rights movements, did not do this. While farm bureau women's clubs studied "-isms" and how recognize the drift toward socialism, IFU women maintained that there were, in fact, differences between socialism and liberalism, the latter being perfectly compatible with American democracy. In August 1951, nearly a year into the public flight between Stover and Patton, several IFU women circulated petitions to repeal the 1950 Internal Security Act, or McCarran Act, a Congressional measure that forced communist organizations to register with the government. These women asserted that measures like the Internal Security Act inhibited personal freedoms and actually thwarted democratic goals by favoring big business and corporate power.[10]

In the postwar period IFU women devised similar rhetorical strategies as the IFBFWC, upholding women's graduation into new political and public roles, but they were required to do so in integrated spaces. From the IFU's beginning, memberships were sold in family units, with the head of the household listed as the primary member and voter on matters related to the organization. In general, women were welcomed as organizers and educators, giving them an "integral position of power within the organization." The NFU had consistently been more intentional about including women in leadership positions than had the Farm Bureau, and in 1946 the NFU amended its constitution to broaden membership and grant women the opportunity to vote as individuals, even if they joined with a family membership. They hoped that the promise of greater gender equality would bring more women into the general membership, and they encouraged state affiliates to elect more women into leadership positions by rewarding those states with extra national convention votes.[11]

Initially, women of the IFU strongly resisted the inclusive strategies imposed by national leaders because they viewed inclusive strategies as an imposition and an effort to actually negate women's voices. The decision to dissolve the ladies auxiliary did not come easily, consuming much of the two-day state convention in September 1948. Board members alternated discussions of programming for the coming year with debates on whether to end the auxiliary system all together. In one report the constitution and by-laws committee recommended that the local auxiliaries become more like informal social clubs. The committee advised local units to remain staunchly nonpartisan and "omit all political issues from discussion." This was immediately followed by a report by the legislative committee that all suggested local auxiliaries secure the voting records of their state legislators and "keep informed on pending state legislation and discuss at meetings." The IFU elected new officers and continued to pass resolutions in support of broader political and social issues, including one that dedicated the organization to promoting peace in an "atomic age," but all these future plans were prefaced with statements such as "should the auxiliary continue" or "only if the State auxiliary sees fit to carry on." Ultimately, the debate was settled by setting a date for a November referendum that allowed members of local auxiliaries to decide their fate.[12]

In the weeks leading up to the referendum, state IFU secretary Betty Lownes confided to Mary Nicoletto, the state director of education, that she found the situation "exciting" but frustrating for many IFU members who believed that women, on the verge of a breakthrough in liberal agrarian politics, would be silenced in the larger organization. They did not fear losing the bonds of friendship forged through club work because that was not difficult to preserve. Many local groups simply functioned as a central meeting point for the informal support networks that had long defined rural women's lives, a task that could be easily carried on without a formal organization. In May 1946, for example, the women of one local chapter near Grinnell each donated one hen to a fellow member whose hen house, along with 200 hens, had been lost in a fire. This was the primary business of their meeting, but it was something they certainly would have done even without gathering under the auspices of the IFU. Other clubs had already disbanded on their own accord, some as early as the 1930s, and remained active as unaffiliated social groups. In 1932 members of the Women's Auxiliary No. 40 near Baxter, Iowa, changed their organization's name to the Ever Ready Club and voted to dissolve their ties with the state organization. They remained an active social organization until the 1980s, with founding members maintaining their memberships over several decades. As the last chapter demonstrated, this was certainly a viable option for women simply interested in retaining social and supportive relationships. Those against dissolution of the IFU women's auxiliary actually feared that the end of the auxiliary system would destabilize women's authority when working in mixed groups. Betty Lownes heard one disappointed local member quip sarcastically, "Yes, let [the auxiliary] go. No one has anything to say anymore anyway."[13]

While it is difficult to assess the exact consequences of ending the auxiliary system and integrating women into the general organization, it is clear that having women serve in leadership capacities was something of a novelty. In January 1949, Edna Untiedt took it upon herself to organize women and increase their participation in the main organization. While participating in a statewide membership drive, she wrote a general letter to members in which she stated that she and other women had already been out canvassing rural neighborhoods. She seemed to see it as unusual but also as an opportunity for women to prove their worth when she wrote, "Come on ladies. Let's show the men what we can do. We have real leadership at the top of our organization. Let's do all in our power to keep it there. Let's all work together for a better Iowa Farmers Union."[14]

Later that year, when Untiedt became the first woman elected to the state board of directors, the *Iowa Union Farmer* reported on the exceptional nature of this event, as well as the state's compliance with national policy. Iowa merely followed "the lead set by other states who have placed women on their State Board of Directors." On one level, integration allowed women to pursue individual interests, focus on educational or junior activities, or seek elected office within the general organization. Bylaws were not prohibitive of women holding leadership roles, and women often served as field organizers, secretaries, and educational leaders at the state level, but overall inclusivity did little to erode engrained beliefs about proper gender roles. In 1950, when the IFU sent ninety-one members to lobby Congress in Washington, D.C., there were only twenty-four women among them. Mary Nicoletto, director of education, found that more men would have "taken along their wives had they known that there were women among the expeditioners." She hoped that more women would go on future trips, but her observations seem to imply that the men did not think to include their wives in their organizational work. Women may have also believed that the trip was exclusively for members and because they had no auxiliary or space to call their own, they were not included as full members.[15]

Mixed messages like this were common and both women and men were unsure how to translate inclusive policies. With the family labor system at the heart of its message, NFU and IFU recruiting pamphlets always highlighted family membership and women's participation as a benefit of belonging. By the 1930s female leaders at the national level, including the Assistant National Secretary, Mary C. Pancke of Kankakee, Illinois, called for greater female involvement as a simple and easy way to grow the organization. She identified women as especially skilled with building and sustaining members, but she utilized a highly militarized rhetoric that called on women to "fight" alongside the men in a "war to preserve agriculture." After 1945 much of this rhetoric was muted in favor of simply having women work alongside men as they would on the farm. The impetus for integration in this period came from Gladys Talbott Edwards, whose father served as president of the North Dakota Farmers Union and was a strong proponent of ending racial barriers to membership during the late 1930s. Edwards, who became North Dakota's first director of education in 1937, considered the elevation of women's status in the organization to be an extension of her father's work toward inclusivity. She moved to Denver after 1945 to further develop the national program, expand the junior division, and improve adult education on politics, cooperative marketing, and agricultural policy. She wrote and edited several books designed to educate farm families and always took care to include women in very visible and meaningful ways in order to portray educational and social activities as part of the overall NFU program and move them beyond auxiliary status.[16]

Edwards's commitment to promoting female membership was exemplified in an edited volume of collected writings from ordinary Farmers Union members titled *This Is the Farmers Union*. Published in 1951, the booklet featured letters written in response to the prompt, "What the Farmers Union means to me." Edwards selected writings that stressed inclusivity and education, using the words of members at the local level to give voice to national policies. Writing about religious and racial equality, several women encouraged Farmers Union members to lobby for civil rights legislation. A small handful of women also addressed gender, primarily in terms of pay. One grandmother, whose children and grandchildren were "ardent" members, wrote, "I think women should get equal pay with men if they do an equal job, and more if they do superior work." Edwards prominently featured farm wives in elected leadership positions, making their work appear ordinary and acceptable. These women discussed attending county, state, and even national conventions as elected delegates, serving as secretaries or educational directors, and even local presidents. One young woman guessed that she was "the first woman in the state to be president of a Local." She served in the position for two years, building membership by offering a strong social program, before stepping down when her first son was born. Selections emphasized the idea that organizational work made the women better wives and mothers and in some cases offered an education otherwise denied them by poverty. One farm wife wrote that she felt ashamed for never having finished school but that the Farmers Union had "helped me gain the education I have missed." Their words and experiences leave little doubt that many women found participation not only meaningful but manageable and complementary to their work at home.[17]

There were limits to Edwards's portrayal of women and in NFU materials more generally. Implicit within images of the traditional "family farm" espoused by the organization was the overriding importance of the nuclear family, the heterosexual marriage, and a gendered hierarchy within families. NFU literature heavily emphasized the mutual valuation of gendered labor, but it never suggested full gender equality. *The Handbook for Farmers Union Locals and Counties*, distributed in the early 1950s, affirmed women's interests when it stated that "housework, tending the garden, caring for the chickens, feeding the pigs, milking the cows, and doing all the other chores around the farm is just as much a part of farm work as riding the tractor, driving the truck, or chopping the cotton." Housework has value in this statement, but the description of farm work clearly delineates tasks by gender and assumes that women are primarily responsible for "chores" as opposed to "work." Women's important but surreptitious roles were also clearly outlined in a pamphlet from the early 1950s titled "Advice to the Young Lady Considering Marriage." Following a series of questions about the prospective groom's productivity and knowledge of farming that upheld men as leaders, workers, and providers, the pamphlet ultimately asked, "Does your man belong to the Farmers Union?" If the answer was no, then it was the woman's "job to reform him."[18]

Materials that portrayed women as agricultural producers cast them in supportive roles, usually as advisors to uncertain husbands. In 1955 an informational novella told the story of a newly married North Dakota farm couple, David and Susan Lindhorst. They systematically learned about the local Farmers Union by speaking with their Lutheran pastor, an extension agent, an FHA representative, and members of the Farmer's Union. The conversations focused on David's questions, but Susan was almost always with him, interjecting her concerns and tempering David's desires for immediate change. When David idealized the family labor system on North Dakota farms, Susan gently reminded him that, "this may have been right a few years ago when prices were around parity. Right now I don't think our neighbors are doing so good. They're worried about falling prices." Scenes like this portrayed Susan as a trusted advisor who was entirely satisfied with this role. When an NFU field organizer visited the Lindhorsts, Susan commented that, "it doesn't seem to be an organization just for menfolk. Wives and young people get right in too." The organizer affirmed her perception and replied, "The family farm emphasis has been strengthened by our refusal to set the women apart in a separate auxiliary."[19]

In some ways, the structure of the IFU fostered family cooperation because entire families — men, women, and children — could attend monthly meetings where all family members over the age of sixteen were entitled to vote. Once they arrived, though, family members potentially had very separate roles, which complicated the unity espoused in NFU pamphlets. Meetings were divided into two parts: a business and informational session and then a leisure session where members enjoyed dinner, singing, a play, an informal presentation, or some other form of entertainment. At the same time the junior division met separately. In the spirit of cooperation and shared work, members of a local "action group," set the agenda. The action group typically consisted of the president, vice president, and secretary, as well as the directors of education, legislation, cooperation, junior activities, publicity, and recreation. Women often held some of these positions, but again official NFU materials portrayed the jobs as more suitable to one gender. The cover illustration on an early 1950s planning manual, "A Guide For Farmers Union Action Officials," featured only men sitting around a table engaged in a vigorous debate. The manual described the specific job of each officer, with illustrations of men for the directors of education, legislation, cooperation, and organization. Illustrations of women accompanied descriptions for the publicity, junior, and recreational directors. These jobs were defined as more intuitive and simple compared with the others, and they were clearly identified as "helping" the main organization. Publicity directors were encouraged to contact local newspapers to advertise meetings but never to "editorialize" their opinions. Likewise, recreation directors were charged with helping members "learn to work together" through fun leisure activities.[20]

During the business and informational session of the monthly meeting, the adults heard guest speakers, discussed agricultural issues, and handled IFU business. As this occurred, women typically prepared the meal or arranged the entertainment. State leaders considered this normal, expecting the women to provide refreshments at local meetings. In 1948, when planning a two-day, multicounty leadership conference in Grand Mound, Iowa, the state director of education, Mary Nicoletto, called on local ladies auxiliary member Pearl Green. Although Green had once been the president of the state ladies auxiliary and had extensive experience with local organizing and community service, Nicoletto only asked for her advice on refreshments and entertainment. Women were also in charge of leading junior division activities for children and young people between the ages of six and twenty-one. Boys and girls met together and studied the IFU "creed," then worked on separate, gendered, and age-appropriate projects. Again, IFU members took for granted that women should lead the junior division. In May 1950 Richard Ronfeldt of Hornick, Iowa, organized a new local chapter and sought Nicoletto's advice on how to set up youth activities. Nicoletto encouraged him to have the local executive committee appoint an adult junior division leader. The ideal leader, she indicated, "is usually the wife of one of the members, or an older daughter. However, it is not necessary that it be either, it can be one of the active members." Nicoletto's description implies that "wives" and "older daughters" were not necessarily active members but rather women serving in appropriately gendered positions.[21]

The structure of the meeting was clearly prohibitive for some women. In

1950, when she was supposed to serve as a member of the state board, help build local chapters, secure well-known speakers for conferences, and recruit more women to work with the general organization, Edna Untiedt found her efforts hampered by her role as the Scott County junior division leader. "Sometimes I wish I did not have the Junior work. . . . I could do more if I were in the meetings," she wrote to Stover. "I love the work, it's true. But one can't be in the local meeting and Jr. meeting at the same time." One evening, Untiedt desperately wanted to join a heated debate that was occurring during the business meeting; instead, she found herself making and serving a goulash supper. Male members of the county executive committee simply sat down to dinner after the business meeting and waited for service. Tired of waiting on others and then eating "leftovers," Untiedt informed Stover that, "from now on some of the others can be the goats." At several points she chided herself for complaining, but she finally found fault with the other members when she wrote, "If Edna will not be the fall guy, then no one else will do it either."[22]

The position of secretary was the one job that afforded women opportunities to become directly involved with IFU business. Secretaries for local chapters took minutes at meetings, handled money and dues, and submitted regular reports of meetings, usually in the form of a letter to Stover or the state secretary. This brought them in much closer contact with county and state leaders, whose response further affected women's perceptions as to the importance of their work. Letters from local secretaries had a distinct informality that included descriptions of meetings, political statements or pointed criticisms of the farm bureau, and some discussions of personal circumstances. Eleanor Biederman's February 1949 report to Stover was typical. Biederman, a farm wife and IFU secretary from Mitchell, Iowa, submitted dues and told of a "pretty good" meeting where members elected officers and heard a guest speaker talk about parity. Rather than a formal report, she sprinkled the narrative with questions and comments. She asked Stover for suggestions for future meetings, then criticized IFBF president Howard Hill's stance on economic policies. Biederman concluded by sharing her concerns about the falling price of cattle, wondering whether she and her husband would have to "give them away." Stover took letters from local secretaries seriously, responding promptly and addressing each point. In Biederman's case he enclosed several press releases on parity and offered the use of a "wire recorder" so that members could listen to convention speeches at their meeting. He assured Biederman that, as president of the IFU, he was demonstrating leadership in their crusade to expose the Farm

Bureau as uninterested in small, family farmers. He wrote excitedly about his recent opportunities to "clash with the big shots of the Farm Bureau" at a panel presentation on price supports and then concluded with the simple instruction to "tell the rest of the folks 'hello' for me." His tone and language made it clear that he considered Biederman to be a member of the IFU, that her concerns were legitimate, and that they shared a common goal in promoting the IFU's political ideology.[23]

Stover consistently assured women in leadership positions that their work was worthwhile. His attention to personal problems and opinions is significant because the letters from local secretaries also reveal that women often struggled with demanding schedules and diverse roles that inhibited their involvement. In November 1951 Alice Sponheim, of Osage, Iowa, wrote a detailed report of Mitchell County's annual meeting. She had high words of praise for the speakers but regretted that she could not be present for voting on resolutions. She had hoped that the county membership would pass a peace resolution in favor of ending the Korean conflict, but during the vote she had other commitments. "I had a baby-sitting job that night," she wrote, "so I failed again—see why I want no important jobs?" For Sponheim, family and work obligations came before the IFU, leading her to conclude that she had "failed" and was perhaps unworthy of more responsibility.[24]

Even women in the top state leadership positions often discussed tensions between the demands of organizational work and family. Their duties as wives and mothers were of the utmost importance and sometimes complicated their ability to accomplish their goals with the IFU. As part of her job, state secretary Betty Lownes only worked in the Des Moines office one day each month, but she devoted several hours each week to working from home, and she traveled extensively with Stover and other officers to organizing events and leadership conferences. In January 1948 the state education director, Mary Nicoletto, asked Lownes to participate in a regional leadership conference. Her response indicates that accepting the invitation was not her decision alone. Lownes had "talked" the conference over with her husband and "he thought I might be able to get away." The mother of three children, who also served as president of her local Farmers Union in Denison, Iowa, maintained an extensive correspondence with Nicoletto that was generally positive and optimistically ambitious. Yet Lownes left little doubt that she needed to use every minute of the day productively. One Christmas Eve, Lownes held her drowsy, feverish daughter, Linda Kay, as she wrote to Nicoletto, "I am almost too busy to write, but some things must be done." She managed to dash off a hastily written, one-page report of a local chap-

ter meeting before she suddenly concluded, "Linda Kay is awake now, so
here we go again." Since joining in 1941 and assuming the role of secretary-
treasurer in 1946, Lownes had been a devoted member, who continued to
work with Stover over the course of several decades, but her activity was
often done in short segments, as her children napped or in the evenings.[25]

Neither Sponheim nor Lownes considered the various demands placed
on them to be a gendered problem. They generally accepted the fact of
having to take on a variety of roles throughout the day and in one's life,
and as a result they sought positions in keeping with their abilities and their
schedules. Stover's familiar leadership style and regard for the local membership provided this flexible outlet for women's voices on the topics of agriculture and politics, although he would eventually ask them to begin redefining
those roles to meet a worsening crisis. By the summer of 1950, Stover's commitment to pacifism in an increasingly volatile Cold War generated allegations of subversion and insubordination to the national leadership.

As proposals to extend wartime price supports floundered in Congress
throughout the late 1940s, the liberal positions of the NFU leadership that
favored enhancing those price supports on a more permanent basis spurred
investigations by the FBI, the State Department, and the House Un-American
Activities Committee (HUAC). These in turn fueled public suspicion of the
NFU and its regional affiliates. New Hampshire Senator Styles Bridges struck
a damaging blow on the Senate floor in September 1950 when he identified
the leaders as communist, calling on Patton and Stover by name. The NFU
certainly had a small minority of communist members who were "not always
considered pariahs" during the early 1940s, but the organization as a whole
was hardly "Communist-dominated or a Communist front." Throughout the
late 1940s Patton had actually resisted demands to expel communist sym-
pathizers, but with the beginning of the Korean War, he initiated efforts to
purge the NFU of controversial figures as a means to demonstrate the NFU's
commitment to American democracy. State leaders in Montana and North
Dakota followed suit by dismissing communists in leadership positions. Two
weeks after Bridges's speech, Patton took his case to the public, issuing statements to the *Des Moines Register* and the delegates attending the 1950 IFU
state convention in Des Moines. Patton did not label Stover as communist,
but he criticized the IFU for refusing to support American actions in Korea.
Threatening to revoke Iowa's charter for noncompliance with national policies, Patton urged conference delegates to vote in step with the NFU. He attempted to present these threats in a positive light, portraying Stover as an
unpopular leader presiding over an uncertain membership.[26]

On the eve of the state convention, Stover mustered his supporters to prepare for what he anticipated would be "the most trying convention in the history of the Farmers Union." He carefully selected members for the resolutions committee — several of them being prominent female members — to maintain some control over the agenda. At the end of August 1950, he asked M. Ida Rink, who farmed with her brother's family in Greene County, to join the resolutions committee. Stover cited Rink's extensive experience with the IFU and her abilities as a negotiator. Referring to a heated conflict over tuberculosis testing in cattle during the 1930s, Stover wrote, "Knowing a little about your 'slugging out' performances in the old cow war days, I am counting on you very, very much." This strategy proved successful: an overwhelming majority of the delegates at the convention approved resolutions to denounce the Korean conflict, decry economic imperialism, condemn war as a means to promote demand for agricultural goods, and protest a military draft that "siphoned" young, able-bodied men from American farms. Their affirmation of Stover's position confirmed a moment of solidarity within the IFU, but it did little to win public sympathies. Within the NFU Stover also faced a disapproving majority. Only the leadership of the eastern division (Pennsylvania, New York, and New Jersey) shared Stover's ardent pacifism.[27]

Stover never identified as a communist, and throughout his life he fought vehemently against any such allegations to no avail. In Iowa he had a tenuous relationship with the state's primary newspaper, the *Des Moines Register*. Editors accused the IFU of "fellow traveling" and published cartoons of Stover dragging IFU members into a "communist international line." Such notions permeated the local levels, where some members expressed a clear disdain for Stover's position on the Korean conflict. Ida Guernsey, a longtime member from Woden, Iowa, informed Stover that she would resign from her committee appointments and cancel her trip to the annual state convention on account of his antiwar stance. Guernsey sided with Henry A. Wallace, the former vice president and presidential candidate for the Progressive Party, who had long criticized Truman's foreign policy but supported the United Nations in Korea. She informed Stover that "if Henry Wallace says the Russians are to blame in starting the war, then they are." Concerned about the communist infiltration of the Progressive Party and the IFU, she warned, "I am sure that the day will come, and it may not be so far distant, when you will bitterly regret your actions. . . . You see, I have believed in you like I believe in Wallace. Now I don't know which way to turn or what to think." Guernsey could not have been alone. In this time period many more members let their memberships slip away than wrote to Stover about their concerns, but certainly farm women were concerned about how their organizational activities affected the status of their families in local neighborhoods and towns. As Americans confused the concepts of liberalism, socialism, and communism, and deemed pacifism as unpatriotic, any association with Stover could mean alienation for IFU members.[28]

NFU field organizers constantly encountered misconceptions and confronted suspicions among the farmers they were trying to recruit. Lois Linse Gleiter, a field organizer in the Midwest, recalled that as she traveled through the region during the early 1950s, most rural residents labeled the NFU as communist. As a result of Cold War tensions, Gleiter asserted that "the Farmers Union was definitely harmed. Just the name, Farmers Union, was not accepted. . . . It was a very hard thing to come to a meeting and be a representative of the Farmers Union because there were many questions that were asked." Gleiter stressed the importance of reaching out to local chapters and "trusting" members to tell the truth about controversial situations, such as Red-baiting, that compromised their membership. Similarly, one organizer in North Dakota believed that women were especially cautious about affiliating with any group deemed "communist" because "they feared their children would be harassed at school."[29]

With the vote in his favor at the 1950 state convention, Stover was confident that most members supported his position, but he wondered how long they would continue to do so. Membership began to waver by the end of October 1950, when a small group of IFU regulars, led by Stover's vice president, Leonard Hoffman, circulated letters and materials accusing Stover of following "the Moscow line." On his visits to local chapters across the state, Stover found organizers "working overtime" to answer members' questions and quell rumors spurred by these letters. He confided to one county organizer that false rumors of his communist sympathies and poor leadership were "effective among . . . our membership." He campaigned eagerly at the local levels, assuring members that he believed in "getting both sides of the controversy" through "free and open discussions." He frequently appeared at informal meetings with local leaders and members across the state at county-level meetings. Rather than making speeches, he ran the meetings as question-and-answer sessions in order to "clear up some of the confusion."[30]

When dealing with dissenting opinions, Stover believed that personal interaction and reasonable discussion would resolve any conflicts and help others see his opinion as being in the right. His response to Ida Guernsey's letter in September 1950 lends some insight into how he handled angry or frustrated members. After Guernsey asserted that he was wrong to disagree with Henry Wallace, Stover replied that he wished they could simply sit down and "have a good long visit sometime and go through all the phases of the matter." He addressed her concerns point by point and explained his rationale for opposing the war, but most striking was his appeal to her personally. He wrote that her angry letter was "not quite like you, Mrs. Guernsey. . . . I want you to know that I have a profound respect for your intense sincerity, your real unselfishness, and the purity of your personality." He encouraged her to read more about international relations, investigate the situation, and draw her own opinions, rather than rely on either Wallace or himself. Stover also made some jokes and attempted to lighten the situation by asking Guernsey not to get swept up in anticommunist hysteria. He wrote, "Americans are trying so hard now-a-days to be different from Russia and communists in every way that it shouldn't surprise us if a lot of Americans . . . will become nudists simply because they found out that the communists wear clothes." He concluded by extending an invitation to the state convention and the possibility of a personal visit if she did not attend. Stover wanted to cultivate personal relationships, as well as organizational loyalty, and did so by passively telling members to think for themselves, read the material, and trust that he would not print anything in the *Iowa Union Farmer* that was untrue.[31]

Throughout 1951 the controversy became even more heated, as Hoffman and Stover allowed the courts to decide the rightful president of the IFU. Hoffman asserted that because Stover had served as chair of the Progressive Party in 1948, he had engaged in partisan political activity and violated the bylaws of the IFU that prohibited such conflicts of interest. Edna Untiedt and Betty Lownes testified at the trial, where they demonstrated a fierce loyalty to Stover. During cross-examination, Untiedt recounted a board meeting in October 1951 where Hoffman attempted to take over but eventually left with his supporters to hold a separate meeting. When asked why she did not join them, she replied simply, "I attended the legal meeting of the Farmers Union." As the trial proceeded, IFU assets were frozen, and the NFU withheld funds, thereby allowing activities to wither. M. W. Thatcher, head of the Farmers Union Grain Terminal Association, the NFU's primary cooperative, refused to distribute funds for educational activities to the Iowa chapter because, he asserted, Iowa's members were not acting "in the best interests of agriculture." The Iowa Farmers Union Seed Service, another primary distributor of educational funds, also began to distance itself from Stover and eventually cut off funds entirely in 1954. The loss of educational funds was especially damaging to female members, placing severe limitations on the junior division activities and the support services they typically coordinated. The Iowa courts ultimately upheld Stover's presidency in April 1951, but the decision failed to resolve the issue and left the membership divided. At that point Patton and the dissenters in Iowa decided to pursue revocation of Iowa's charter so that the IFU could be abolished and reconstituted under new leadership. Member Leo Paulson of Crystal Lake complained that, as news of Patton's new strategy spread, members left local chapters in droves, making it impossible for the IFU to "build an effective organization." By 1953 overall membership had declined by 43 percent to just 1,311 members.[32]

Throughout this difficult period Stover's closest advisors included several women who actively worked on his behalf. Shortly after the verdict came back in favor of Stover, Untiedt and Lownes accompanied him to the 1951 NFU conference in Denver, where they appealed to Patton personally but left disappointed. Lownes asserted that the democracy she thought existed "seemed to be gone." She recounted how Patton said the women wouldn't "get anywhere by yat yatting at him." Critical of his condescending tone, she wrote, "I didn't think we were yat yatting, we only asked him a question, . . . the first one I had ever asked him. When members of an organization cannot ask their leaders questions, whoever they are, then the whole organization suffers." Lownes was not alone in her disappointment. As the NFU pursued the revocation of Iowa's charter, letters of support poured in from women in Iowa and across the Midwest. Interestingly, in the letters Stover retained from this period, women penned most of the positive statements. They sought an active role in helping him retain his leadership, often citing their personal faith in his abilities and their gratitude for his willingness to speak a truth in keeping with their world view. One of the most impassioned letters came from Edna Untiedt, who assured Stover that the IFU was her "first love outside my family and home." She refused to let Leonard Hoffman and the dissenting members "hurt" Stover, promising to "do all I can to help in any way." Fearing that he might get discouraged, she wrote, "Fred, just remember that I have all the faith in the world in you." Likewise, Myrtle Locken of Webster, South Dakota, congratulated Stover for taking a "courageous and enlightening stand on the issue of world peace." Locken, like most letter writers, requested recent copies of the *Iowa Union Farmer* for herself and several friends so they could get "the facts on today's inhumane conflict."[33]

In their letters these women offered assistance, not passive praise. The services they proposed were those deemed appropriate for women, gained through their participation in auxiliaries or as local secretaries. They offered to write and publish works on his behalf, canvass neighborhoods, and provide other support services. Longtime member M. Ida Rink headed the Farmers Union Defense Committee, which published and distributed materials in support of Stover. In one publication Rink featured letters from ordinary members in Iowa and elsewhere showing their support. One letter from Myrtle Locken, originally written to Jim Patton nearly two months after her letter to Stover, appealed for reason and compassion. She asked, "Since when in Farmers Union circles has it become something less than a virtue to be sensitive to oppression?" She warned Patton that he had "greatly underestimated" the interest that Iowa farmers had in international affairs and their support of Stover's antiwar position.[34]

Similarly, in November 1951 Mrs. Carl Benna of Marathon, Iowa, asked for membership blanks and recruiting materials that expressly supported Stover. She planned to canvass her neighborhood and hoped to generate interest among her friends. Lucille Olson of Bergen, North Dakota, reported to Stover that she and her husband had distributed 700 copies of Stover's pamphlet "People vs. Plunderers." As the parents of two young boys, Olson and her husband objected to the draft and "American imperialism." She believed Stover to be a more honest leader than those of the North Dakota Farmers Union. "Too bad we don't have a leader like you in our state," she wrote. "It wouldn't take long to organize then. We do admire *your* courage!" A few months later, in April 1952, Susie Stageberg, of Red Wing, Minnesota, not only requested several subscriptions of the *Iowa Union Farmer*, but she offered to write a regular column. She wrote, "I as a former Iowan feel tremendously interested in Iowa's 'fearless farm organization' and I want to do all I can to help you." Stover gratefully accepted her offer and hoped that her writing would "make a real contribution to the cause."[35]

Through their supportive services, women were able to apply the social feminisms and feminine organizing strategies that they had carefully developed over several decades. Caution was warranted because speaking publicly carried significant risk, especially for those with husbands active in the IFU. In Wisconsin the state president removed local officers deemed "communist" and let go state office workers with liberal political views. In 1951 Patton fired Clifford Durr from his job at the NFU office in Denver simply because his wife, Virginia, signed an antiwar petition circulated by the American Peace Crusade. Working on Stover's behalf, especially when circulating materials, signing one's name, and offering help, would have required women to either act with complete independence or with the consent of family and neighbors. This is further evidenced by the fact that the most vocal Stover supporters were older women who had been active in the Farmers Union for decades, who had held leadership positions, and whose financial and familial situations were fairly stable.[36]

Women leaving the safety of all-female spaces cited a particular sense of urgency in protecting not just Stover but their own liberal beliefs that had come under suspicion in the Cold War era. Although none of the women who wrote letters to Stover ever indicated any severe problems with friends or neighbors on account of their political activities, they were well aware that their beliefs were not popular. Building and sustaining membership was the most important job that women could perform on Stover's behalf because at the 1952 NFU convention in Dallas, Patton announced that the minimum membership for state affiliates would be raised from 1,000 to 3,500. Any state that failed to meet the minimum by the end of the fiscal year in 1953 would have its charter revoked. Patton wanted to avoid revoking state charters on ideological grounds, but his motives were made clear by the national board's recommendation that Texas, Michigan, and Oregon, the three other states falling below the minimum, be given assistance in building membership. In their official report on the matter, members of the national board issued a statement that "liberty is not a license and the improper and dangerous actions and methods of a relatively small minority within the organization may no longer be tolerated." They identified Iowa as a problematic state where ordinary farmers shied away from Stover's leadership and would not join the FU "as it is presently constituted." In other words, Iowa's farmers were fearful of joining an organization mired in controversy and labeled as too liberal—or even communist. They recommended revocation and asserted that a "fresh organizational start in Iowa would receive wide and effective farmer support."[37]

Stover again turned to female leadership as he attempted to reason with the national leadership. In March 1952 Lownes and Untiedt accompanied Stover to the national convention in Dallas, Texas, where they offered their support as members of the newly formed Rank and File Committee of the Farmers Union Members. This small group was dedicated to preserving liberal voices in the organization, defeating the proposed membership requirements, and keeping "the Farmers Union on its traditional course of fighting for the common people." Lownes passed "mimeographed resolutions" to conference attendees that emphasized a cease-fire in Korea, a condemnation of racial discrimination in the United States, and a criticism of the "monopoly enterprise system" that was responsible for political corruption and economic uncertainty. The Rank and File Committee also ran candidates for national offices, including Marie Holt of Bergen, North Dakota, for national vice president. The election returns, which garnered 9,920 votes for Holt and 303,957 for the incumbent, demonstrated that the Rank and File Committee represented only a fraction of the entire NFU. Nonetheless, Untiedt continued to agitate for recognition during the open debate over membership requirements. Speaking to the entire membership, she explained how the NFU used underhanded tactics to divide the IFU membership and hamper Stover's leadership. When she demanded more transparency in the organization, Untiedt was ruled out of order midway through her comments and removed from the floor.[38]

The national convention in Dallas was a major defeat for Stover and the Rank and File Committee. The *Des Moines Register* reported that the IFU was about to get a "good housecleaning." Stover and his supporters responded with a stubborn determination to launch membership drives, continue personal visits with local chapters, and devise new strategies for the economic security of the IFU. The Rank and File Committee, for which Untiedt served as the secretary-treasurer and primary contact, published a critical pamphlet titled "Whither the National Farmers Union?" Drawing on a rhetoric shaped by agrarian romanticism, the pamphlet claimed that the NFU had always stood for "true democracy" and called the events at the Dallas convention a "complete violation of the traditions and history of everything the organization once stood for." It carefully outlined the Rank and File Committee's objection to war, civil-rights violations, and federal limitations on cooperatives, and it presented these arguments to readers as "evidence" that would prove, beyond a doubt, that Patton was taking the NFU in the wrong direction.[39]

Convincing Iowa's farmers would require more than a pamphlet. On May 15, two months after the Dallas convention, Pauline and Elmer Gustafson wrote that someone at a recent meeting of a Boone County local had directly challenged Stover's leadership. Stover reassured them that the person (whom he knew) was not a member, adding that "I think we can trust the members to save the Farmers Union." He urged them to disregard that one person and to build "membership as far as we can everywhere." Stover optimistically reported to the Gustafsons that he had just returned from an organizing trip to Monona where they would form a new county organization "with several hundred members in the very near future." Yet many of these drives were not especially successful. In June Horton Gilbert, a member from Henry County, informed Stover that he was "entirely alone" and facing an increasingly hostile membership. In response, Stover assured

Gilbert that he and several other state leaders would soon visit personally to clear up any misconceptions. Upon hearing his side of the story, Stover was sure the people of Henry County would "line up on our side pretty fast." Certainly, Gilbert was not alone but only in the sense that he was among a growing number of discouraged organizers. In November 1952 Earl Ronfeldt of Smithland, Iowa, reported his "failed" membership drive. Members did not feel comfortable participating in the drive, and farmers simply did not want to join. "I am at a loss to know where you start," Ronfeldt wrote apologetically. "I hope other locals have done much better than we have on this drive." He wondered whether improving junior activities and reviving a women's auxiliary would help, recognizing that most prospective members were also looking for a social element to the organization. He promised Stover that he would begin canvassing the next week, as soon as he had harvested his corn.[40]

Without the financial backing of the NFU or its cooperatives, Ronfeldt's ideas to enhance the social activities would be nearly impossible to achieve. By January 1953, as revocation appeared imminent and the IFU faced "very serious and immediate difficulties," Stover organized a new finance and promotion committee of five seasoned members to raise money "in addition to membership dues." The committee included three women, Pauline Gustafson, Frances Hendricks, and Bernice Strubble, all of whom brought years of experience in both the ladies auxiliary and in the general organization. Stover hoped this would allow the organization to operate independently of national oversight, and over the following year membership actually increased by 34 percent. Edna Untiedt was actively recruiting members until the last hour, even giving up her poultry operation that year to spend more time traveling to various counties. This was not enough to reach the new minimums, however, and the NFU formally revoked Iowa's charter in March of 1954. Stover, who turned down Patton's suggestion to resign, continued to publish the *Iowa Union Farmer* and operate under the auspices of the Iowa Farmers Union. In February 1955 the NFU filed suit against Stover for unfair competition, falsely representing the organization, and the illegal use of trademarks.[41]

Without adequate financing, the most that Stover's IFU could do was to promote a liberal ideology through a modest publicity campaign. Untiedt again began traveling to neighboring counties to hold meetings and assess member attitudes. By July 1956 she assured Stover that the members of Lee County "are still with you and ready to carry on." The state board of directors also organized the Educational and Advisory Committee, which consisted of five women, to produce and distribute materials in Stover's defense. Members of the committee, Margaret Andregg, Martha Joens, M. Ida Rink, Alice Sponheim, and Julia Wharam, were all older women who had been members for nearly thirty years. Their age and experience allowed them to speak with some authority, and their relative stability on farms, in families, and in marriages insulated them from neighborly suspicion. They utilized feminine strategies by emphasizing education and information, as well as a shared sense of urgency about their immediate community. They wrote letters to newspapers and produced pamphlets, including a thirty-one-page booklet titled "What Farmers Should Know About the Farmers Union: The Inside Story of Outside Interference in the Iowa Farmers Union." The pamphlet assured readers that the IFU "does exist" and then, with sophisticated writing and analysis, detailed the conflict between Stover and the NFU. The ultimate solution was simply staying together, trusting Stover's organization, and working for peace and prosperity through legislative action.[42]

Stover often expressed his personal gratitude to those who dedicated time and resources to supporting his cause. In December 1955, after the Scott County Farmers Union sent a letter of support to the *Des Moines Register*, Stover promised to "throw a party for the Scott County FU. He cited their "unusual amount of courage" in defending "a highly controversial and beleaguered individual like your humble servant." But despite their efforts, and the efforts of the Educational and Advisory Committee, the courts sided with the NFU in August 1957 and barred Stover from using any trademarks, insignias, or references to the IFU.[43]

In supporting Stover over the course of seven years, a small number of women had, in many ways, fulfilled the NFU mandate for greater inclusivity. They served in leadership positions, helped to organize and educate members, attended state and national conferences, volunteered for committees, and made themselves the public face of a heated controversy. They were not motivated by any desire to promote gender equality or even to utilize entirely new organizing strategies, but they were willing to take new risks in order to support a leadership that was respectful of their talents and experiences. Interestingly, in the fallout of Stover's defeat, many of these women were perfectly willing to retreat. Untiedt expressed great excitement as Stover reorganized his supporters into what would become the U.S. Farmers Association (USFA). Now facing the limitations of age, she hoped to find a tenant to work part of her land and in order to devote more time to organizing and finding new members for a "real down to earth [organization]." On the other hand, she shied away from taking on any leadership roles. Although she was dissatisfied with the man they elected as county president of their new USFA chapter, she had decided not to run herself. "I felt it was a position for a man," she wrote, citing the fact that a woman might be too controversial among the "business class of the county." Well aware of gendered expectations for women in organizations, she wrote that no businesses would "recognize me as the head of a group. Sec-treas or such position, yes, that would be a little different." Her years of travel, organizing, speaking to members, testifying in court, attending national conventions, and even being removed from the floor of the Dallas convention, had not changed Untiedt's understanding of how she should behave—or at least how others might perceive her behavior. Her actions had been acceptable so long as she was working on behalf of Stover in a crisis situation, but as tensions eased she had to rethink her role in the new organization.[44]

The women who worked on his behalf had been inspired by Stover's ideology and commitment to his beliefs. Yet they acted because, as a leader, he sought out and fostered female voices, harnessing women's transformative experiences as members of the ladies auxiliaries and utilizing a highly personal approach in retaining their support. These dynamics, based on the active support of male leadership, made possible women's entry into more public spaces. In Stover's IFU women's work was highly valued, and they were encouraged to aggressively employ the inclusive rhetoric set forth by national leaders. As much as a few women gained, it is certain that many ended their affiliation with the IFU and shied away from the controversy that put unwanted attention on the members' liberal political beliefs. As farm wives, women often had some say in which organizations the family would join, and that choice quite often depended on the services and social opportunities offered. To join the IFU during the 1950s carried some risk, although for the most part women's voices on this side of the story are largely silent.

Understanding Stover's strategies and leadership style is significant in understanding how women were able to integrate themselves into male-dominated organizations. The limits of inclusive rhetoric, as a means to change deeply engrained beliefs about gendered divisions of labor, are evident in the IFU as it reemerged as a more stable organization in 1957. Immediately following its legal victory, the NFU initiated efforts to reorganize a new Iowa affiliate under the leadership of a carefully selected and closely supervised president. By 1958 more than 5,000 members had joined. But membership lists featured only male names, and women were still primarily in charge of the junior division and the entertainment. Few regularly attended meetings. Local meeting reports from nine counties during 1958 and 1959 show that women made up only 16.3 percent of those in attendance. Children and juniors (under the age of sixteen) comprised another 19.5 percent. These local meetings were largely male dominated, although more women attended meetings regarding membership drives or social events such as parties and picnics. Official publications began featuring women's sections and household hints, while female leadership was reported with some novelty. In 1965, when Florence Dimmitt became the first female president of the Wapello County Farmers Union, the *Iowa Farmers Union Spotlight* declared that she was "making history" as the first woman to serve in that position.[45]

The stories of the women of the Iowa Farmers Union, Fred Stover, and Cold War politics reveal the various trajectories of social feminisms. When compared with the Iowa Farm Bureau Federation, the IFU demonstrates that the marginalization of women was not inevitable, but inclusivity also proved complex and largely incompatible with farm families' understanding of gender roles. Between the 1920s and 1940s women of the IFU and the Iowa Farm Bureau Federation utilized similar strategies that grew out of social feminisms, a maternal rhetoric, and a commitment to transformative leadership and community service. The postwar period brought very different challenges to these groups, and in contrast to the IFBF, the IFU chose to foster an inclusive rhetoric and to actually remove women from their all-female spaces. By the end of the decade, it had become clear that this strategy also had significant limitations. Women were able to act only in an environment that welcomed their approach to organizational involvement, one that valued education and community. Furthermore, the women who thrived in this situation tended to be older, enjoy supportive relationships with their husbands, and have a firm standing in the community. They could safely respond to a divisive crisis as willing workers, but once the situation had been resolved, their roles were less certain.

For women interested in agricultural activism, then, Iowa's second-largest farm organization offered few practical outlets that fully utilized their voices and talents to influence policy or garner public attention. By the end of the 1950s, the IFU also had a new competitor, the National Farm Organization (NFO). Formed in 1955 as a group committed to collective bargaining, the NFO did not shy away from controversy and provided experiences for its members that, in conjunction with a new rhetoric of rural decline and equality under the law, proved startlingly transformative. It too promoted membership for entire families and claimed to utilize women's voices, but it did so in ways that firmly embraced established gender roles in integrated settings and utilized a militarized rhetoric that encouraged women to work on behalf of the organization in public settings, rather than within the organization itself.

CHAPTER FOUR

Because Somebody Had to Do It

Women, Families, and the National Farmers Organization

DURING THE LATE WINTER OF 1958, Luella Zmolek's husband, Don, announced that he was going to a "farm meeting." Don had never joined an agricultural organization or even expressed interest in farm politics, but Luella was so caught up with her chores that she did not stop to question him. The following day, when Don attended another meeting, she began to think it was a little bit strange. She and Don had been married for nearly thirteen years and, along with their three daughters and three sons, had enjoyed several prosperous years on an eighty-acre farm in Black Hawk County, Iowa. In 1955, however, after commodity prices fell dramatically, their eighty acres and purebred Angus herd were in jeopardy. She and Don found work in Cedar Falls, Iowa, to provide for the family, but working for wages was not a long-term solution. So, in 1958, after Don had attended the two meetings, he approached Luella with a copy of the NFO *Reporter*, the official newspaper of the National Farmers Organization (NFO). Intrigued by the NFO's plan for collective bargaining in agriculture, Luella reasoned that if they worked to improve commodity prices, she could quit her job and devote herself entirely to the farm. At twenty-five dollars, membership dues seemed high, but she told Don they should give their money to "anyone who would try."[1]

Midwestern farm women like Luella Zmolek found their expectations for farm life, marriage, and family disrupted by rapid modernization and economic instability. Along with their husbands, many placed their hope in new, specialized farm organizations that emerged after 1945 to promote specific production and marketing methods. By joining these groups, women began to imagine new forms of community based on personal experience. In a period when communities defined by geography, ethnicity, and kinship were slipping away, organizations like the NFO played a pivotal role in the development of agrarian feminisms by promoting politicized, public identities for farm women. In the same period when Betty Friedan posed "the problem that has no name" to white, urban, middle-class housewives and attacked institutional sexism, farm women of the American Midwest also developed feminist approaches to a much different but similarly unexplained "farm problem." Most farm families experienced depopulation, economic uncertainty, and modernization as an endless progression of personal decisions. They believed that the ultimate outcome reflected their character and ability, with devastating consequences for those who failed. Formed in 1955, the NFO provided an explanation for the crisis in agriculture that permitted its members to shift the blame and identify their daily struggles as part of systemic social and political inequalities in American society, lifting the burden of blame from individuals and placing it on the system. The NFO also promised that farmers could obtain consistent and fair commodity prices through collective bargaining. Just as Second Wave activists acquired a feminist consciousness through participation in movements for peace or civil rights, membership in the NFO did not necessarily present a venue to challenge sexism, but it provided a transformative experience that linked women's legal, political, and social rights directly to the well-being of the family and their farm.

Identifying corporations, food processors, and financial institutions as outside threats to their way of life allowed women to mute social feminisms and formulate early manifestations of a politics of dependence that emphasized women's vital roles in times of economic urgency. In contrast to the rhetoric of rural uplift supplied by the Farm Bureau and the Farmers Union, women harnessed a newly emerging narrative of rural decline that required solutions far more complex than the better housekeeping promoted within social feminisms. Members of the NFO held fast to gendered divisions of labor, but they also understood that economic conditions and the demands of the organization required families to rethink those boundaries. Framed within a militaristic rhetoric that upheld women as Rosie-the-Riveter-type figures, this idea was represented in terms of families, especially women, who were sacrificing individual aspirations to work on the farm, in town, or in NFO offices only "for the duration," or until they secured higher prices.[2]

Women's experiences with the NFO during the 1950s and 1960s underscore the significance of work, family, and activism when tracing the development of agrarian feminisms that permitted women to quietly question patriarchy while defending gendered divisions of labor and the integrity of the nuclear family. Women challenged the male-dominated power structures within corporations and government but not necessarily within their own lives because they believed themselves and their husbands to be equally oppressed by these distant entities. In many ways this mirrors developments within the civil rights movement and the efforts of early Second Wave leaders, including Friedan and the founders of the National Organization for Women

(NOW) who "militantly demanded equality in the public realm," but not in their private lives. In movements for civil rights, women — particularly white women working with student groups like the Student Non-Violent Coordinating Committee (SNCC) — took on feminized roles and were barred from leadership positions. When they challenged male leadership in 1965, men labeled gender issues a distraction from matters of race and "too threatening to discuss." Women who dared to speak out were ridiculed and rebuffed by male activists claiming to value equal rights for all. According to historian Sara Evans, working for organizations like NOW and SNCC marked important turning points in the lives of many female activists, who acquired the language and skills they needed to contest gendered oppression. Thus, while the women of the NFO did not directly challenge gendered thinking, such confrontations were rare in social movements overall during this period. But by the end of the 1960s, NFO women, like female civil-rights and peace activists, had emerged as very different people with a new confidence that women had the right and the ability to act publicly.[3]

Farm women were even less likely than civil-rights activists, and obviously feminists, to point out the gendered disparities between men and women. The primary difference between the feminism of NOW and agrarian feminism was that the former focused on individual rights, while the latter emphasized the community. In her groundbreaking work, *The Feminine Mystique*, Betty Friedan encouraged women to escape the drudgery of housework and prescribed paid employment outside the home as a means to personal fulfillment and economic security. As historian Monda Halpern pointed out, however, farm women tended to view off-farm work as oppressive. Unless they had teaching, nursing, or secretarial skills to land the most socially respectable jobs, farm women had few choices and would likely end up working for extremely low wages. Housework was actually optimal for these women in that they wanted to maintain some degree of autonomy and contribute as helpers on the farm. Farm women were integrated into their husband's work spaces, and perhaps for this reason they tended to value community before individualism. Their integral role in the farm's success gave many women a strong sense of responsibility for their own and their community's economic well-being. As they came together in organizations, they also began to understand that women could contribute a more holistic view of policy, politics, and daily life to public debates about agriculture. The NFO encouraged farm women to make the personal political by politicizing the entire family and making stringent demands on women to undertake an array of roles both on and off the farm. The resulting transformative experiences connected women's legal, political, and social rights to human rights and to the well-being of the entire community.[4]

The NFO has its roots in the period of economic readjustment following the Second World War. As postwar reconstruction projects continued around the globe and the Korean conflict propped up the demand for animal byproducts, many Midwestern farmers increased hog production in an attempt to offset losses triggered by reduced federal supports and drought conditions that decreased crop yields. This was disastrous for many families, as overproduction led to a rapid decline in hog prices. In April 1953, just before the end of hostilities in Korea, the price of hogs reached a record high of $26.40 per hundredweight but then bottomed out at $10.60 per hundredweight in December of 1955. During the fall of 1955, Jay Loghry, a fifty-five-year-old feed salesman from Corning, Iowa, observed that many of his customers were on the brink of foreclosure. Having lost his own farm to foreclosure in 1932, Loghry began holding meetings that attracted hundreds of anxious farmers and their families seeking solutions to faltering commodity prices. In response to vocal calls for action, on October 20, 1955, Loghry hosted a regional conference in Corning for farmers from Missouri and Iowa, where they decided to form the National Farmers Organization.[5]

By the end of the 1950s, NFO leaders, with longtime president Oren Lee Staley at the head, had formulated the clear goal of organizing farmers to bargain collectively for fair prices on their products. Seeking strength in numbers, the NFO recruited aggressively in the Midwest and quickly established chapters in Missouri, Nebraska, Minnesota, Illinois, and Wisconsin. Thirty-seven state chapters had been established by the mid-1970s, although exact membership numbers remain elusive because Staley kept statistics confidential in order to enhance the group's bargaining power. Organizers estimated that in any given county the NFO needed just 25 to 30 percent of the farmers to join in order to successfully bargain with processors for higher prices, but they hoped processors would believe the numbers to be much higher. Most estimates for the 1950s and 1960s range from 150,000 to 300,000 families nationwide, making the NFO a fierce competitor with the National Farmers Union.[6]

Inspired by organized labor, members of the NFO had few real connections to urban workers. They identified as farmers committed to preserving agriculture as a way of life and the family farm as the ideal mode of production. By the 1970s and 1980s many members of the NFO recognized that they had not been successful in this mission, although for several critical years in the 1950s and 1960s, the NFO at least offered farmers a means to resist what they viewed as corporate control over agriculture. Collective bargaining seemed to remedy the situation by allowing farmers to modernize and specialize on their own terms while holding fast to community ideals. As historian Linda Tvrdy explains, "The NFO tried to convince farmers that collective bargaining, not individual begging, would give them the power to save themselves and their rural communities from the increasing corporatization and concentration of American agriculture." Throughout the early 1960s this played out in the formation of cooperatives, as well as holding actions, in which farm families withheld hogs, milk, and other products to influence market prices. The goal was to secure comfort and security, not excessive wealth, for members. In 1962 member Don Henry from Nemaha County, Kansas, explained that he simply did not have the capital to invest in mechanizing his dairy farm, nor did he have the physical strength to milk thirty cows by hand every day. He feared that continual hard labor would make him "one of the youngest farmers in the cemetery." If dairy prices improved, however, he could reduce his herd and "take life easier."[7]

As a burgeoning organization dependent on grassroots activism, the very nature of the NFO necessitated the development of new strategies for women. Most who became active members had previous experience with township homemakers clubs, women's auxiliaries, extension groups, and 4-H clubs, but their exact roles in a collective bargaining organization were not immediately apparent. In specialized groups more generally women had carved out roles that were fluid, flexible, and reflective of their own interests because becoming active members meant emphasizing their skills as bookkeepers, producers, and farm managers. These organizations often attracted women who already possessed some degree of confidence in their abilities and shared in business decisions with their husbands. Women were openly invited to attend meetings and work in tandem with their husbands, but there were few roles especially delineated as female specific. Aside from local social events and fundraisers, there were no auxiliaries, youth groups, or educational activities that women could call their own. Some took on leadership at the local level or worked in supportive roles — as bookkeepers at checkpoints where farmers gathered their livestock for sale, as secretaries at an office, or as organizers of social functions. During holding actions some maintained vital networks through telephone trees. Women called into radio shows, made television appearances, and gave public presentations. Still, for others participation meant running the farm and overseeing the family while their husbands pursued leadership positions.

Women's experiences in the NFO are representative of larger trends that

developed as Midwestern agriculture transitioned into a more capital intensive business, creating new demands for farm families and alternative
labor strategies for women. Whereas women of the previous generation had
shared a general set of tasks, such as poultry, gardening, sewing, and cooking, by 1960 women enjoyed broader choices about how they contributed
to family farming operations, whether it be field work, bookkeeping, homemaking, or off-farm work. These were not simple choices, and farm women
often received conflicting advice in farm periodicals. Anthropologist Jane
Adams found that rural women were not immune to the "feminine mystique" that shaped the public discourse during the 1950s and upheld domesticity and leisure as ideals for women. Farm periodicals increasingly focused
on domestic issues and considered women's economic contributions to the
farm as "'a sideline' providing money for luxuries and extras." This hardly
reflected the reality of most readers. In 1960 an article in *Wallace's Farmer*
declared that wives had taken the place of hired men in the field and quoted
one young farm wife in Washington County, Iowa, who asserted that she
could set her own hours and "make more money for us by working in the
fields than many women can by working in town." Whether women's farm
work fostered or detracted from gendered equality for farm women has been
a matter of debate, but a 1962 *Wallace's Farmer* poll of Iowa farm wives found
that 82 percent of those aged twenty-one to thirty-four, and 79 percent of
those aged thirty-five to forty-nine expected to discuss farm purchases with
their husbands. "Times have changed," the article declared, and "husbands
who consult their wives . . . are in the majority." Farm periodicals were suddenly full of articles designed to help men integrate their wives into the work
routines and women to navigate options for housework and childcare as
they took on field work, wage labor, or even courses on agriculture and accounting to be better farm managers for their husbands.[8]

The countless choices available to women were important to the development of agrarian feminisms, which increasingly appeared in more public
arenas as women also had more options for expressing their political identities in specialized farm organizations. Women interested in consumer relations, for example, might become active in a commodity organization like
the Iowa Porkettes. Women interested in marketing might lean more toward
the NFO. Just how they should contribute, however, was not immediately
obvious. For female members of the NFO, changing established marketing
practices required women to rethink how their homemaking or bookkeeping skills might be applied in an office setting. It meant pitching in when
asked and partaking in a culture of sacrifice that necessitated giving up ma-

terial comforts for the good of all members. Perhaps most difficult was re-thinking trust in neighbors, authority figures, the media, and how one should present oneself as an activist in public settings.

Women most often worked behind the scenes by tending to farms and mundane office work, but their experiences highlight members' motivations in an organization whose history is rife with controversy. In evaluating the group, social scientists have primarily focused on the economic aspects of collective bargaining and whether this idea of organizing farmers into a single bargaining unit could actually work in a free-market economy. Journalists, politicians, and observers have more generally preferred to emphasize the NFO's strategy of withholding or destroying agricultural commodities through holding actions. These holding actions were accompanied by federal lawsuits against the NFO and acts of violence against farmers who did not participate in withholding their products from the market. Such militant activities of the NFO long provided sensational news stories for journalists, as well as scandalous fuel for opponents hoping to discredit the organization. Writing primarily from journalistic accounts, historians have likewise described the NFO as an ineffective organization for the militant farmer, with no lasting influence in the countryside. Historian R. Douglas Hurt described the NFO as a small, politically insignificant, "radical" organization that attracted negative media attention and merely "dramatized . . . the economic plight of many farmers."[9]

In 2001, as NFO member Martha Linn reflected on her life as a farm wife near Villisca, Iowa, she painted a very different picture of this controversial organization. As farmers invested in more machinery, chemicals, and land, they fostered a "get big or get out" mentality. Linn asserted that by working for better prices, the NFO promised a new economic model that stemmed the growth of agribusiness and allowed small family farms to remain viable for future generations. She described the NFO philosophy as one that valued cooperation over competition and said, "I think the NFO is trying to show a whole philosophy of learning to work together with your neighbor. . . . It was to, you know, put your crop together and put your livestock together so you had some clout at the marketplace." With these words, Linn echoed a common attitude among NFO members who sought to change the marketplace in order to maintain the family farm ideal, thereby upholding traditional rural values.[10]

With members like Linn in mind, historian Linda Tvrdy offered a new interpretation that identified members of the NFO as "authors of a social movement." The overall mission of the NFO, she asserted, defied the standard historical narrative in which the loss of the family farm and the rise of corporate farms are viewed "as an almost inevitable by-product of free-market realities and technological progress." The NFO proposed an alternative, economically feasible vision of modern agriculture in which independent farm families served as proud stewards of the land, who emphasized sustainability, practiced careful soil conservation, and treated livestock humanely. Members of the NFO warned Americans that this was "something faceless corporations could and would not do." Saving the family farm, therefore, meant preserving and even strengthening the gendered divisions of labor that defined the family farming system. As Zmolek explained, the family farm ideal is what "kept them going" in their support of collective bargaining.[11]

Official NFO publications sold the organization as one for the entire family, but in reality women depended entirely on their husbands for access to the organization. When the NFO *Reporter* appeared in 1956 as a monthly newspaper, there was no separate section for articles of interest to women. National leaders made no provisions for women's auxiliaries, although some members organized women's groups according to local preferences. In March 1957 the NFO *Reporter* featured a photograph of approximately 100 women of Johnson County, Missouri, who met in Warrensburg, the county seat, to form the Johnson County NFO Ladies' Auxiliary. But such reports were extremely rare. Between 1957 and 1963 the *Reporter* mentioned only two other auxiliaries: one in Webster County, Iowa, and another in Macoupin County, Illinois. For the women of Webster County, their activities were in keeping with farm bureau women's clubs in that they were primarily social and focused on leisure. In June 1962 the Webster County NFO auxiliary took a bus tour to Minneapolis and St. Paul, where the members saw the zoo and went shopping. The excursion included fifty women, but most of these were women from other counties where no auxiliary existed.[12]

Most of the women who became active in the NFO saw little need for an auxiliary because they had a genuine interest in marketing that they shared with their husbands. Monica Tvrdy of Ashland, Nebraska, who joined with her husband, Edwin, in the early 1960s, explained that women were just as interested in collective bargaining as the men. As a result, "we were so busy with the one organization, we didn't need an [auxiliary] to socialize." And just as Don approached Luella Zmolek before joining the NFO, membership was often a joint decision between husbands and wives because it involved managing farm income and a family's overall economic stability. Members were landowners, or tenants aspiring to landownership, who considered themselves educated, upwardly mobile Midwestern farmers. They did not want to gamble with the assets they had acquired. Married in 1941, Mabel Schweers and her husband, Art, farmed 400 acres in Adams County, Iowa. They promised each of their eleven children one year of paid tuition at the college of their choosing and expected their farm income would fulfill this promise. Schweers described their diversified farm as productive and stable. She earned cash income through the sale of eggs, provided much of the family's food through gardening and canning, and sewed most of the family's clothing. The NFO did not necessarily offer the Schweers greater prosperity, but it did offer protection from falling prices that threatened their economic stability. And working for that stability was just as much a concern for Schweers as it was for her husband. She believed men and women worked equally hard, saying, "On the farm, the women had just as big a part to play as the men. My daughters milked just like my sons did. They loaded bales. They could do anything. They could drive the tractor. They could do anything."[13]

Still, women's active participation and access to the NFO required the approval of husbands, who often determined the couples' level of involvement. Women who became active members tended to have confidence in their abilities, and they were more likely to have stable, civil marriages in which they shared financial and marketing decisions with their husbands. Such was the case for Ilo Rhines, who began farming in 1950 with her husband, Don, on his family's farm near Edgewood, Iowa. One summer afternoon in 1958, she took a break from her work and "sat down on the grass alongside the barn" with her brother, Willis Rowell, to discuss family news. It was just like any other family visit until Rowell brought up "this new organization that he was excited about." Rhines was initially skeptical, but she and Don quickly became "willing workers" for the NFO.[14]

For Ilo Rhines, like Mabel Schweers, mutual decision making was a normal part of her married life, as it was for many of the women who became active members. As the family bookkeeper, or "the watchdog on the money," Rhines related several humorous stories about her husband purchasing farm equipment at auctions and then asking friends to accompany him home because "he was afraid of what I was going to say." When it came to the NFO, Rhines found that "the women were just about as active with some of the decision making and whether they [the family] were joining or not." Certainly, not all women enjoyed such deference from their husbands, but Luella Zmolek knew of only a few men whose wives were not involved in the NFO. Zmolek explained that for men to take on leadership responsibilities and become active in the organization, they needed their wives' support. She said, laughing, "[The men] had to do so much volunteer work and all that sort of thing and be gone so much, that if the wife wasn't involved also, then, you know, it would not work."[15]

In some cases women approved only because they trusted their husbands to make good choices for the farm. Martha Linn, who grew up in the town of Villisca, Iowa, first lived on a farm when she married her husband, Darwin, in 1957. The couple started out on rented land near Villisca, and Linn clearly recalled the day, shortly after they were married, when Darwin came home energized from a local NFO meeting. Having grown up in town, Linn had little knowledge of farming or marketing, but she knew "we didn't have a lot of money," and she trusted her husband's judgment. Doubtless, there were numbers of women who objected, who distanced themselves from the organization, and who suffered as a result of their husband's associations with the NFO. Historian Sara Evans noted that the social movements of the early 1960s required women to reach "beyond themselves day after day." Some who had once been active "just disappeared" when they were pushed too far. These women remain hidden, not typically identified in the historical record or questioned for oral history interviews.[16]

In his memoirs as an NFO organizer, Willis Rowell praised the women who supported their husbands in the NFO, but he found that "wives could also be a hindrance." As he recruited members during the late 1950s and early 1960s, Rowell encountered men who refused to join because their wives objected. In one instance a woman demanded that Rowell stop talking to her husband and go home. "He and I both knew that she meant just what she said," Rowell recalled. Months later, Rowell met the man in town, where he explained that the family had fallen on hard times and his wife was afraid he might spend their last $25 on NFO dues. Rowell concluded, "Who could blame her for feeling the way she did? Times were tough on the farm."[17]

If many of the women who joined already enjoyed mutual and reciprocal relationships with their husbands, they also had the tenacity to integrate themselves into an organization that emphasized their talents. The NFO politicized women's work by offering an array of options to women and validating women's work within a framework of urgency, as opposed to mutuality, as did the IFBF and the IFU. Publications utilized a militarized rhetoric and often equated organizational activities with battles and wars. They urged members to sacrifice for the good of the organization, whether it was money, time, or resources. In September 1956 President Oren Lee Staley prepared members for "the last battle for agriculture." He warned readers that if they lost this "battle," current trends would lead to "corporation farms and ghost towns in the agricultural areas of America." He offered hope and attempted to inspire action by empowering farmers to see themselves as an "economic force." Women were fully integrated into this rhetoric as members of a society engaged in a battle for its own survival. Rowell identified women as "the front-line troops" and "a force to be reckoned with during holding actions," as they dumped milk, churned butter to preserve the cream, and maintained the NFO's Minuteman system, or telephone tree.[18]

Stories in the NFO *Reporter* often justified women's participation, especially their public activities, by noting that women's work was an essential part of a "war effort." In March 1962 a story in the NFO *Reporter* declared, "We Salute Our Wives." The writer told the story of one anonymous farm woman who managed three young children, 400 acres, seventy ewes, forty sows, six cows, three calves, "innumerable cats and a horse." She performed strenuous farm work, isolated in her home "thirty-five miles from their doctor, a half-mile from any neighbor, and nineteen miles from the nearest relative." Two photographs accompanied the article, showing her in deep snow feeding sheep and filling a hog feeder. Her experiences served as an example to other NFO women and upheld her hardships as a necessary sacrifice for the good of the whole group. In militarized rhetoric, reminiscent of home front propaganda during the Second World War, the article concluded: "The NFO salutes these thousands of women like her, who, by their courage and uncomplaining devotion, hard work, and self-sacrifice, make it possible for their menfolk to carry on the fight to get farmers in a position to price their products at the market place." These images reinforced gender roles by identifying men as warriors and women as devoted supporters, but unlike more established farm organizations, the NFO recognized women's support as absolutely essential to the overall administration of the organization. Without women, the male leaders asserted, the NFO simply could not function.[19]

This argument appealed to women because the "fight" was only meant to be temporary, and once the crisis was past, they would no longer be asked to step outside their appropriately gendered roles. Several articles and features motivated members by promising that once they achieved higher commodity prices, NFO members could become full-time farmers and their wives could be full-time homemakers. A two-page spread in February 1962 featured Mrs. Charles Salyer, the wife of an NFO organizer in Clinton County, Missouri. She had a vested interest in raising prices because not only could she "quit feeding hogs," but "when hogs bring in enough we can hire a man to feed them and my husband can spend more time at home." Following these comments, the editor of the NFO *Reporter* added that Mrs. Salyer was not alone. He wrote, "Thousands of NFO wives will echo this sentiment—and thousands of them are feeding hogs and milking cows to make it come true that much sooner."[20]

Placing women's aspirations for comfortable living on the frontlines of the NFO's mission was designed to motivate all members, men and women, to change their marketing practices. NFO events with mixed audiences often featured female speakers who spoke on behalf of the entire organization and emphasized the simplicity of the NFO's plan. Mrs. Ralph Labertew, whose husband was the president of the Appanoose County NFO, went on a speaking tour throughout Iowa after she delivered an address at the 1960 national NFO convention. She spoke of the false ideal of individual independence in agriculture, stating, "A farmer is his own boss, he can work as many hours as he chooses, he can produce as much as he likes. He can over produce, he can flood the market. But when he takes his product to the processor his independence has suddenly left for then he is told how much will be given him."[21]

As members developed a rhetoric framed by exigency, women found that this also provided flexibility and mobility within the organization. Acting in unusual circumstances allowed them to speak publicly and emphasize their skills as agricultural producers and farm managers. Mrs. A. Van Vooren of Buchanan County, Iowa, made an appeal in the pages of the NFO *Reporter* for women to shed preconceived notions about women's proper roles when she wrote, "Let's put aside our pride, ladies, and tell the world we need a better living and income for our family. . . . Let's attend meetings with our husbands and be informed on the NFO program so we too can explain it and pass it along." Van Vooren situated herself and other women within heterosexual marriages, but she made a significant departure when she urged real cooperation between men and women.[22]

By the mid- to late 1960s, women appeared more frequently in public roles, speaking on behalf of the entire organization, and they linked women's concerns directly to the specific goals of the group. Mrs. Kenneth Johnson, a young farmer's wife who worked with her husband to lobby the Iowa legislature, appeared on the NFO's weekly television program, *U.S. Farm Report*, with two other female panelists in 1965. Johnson spoke of her conversations with politicians, but she attempted to relate to women in the audience by speaking about the sacrifices she made on behalf of the NFO. Because she was away from home so often, Johnson believed her children suffered for her work. Yet it was worthwhile because her children would have no future in farming "unless things change."[23]

More than emphasizing their maternal roles, women speaking in public usually upheld the farm wife as a full partner in the farming enterprise. In July 1966 the *U.S. Farm Report* again featured a panel of three Iowa women, including Luella Berstler of Emmetsburg, Iowa. The mother of five sons and two daughters operated a diversified farm with her husband and compared women's work in the NFO to helping men in the fields. She said, "There isn't a wife who won't help her husband any day in the field when they're busy, and I think they can work just as hard on marketing and getting an adequate income, and creating new wealth that the nation deserves." Later that year, in November 1966, the *U.S. Farm Report* featured another panel of women from Tennessee. Mrs. William Stone, whose husband was the county NFO president, instructed women to use their social networks to build membership. She said, "A woman can't keep a secret, this is the time to talk, girls. We should take every opportunity to help. We can talk to our neighbors about NFO. We have home demonstration clubs, and if you drop in for a cup of coffee, talk about the NFO."[24]

Berstler's and Stone's suggestions resonated with women active at the local levels, who typically pursued gender-appropriate activities based on personal interests while fulfilling the needs of the local chapter. Many women looked forward to chapter meetings as opportunities to form new friendships and for couples, friends, and neighbors to meet and discuss "the farm problem." Luella Zmolek recalled that initially, "there weren't too many farm women who would come," but more began attending as membership grew. She explained that the women in the group formed a close bond based on their mutual interest in the NFO, and "you'd almost feel closer than you did to your brothers and sisters because they understood what we were doing, and we just understood each other so much." Likewise, Martha Linn, who had never farmed prior to her marriage and who struggled to understand the business of agriculture, found great support and encouragement from those she met in the NFO. Linn said, "That was probably one of the nicest things about belonging to the NFO, you got to meet all the people who were sharing the same philosophy and way of thinking about farming as you were."[25]

Nearly all women engaged in the gender-specific task of preparing and serving food during the social period of the meeting, but this did not necessarily hinder involvement in the business portion. Mabel Schweers, who began attending meetings with her husband after reading a newspaper article about the NFO, found that men and women worked well together as couples. Schweers described the NFO as a "community of farmers" and stated that although men "were the ones that made [the NFO] work," wives

Women and a printing press. Special Collections Department, Iowa State University Library.

usually attended meetings and provided input. She said, "If [women] had something they wanted to say, they would. I mean, we were not shy at all. We said what we thought." Such comments denote an expectation that women could and should play an important role in the organization, and interestingly, all the women interviewed made similar remarks about women's inclusion. Although they did not make any overt connections to Second Wave feminisms and they never spoke in terms of complete gender equality, they consistently promoted women's involvement as a positive aspect of membership.[26]

Meeting attendance was only a small part of membership, and as they came to see collective bargaining as the answer to unstable commodity prices, several women expressed a new sense of empowerment. When asked whether the NFO was strictly a "man's organization," Ilo Rhines explained that participating in the NFO required the efforts of an entire family. She said that "other than the men's signing the contract, it was their name on it, you know [laughing], . . . it was a whole family-type project." Women typically sought elected office as secretaries and took charge of managing information and membership. Wilma Embree farmed 160 acres in Adams County, Iowa, with her husband, Stanley, and their two children. Married in 1945, Embree quit her job as an elementary-school teacher to become a full-time farm wife. When commodity prices dropped in 1955, she returned to teaching and became active in the NFO. Seeing a very real need for better communication at the local level, in 1960 she decided to use her writing skills to start a county newsletter and help coordinate activities. Along with Mabel Schweers, Embree and several other women wrote stories about events and members in the county, and they summarized information from the NFO *Reporter* before printing and mailing it out.[27]

Embree was not simply bringing members together for social activities but actually engaging the collective bargaining process by publishing meeting times and locations for members to market their products cooperatively. Members marking hogs, for example, would negotiate prices with a processer, then meet at a "check point" to load their hogs on to one semitrailer. Before they delivered the hogs to the processing plant, they enhanced their bargaining power by weighing individual hogs, measuring the back fat, and determining the grade of the meat. Women often worked alongside men at checkpoints, and Mabel Schweers recalled the empowering nature of the process as they negotiated better prices. She said, "The scales were one of the biggest advantages because we knew how much [the hogs] weighed before they went to the packing plant. They couldn't cheat us on weight, so that was a big advantage. We were feeling like we were getting in command. We could set some prices ourselves. . . . It was a good feeling."

Collective marketing efforts allowed women like Schweers to take their bookkeeping expertise and their interest in livestock into public spaces where they applied their knowledge to furthering the goals of the entire organization.

Occasionally, these skills also transferred to full-time employment at county NFO offices or even the national headquarters in Corning, Iowa. In 1968, as her children began leaving for college, Embree decided that working at the NFO office would not be as "demanding as [teaching] school." Working from eight to four, she managed new memberships, handled membership dues, and started files on new members. In general, she viewed her work with the NFO as one more thing that she could do to help her husband. Embree equated office work with farm work when she said, "We lived in a farming community, and everybody helped their husbands. Some of them worked in fields and did chores and did those things, and that was a way to help them maybe farm more land even. To expand and get better machinery in that way." Not all paid employment for the NFO provided such positive experiences, though, and Embree confessed that at times office work could be "mundane." It provided more income than personal fulfillment, and as it did for many women, wage work took her away from responsibilities at home. Other women felt as though they had been conscripted to work in the office simply because no one else was available and their husbands had volunteered their wives.[28]

The friendships and opportunities afforded by the NFO were essential in keeping women active because membership sometimes created tense divisions with nonmembers in neighborhoods, organizations, and families. The men and women who joined had to justify their membership in an increasingly controversial organization, and they turned to one another for support. This was especially important for women who relied on social networks to fulfill many of their basic needs, such as shared work, child care, transportation, and assistance in times of illness, childbirth, and death. In most farming communities collective bargaining was counterintuitive to traditional marketing practices that emphasized individual success in selling at just the right time for the best price.

Early on NFO members fully expected to cooperate with established groups, like the Farm Bureau and the Farmers Union, partly because they believed the NFO's message was universal and partly because they were also members of those groups. Relationships were most strained with the Iowa Farmers Union, which by 1957 had returned under new leadership and tighter national oversight. The state director, Kenneth Schumann, considered the NFO a direct threat to IFU cooperatives and their efforts to rebuild membership in the state. At the local level many IFU members saw the two organizations as highly compatible and even suggested that they collaborate on holding actions. In 1959 the Jackson County IFU president, Harvey Rickert, wrote that the "NFO idea seems to be kindling the imagination here." But Schumann never endorsed the idea since his primary job in Iowa was to rebuild the IFU as a more conservative political, social, and marketing group.[29]

This isolated some members like Wilma and Lloyd Zubrod of Chickasaw County, Iowa, who canceled their long-standing membership in the IFU in 1960. The Zubrods held local leadership positions in both groups, and Lloyd often coordinated joint activities. In October 1960, however, Wilma wrote to Kenneth Schumann questioning whether he was "interested in the farmers and their problems at all." Unable to comprehend why he would want to undermine the NFO, she admonished Schumann, stating, "When you change your tactics and decide to get along with the NFO, we will again join the Farmers Union." In their case Lloyd worked as an organizer, but Wilma was clearly invested in their organizational activities and was willing to break ties with the IFU, possibly risking friendships and neighborhood ties.[30]

Divisions between the NFO and other organizations took Luella Zmolek by surprise, and like Wilma Zubrod she was disappointed to hear "their leaders say, 'You know, that isn't a good thing to join,' and so on. . . . We just assumed other farm organizations would help us out, but then it turned out that wasn't the case at all." Mabel Schweers, a longtime Farm Bureau member, deduced that major agricultural organizations, along with "the government, and large corporations like the large grain companies, the large packing plants," actually benefited from keeping commodity prices—and thereby consumer prices—down. And for Schweers, whose brother worked on their parents' farm in Adams County, Iowa, the tensions between the NFO and the Farm Bureau even caused friction in her own family. Her brother refused to join the NFO and intentionally sold cattle during a holding action with the help of Farm Bureau members who assisted farmers "as a protest" against the NFO. As a result Schweers said that she and her brother "didn't speak very friendly for quite a while, but it soon passed." These personal slights or feelings of exclusion were commonplace, which explains why many women placed such tremendous value on the friendships they made through the NFO. As members of a specialized organization focused on a single issue, these women came together through an economic and political ideology, rather than by the happenstance of geography. In times when neighbors and families disapproved of NFO membership, these friendships provided women with a new community of like-minded people to provide support.[31]

Day-to-day membership clearly provided opportunities and challenges. But holding actions provided the most dramatic staging grounds for women's skills and contributions, and it was in these times that women became acutely aware of how challenging inequalities in the countryside could meet with resistance and hostility. Most of the women trusted that their neighbors would understand and that urban consumers would support their efforts, but they quickly found themselves isolated and labeled as radicals. In the weeks that members withheld commodities from the market, women were instrumental in maintaining lines of communication, providing accurate information, and coping with the stress brought on by dispensing with livestock or milk, limiting their income, and confronting negative media attention and the grumblings of disapproving neighbors. All of the skills they had developed by going to meetings, serving as active members, forming friendships, and negotiating tense moments with other organizations came into play. In 1959 the NFO staged its first holding action to keep hogs off the market; this was followed by a similar action in 1960. In 1961 cattle and market lambs were added to the list, and in 1962 the NFO ordered its members to hold all livestock. In the fall of 1964, the NFO sponsored another holding action between August and October on all livestock, and this particular action was characterized by heightened violence. Then, in 1967, the NFO supported milk holding actions, and in 1968 they staged hog kills, resulting in the destruction of 14,083 hogs.[32]

Holding actions usually began following an order from the national office or following a vote from the membership. Once this decision had been made, members then spread word of the holding action by telephone or by visiting with neighbors, a job typically given to women or married couples. According to the NFO *Reporter* members clearly expected women to participate. Following the first major holding action, the front page of the October 1962 issue of the NFO *Reporter* featured a photograph of two women, Mrs. Veldron Hannah and Mrs. Ronald Schweider, at an observation post along U.S. 71 and commended all NFO women who "did a tremendous job staffing information points and observation posts," where they kept tallies of livestock on their way to market. News articles like this reinforced to members the extraordinary nature of holding actions, as well as the exceptional loyalty of NFO members. Again, echoing propaganda from the Second World War, these stories told of women stepping in and doing extraordinary work to ensure victory. In 1962 members of the NFO ladies auxiliary of Macoupin County, Illinois, "took complete charge of manning the office, stood on check points for hours at a time, secured the newsflashes . . . and helped the husbands on the Minuteman system." This meant keeping tabs on who sold their products, how much they sold, and the prices they received. And in June 1967 a photo essay of farmers dumping milk in Herkimer County, New York, included one image of women removing milk containers from the back of a truck and emptying the contents. The caption, perhaps intended to humiliate and motivate male members, read, "Women got into the act as the dumping gathered steam. If anything, they proved to be more active than the men."[33]

Holding commodities from the market required a tremendous amount of work that proved emotionally and physically demanding. Ilo Rhines recalled that, due to the perishable nature of milk, holding at her family's dairy was labor intensive. She said, "Once you opened that spicket [sic] on that tank the milk was gone, and the profit was gone and it wasn't easy to do that,

Dumping out milk. Special Collections Department, Iowa State University Library.

though in the long run it paid off because prices were much different after that for a good number of years." Women on dairy farms hated to see their product go to waste so they fed milk to the hogs or separated the milk and made butter out of the cream before they dumped it. Rhines noted that few farm families actually had butter churns suited to large-scale production so they used antique, gallon butter churns or even tried making butter in old washing machines. They also reached out to NFO women from cattle and grain operations by asking them to help churn and consume the milk or even exercise their gender-appropriate roles as consumers and create local shortages by buying up all the milk from nearby grocery stores.[34]

Holding actions took their toll on entire families, as existing tensions with friends and neighbors intensified and reports in the media misrepresented the intentions of NFO strategies. Luella and Don Zmolek often went to processing plants to see who was selling their livestock, and when they saw those, they knew "there could be very hard feelings because we were trying so hard." Zmolek described holding actions as full of highs and lows. She said, "Pretty soon, you know, it seemed like everyone was holding and we would feel really good about it. . . . And then, all of a sudden, it would start to go the other way again," and some farmers would start selling. Members became even more frustrated when the NFO successfully bargained for higher prices and some nonmembers took advantage of higher prices,

NFO demonstrators. Special Collections Department, Iowa State University Library.

sold their commodities, then glutted the market to drive prices down again. Women whose husbands had county or state leadership roles found it their job to field endless phone calls from anxious members who were unsure about their participation or who had heard false rumors about prices, members selling produce, or even instances of violence. The support networks, based on shared food, work, and space were indispensable in these moments. Wilma Embree recalled that during holding actions she would take "cookies and things" to a country school a half mile from her home. There, NFO members would eat and discuss any news about the holding action, thus quelling rumors and fostering solidarity.[35]

Women's skills at community building helped members to weather holding actions, especially the damaging reports in the media of violence incited by the NFO. Mabel Schweers insisted that from the top down NFO members were told not to incite hostility. She said, "They were admonished and admonished and admonished not to do anything violent." Yet between August 20 and October 1, the *Des Moines Register* blamed the NFO for twenty-two dynamite explosions in Iowa, Illinois, and Wisconsin. Members were also blamed for twenty-three incidents of cutting fences in Iowa and eleven instances of slashed tires in Minnesota, Wisconsin, Illinois, and Missouri. They staged eight separate pickets outside processing plants, and shots were fired in nine unconnected incidents in Nebraska, Missouri, Minnesota, and Iowa. In September 1964 two NFO members were killed as they tried to stop a truck from entering the Equity Livestock Cooperative in Bonduel, Wisconsin. As dramatic and shocking as these events were, direct actions and violence were limited. In 1964 acts of violence and vandalism were concen-

A milk bath. Special Collections Department, Iowa State University Library.

trated in only twenty-two of Iowa's ninety-nine counties. Of these, just five counties reported more than one or two cases.[36]

The *Des Moines Register*, whose editorial staff was largely critical of the NFO, asserted that the violence was widespread but underreported because many farmers were hesitant to discuss vandalism or harassment. Members found such assertions in the media to be unnerving, especially when journalistic accounts portrayed members as greedy, cruel, and socialistic. Members considered themselves to be ordinary, law-abiding American farmers who simply sought economic stability and a voice in the capitalist system. Members participated in dramatic aspects of holding actions, like hog kills and dumping milk, because they expected the news coverage to generate support, especially in urban areas. It quickly became apparent that the NFO had little control over how those events were reported or received by the public. Luella Zmolek hoped that the newspapers would bring public attention to the mission of the NFO, but she found instead that journalists were more interested in the sensational and shocking nature of hog kills. She recalled that urban journalists were disgusted by the dead animals, but to farm people this was simply part of dealing with livestock. She asserted, "All you had to do was go to a packing plant and see it was a lot worse than shooting these hogs." And when they attempted to counteract negative media reports by butchering the hogs and giving away the meat, she found that journalists simply were not interested in covering the story.[37]

By the end of the 1960s, it became increasingly clear that despite members' early hopes for a rapid movement toward organizing farmers into collective bargaining units, it was not coming to fruition. Like proponents of many of the social movements for civil rights and feminisms that began the decade with confidence and optimism, the members experienced constant disillusionment. Animosity with other organizations, their own disagreements with neighbors during holding actions, and negative media attention took their toll. Women internalized these struggles by asserting that "somebody had to do it" or family farms across the country would fade away. Alongside the militaristic rhetoric of the NFO *Reporter*, members created for themselves a culture of sacrifice that justified years of struggle before the NFO achieved its mission. Women whose husbands took on leadership positions at the state and national levels best exemplified this culture of sacrifice as they took on work well beyond the bounds of gender-appropriate labor on the farm simply to weather these years of crisis.

Women were most prized as resourceful, hardworking, uncomplaining wives. The March 1961 NFO *Reporter* featured the story of Don Henry, a county organizer from Nemaha County, Kansas. The caption below a photograph of his wife and family chopping wood explained how the family hauled wood to heat their home. Henry's wife hoped the "NFO makes it possible for them to have a furnace. She hand-milks 30 cows while Don is out NFOing." Stories like this abounded—of wives married to county and state workers who spent days and weeks alone on the farm as husbands worked for the NFO. And Willis Rowell, who praised women's extensive involvement in his memoir, ultimately concluded that "perhaps our wives' greatest contribution was keeping the bed warm and friendly no matter what time we organizers got home for a night or a weekend." Male leaders actually recognized this as a hardship for women and did not necessarily believe that women were obliged to help in this way. They asserted that women did so because they believed in them and in the NFO, placing value on women's work and providing a supportive rhetoric to help women justify the situation to themselves, their families, and others.[38]

Women who reflected positively on the NFO in oral history interviews tended to enjoy a mutual valuation of labor with their husbands, as well as joint decision making and generally stable family situations. In some cases, though, NFO membership tested the limits of mutuality as women endured loneliness, frustration, and anxiety during the long absences of husbands who organized other counties or worked at the national office in Corning, Iowa. Shortly after they joined, Don Zmolek became the main organizer in Black Hawk County, Iowa, and spent several days off the farm every week. The job paid only a modest commission of $7.50 for each new member, with limit of $15 per day. He harbored no professional aspirations, but he and Luella both believed his organizing work with the NFO would only require a short-term commitment. Luella recalled, "We always had the feeling that farmers would get behind this and it won't be very long."[39]

When Don began to travel more frequently, Luella quit her job as a secretary in Cedar Falls to take care of the farm full time, creating an even deeper economic hardship for the family. Then, in 1960, Don was asked to work at the national NFO office in Corning, a three-and-a-half-hour drive from their Black Hawk County farm. He initially turned the position down, but as Luella told the story, several men at the national office said, "We're not asking you to do anything that we haven't been doing ourselves." They had all left their families and farms to work in Corning and often discussed their own personal sacrifices at board meetings when it came time to discuss budgets and salaries. The job did not necessarily mean a steady income for the family because, when the NFO was unable to meet its expenses, the employees simply went without a paycheck. By working in Corning, Don "did not make really good wages. He could have made better wages by working locally here in town, but it was just something that we definitely believed in."[40]

To make ends meet Luella found another job as a secretary at an elementary school in Cedar Falls, leaving no one to work the farm. Although they had six children, Luella encouraged them to pursue an education, participate in school activities, and consider professions other than farming. The couple rented their land, divided their Angus herd with another NFO member, and began sharing the "calf crop." Eventually, they sold off the entire herd to another farmer in Grundy County, and as Luella recalled, "It was a very sad day when the last cows went out of the yard." Nonetheless, Luella and Don maintained an attitude of commitment to the NFO, as well as to the idea that "we'll come through this again." Luella moved even farther away from her ideal situation of farming with her husband but believed she would simply weather the crisis until better times came along.[41]

Similarly, in 1970 Martha Linn's husband, Darwin, went to work at the national NFO office as an organizer and manager of collection points, a job that required that he travel throughout Iowa. They had been members since 1957, but in 1970 they moved to Adams County, to a farm close to Corning, where Darwin worked at NFO headquarters. Martha Linn became "the farmer during the week." She and her two daughters took tremendous pride in the fact that they "learned to hay, [and] learned to run the tractors and the pickups." Yet Linn was still anxious when she did not hear from Darwin, especially late at night when he was supposed to be on his way home. She often wondered, "'Well, has he had a wreck?' 'Has he hit a deer?'" Linn added, "It was kind of traumatic in those years," emphasizing that she enjoyed working the farm but often felt lonely when her daughters were at school and Darwin was at work. The couple had just one car, keeping her from attending her women's club. As a result, by 2001 she admitted that during those years she "got rather depressed" and felt something of the "feminine mystique," or a feeling of being unfulfilled, as her husband pursued his career. She escaped into soap operas and books and even confessed to "resenting the NFO a little bit," a rare admission among fiercely loyal NFO women.[42]

Linn coped with the situation by increasing her involvement in the NFO and attending county meetings when Darwin was "off to another meeting in another town." She served as the county secretary for several years and was elected as a delegate to several national conventions, where she served on the credentials committees and others to which she was elected. She was proud of the fact that she attended "national conventions by myself, without my husband" and became part of a growing cohort of women acting independently within the NFO. She estimated that by the mid-1970s men and women attended the national convention in equal numbers, and many of the women did so on their own.[43]

Increasing her independent involvement did not necessarily strengthen a woman's commitment to the organization, however, and by the 1970s growing numbers expressed disillusionment with collective bargaining. For Luella Zmolek tensions came to a head in the early 1970s when the presidency of Oren Lee Staley was repeatedly contested at national conventions. It was following one of these conventions that Zmolek realized, "There is just no way we are going to be able to accomplish this," revealing that her quiet resolve to remain with the NFO was rife with doubt and tension. When he accepted the job in Corning, Don told Luella that if she ever wanted him to quit, he would. So, following one annual convention in the mid-1970s, she asked him to quit, saying that if the organization itself was so divided in selecting its leader, then the NFO would never be able to organize farmers into a collective bargaining unit. Describing the tension between herself and Don, Luella said,

> We came home, and then Don went working outside, doing things out there in the barns, and so on. And then one day, he came in, and he went up and got his suit, went upstairs and came down with his suitcase. And I said, "Where are you going?" And he said, "I'm going back to Corning." [pause] And I could see he was determined, and so I didn't stop him.

It was not just disillusionment, though, that concerned Luella. She had joined the NFO believing that it would bring stability to the family, but it had only brought further hardship. More than her farm, her marriage was now in question since Don's health was suffering from the long hours he put in at the office.[44]

Not long after he arrived back in Corning, Luella's fears became reality when Don suffered a heart attack at just fifty-three years old. By then Luella noted that several of the men working for the NFO had experienced heart attacks because of the long hours and because "the pressure was just really intense on them all the time." Following this episode she begged him to find another job, but again he returned to Corning and worked for another five years before she finally "talked him into quitting." Like many members Zmolek came to believe that the NFO would not be able to organize farmers on a large scale and effectively set commodity prices. Looking back in an oral history interview, however, she had few regrets about their activities with the NFO. For Don, it had provided confidence and leadership experience of which Luella was very proud. She related the story of one memorable meeting in Postville, Iowa, where bad weather delayed Staley, a well-known, fiery orator, and Don had filled in as the guest speaker before an audience of 900 people. Luella said, "He had just gone to high school, he never spoke in public or did anything like this. All of the sudden, he is conducting all these meetings." And in Postville, that night, Don was completely unprepared. She recalled:

> He didn't even have any time to prepare for this at all, no notes to speak of, or anything . . . and [he] did a wonderful job and it was just unbelievable. But I think, would you really believe [pause] [crying] . . . When you become so dedicated that you could do it. And some of them commented afterwards how wonderful it was. And they, it gave them confidence. "It shows" they said, "we can all step up and do what we have to do." And the leadership that came forth from all these farmers, it was just absolutely incredible.

Luella described her time in the NFO as an awakening to the social and political issues that created inequality and hardship for herself and others. Though she did not increase her involvement with the NFO, she found alternative outlets for her activism and interest in pacifism. An active opponent of the Vietnam War, she became involved in the peace organizations Pax Christie and Mothers for Peace, as well as an active group in Cedar Falls, Iowa, called Citizens for Peace. She did this on her own, without Don's involvement, but she credited the NFO with raising her awareness. She said, "I never regret being involved in the NFO because it just changed us completely. And not only that, we became aware of everything that was going on." Though she had her doubts about the effectiveness of the NFO, she could confidently speak of the hardships of agriculture and their connections to processors, corporations, consumers, federal policies, and the greater social, economic, and political systems in which these operated.[45]

None of the women who granted oral history interviews in the early twenty-first century regretted their involvement with the NFO, although all of them looked back with disappointment that the organization was unable to accomplish its goals in organizing farmers to bargain for better prices. Some placed blame on the NFO for failing to push for aggressive change after the mid-1970s. Martha Linn grieved for what could have been when she said that "if the NFO was as active as we all hoped," then rural America would look very different in the early twenty-first century. Her commitment to the ideals of the organization still ran strong when she said,

> *The passion for it was so great. The fact that it didn't really turn out to be what we all dreamed it would be is kinda like, heart rendering sometimes. You just want to sit down and cry about it because in my heart I just feel that if it had been, everybody had done it together, we would not have the problems that we have today . . .*

In its first decade NFO leaders promised that after a few years of hardship their new organization would deliver economic stability, allowing farm families to enjoy modern homes, safe and productive farming operations, and educational opportunities for their children. But the crisis never seemed to pass. Collective bargaining and broad organization simply could not meet the challenges of modernization and depopulation or prevent widespread farm loss.[46]

As a burgeoning, specialized farm organization devoted to collective bargaining, the NFO offered farm women opportunities to increase their public activities by moving away from the rhetoric of mutuality and toward a rhetoric shaped by urgency and demand for their service in the countryside. Expectations for gender-appropriate behavior dictated much of what men and women could do, but organizational needs, along with an overall climate of social and political change during the 1960s, allowed for subtle changes in the way that women approached activism. This new framework still situated women as wives whose participation was largely determined by the level of the husbands' involvement and the couple's valuation of gendered labor. Women did not challenge gender roles because for them economic independence meant living and working within a family unit on a prosperous farm. New strategies also continued to emphasize communal bonds between women by making them primarily responsible for work with membership, public relations, and communications. But, as the women of the NFO demonstrated, communal bonds were essential in keeping women of the organization together through periods of hardship and disillusionment. Friendships with other members sometimes replaced family, friends, and neighbors when tensions ran high. Although NFO women did not organize separately or create exclusively feminine spaces, their extensive memories of friendships illustrate how, in order to feel successful as activists, they needed the support of other women. And here, especially in the stories of women whose husbands were highly involved with the NFO, there is evidence that some farm women were becoming increasingly disillusioned, not only with farm organizations but with male-led farm organizations that placed limitations on opportunities for women.

This strategic shift toward creating a sense of urgency and full participation in solving the farm problem eventually characterized much of farm women's activism after 1970. The agrarian feminisms that emerged in the mid-1970s emphasized shared personal experiences, fears of economic hardship, and disappointments with agricultural policy. Full participation was still largely determined by the level of the husbands' involvement and the couple's valuation of gendered labor, but with the backdrop of the 1960s and the social movements of that decade, women gained a more descriptive rhetoric based both in agrarian traditions and Second Wave feminisms to explain their response to the tenuous economic conditions of the 1970s and 1980s. They intensified arguments based on a "politics of dependence" that justified their activism by claiming that their husbands were too busy or that political activity was simply another part of their jobs as farm wives. They also spoke in terms of permanence, leaving behind the idea that they would abandon their activism and return to gender-appropriate roles once they attained an ambitious goal. Their politics of dependence was ongoing and sustained, as the farm problem appeared to be one that would not resolve itself easily. Women put their experiences and their voices forward because, in the words of NFO women, somebody had to do it.

CHAPTER FIVE

Hop to the Top with the Iowa Chop
The Iowa Porkettes and Transformative Leadership

IN JANUARY 1964, WHEN JAN JACKSON became the first president
of the Iowa Porkettes, the women's auxiliary of the Iowa Pork Producers Association (IPPA), she reflected on her own realization that women played a
vital role in promoting pork consumption. During a visit by "city friends" to
their farm near Lytton, Iowa, Jackson learned that they did not eat pork because of its reputation as unwholesome meat. When Jackson argued otherwise, one of her guests, a "professional man from the city," challenged her
to stand behind her husband's products by serving pork while entertaining
company. Jackson realized that she rarely did so, preferring chicken, roast
beef, or turkey on special occasions. So, at dinner the following evening,
Jackson served French-style green beans with bacon, scalloped potatoes
with ham, and roast pork. The results were nothing short of miraculous. Her
city friends began to eat pork several times each week, and Jackson wrote,
"His wife told me not too long ago that whenever they have company they
[cook] chops, outside weather permitting, and a lot of times he will do them
in the carport."[1]

Jackson's success in marketing pork products was one small step toward
the Iowa Porkettes' greater objective of cultivating new roles for farm women
and integrating women into the male-dominated commercial marketplace.
Over the course of twenty-eight years, between 1964 and 1991, members of
the Iowa Porkettes promoted pork products in order to assert their roles as
agricultural producers, eventually transforming a women's auxiliary into a
female-led commodity organization. Their story provides a key example of
how women's groups adapted to the changing nature of agriculture and utilized the rhetoric and strategies of the Second Wave. Although only a small
minority of Iowa's farm women actually joined the Porkettes (8,366 by the
mid-1980s), their experiences offer insight into broader developments that
enabled farm women's organizations to renegotiate gendered divisions of
labor, claim new public spaces for women, and demand greater recognition
from male agricultural leaders.

Founded in the mid-1960s, the Iowa Porkettes appeared at a key moment in this process, as membership in locally based homemakers' clubs declined and farm women created alternative activist outlets based not on local geography but on common interests in commodities or political issues. The Porkettes believed that, as women, they could increase pork consumption by teaching urban, female consumers about the healthfulness of pork and proper cooking methods. Doing this required that they leave their homes and local communities, the traditional sites of female activism, and work in the male-dominated field of retail sales and agribusiness. Rather than simply serving an organization, as did the other groups in this study, the Porkettes' main focus was public outreach. This proved to be a difficult transition because, as Jan Jackson's example demonstrated, they built upon organizational models employed by generations of farm women. Upon joining the Porkettes, members brought experiences gained through participation with homemakers clubs and auxiliary groups, where they had emphasized separate female groups and social action within a framework of domesticity.

Within a few years of organizing, members of the Porkettes struggled to gain recognition and financial support from the IPPA and came to believe that gender limited their ability to act on behalf of the pork industry. They gradually abandoned maternal and domestic frameworks and began to stress the economic value of their work on the farm and within the IPPA by portraying themselves as agribusiness professionals, instead of farm wives, and by leading large-scale marketing campaigns and fundraising efforts. Their strategy did not carry the same sense of urgency as did that of the women of the National Farmers Organization, but they shared a common rhetoric of stepping in and fulfilling the needs of an organization when men were unable or unavailable to do so. The Porkettes also benefitted from a blossoming farm women's movement that gained momentum both in the United States and in Canada. In her study of Ontario farm women, historian Monda Halpern found that after 1970 women increasingly favored "'modern' equity feminist principles of sexual sameness and integration" over "female specificity . . . women-centered rituals and domesticity." Most members of the Porkettes did not identify as "feminist," but in a 2001 oral history founding member Kathryn Louden recalled that by the time she served as president in 1969 and 1970, members had situated themselves in the context of Second Wave feminism. She said, "It was simply perceived that men were the pork producers, period. We were just at the cutting edge of the 'woman's movement,' in which women were beginning to assert themselves and say, 'I'm here, I'm part of this.'"[2]

Like most of the women cited in this study, members of the Iowa Porkettes gained access to land and resources—and thereby membership in the Porkettes—through marriage. They identified first as pork producers and farmers, a group whose numbers were dwindling by the late twentieth century and who, according to the Porkettes, struggled to survive without women and men collaborating to find markets for their products. What sets the Porkettes apart from the other groups in this study is their representative experience of employing innovative strategies informed by a gendered awareness and a greater, national farm women's movement. Throughout the 1970s this movement developed agrarian feminisms to question the notion of farming as a purely male occupation, as well as women's exclusion from male-led groups like the IPPA. Their efforts set important precedents for women's participation in agricultural organizations in the 1980s and 1990s. They wanted recognition as partners on the farm, regardless of whether they worked directly with livestock, in order to promote their product and maintain family farming as a way of life. Their actions illustrate that Second Wave agrarian feminisms emerged as a homegrown response to the social and economic conditions in the countryside, and they challenge assumptions that Second Wave feminisms diffused from urban centers "to rural peripheries after a time-lag of a decade or more."[3]

Formed on January 8, 1964 as the auxiliary to the Iowa Pork and Swine Producers Association (IPSPA, later renamed the IPPA), the Iowa Porkettes organization was the first state chapter of the National Porkettes, formed in December 1963 as the auxiliary to the National Swine Growers Council (later the National Pork Producers Council, or NPPC). The Iowa Porkettes began with approximately thirty members and several goals: to sponsor Pork Queen contests at the county, district, and state levels; to have a booth and lard baking contest at the state fair; to consult with high-school home economics instructors; to distribute pork pamphlets and promotional materials; and to establish a network of women's organizations at the district and county levels. By the end of the year, they had gained 240 members and made considerable progress toward their goals, having sponsored queen contests and a "Pork in Education" campaign to survey Iowa's high-school home economics teachers. They adopted a mascot, "Lady Loinette"—a smart-looking Disney-type sow donning a lady's business suit and carrying a briefcase—as the ideal companion to the IPPA mascot, "Sir Hamalot." Throughout the next decade, however, membership wavered as the Porkettes encountered resistance from the men of the IPPA and from women who did not consider commodity promotion to be appropriate feminine work.[4]

Commodity organizations like the IPPA and the Iowa Porkettes emerged in an era when a growing emphasis on agribusiness persuaded many farmers to specialize in the large-scale production of specific commodities. For those who raised pigs and hogs, this meant moving livestock from pastures to confinements where farmers could better control feeding, movement, weight gain, and breeding. Investments in confinement systems and antibiotic-infused feed required substantial capital, and hog farming gradually became a specialized business. As a result, between 1940 and 1992, the number of hogs sold in Iowa, the nation's leader in pork production, increased from 9.3 million to 26.8 million. The number of farms that raised hogs, however, fell from 167,342 to just 34,058, while consumer demand wavered. New vegetable oils and synthetic detergents reduced the need for lard and pork by-products, while the growing urban population demonstrated strong preferences for beef and poultry as fears of trichinosis remained in the public consciousness. These conditions fostered a collective identity among the shrinking number of farmers specializing in hogs and pigs, bringing together farmers based on their production activities, rather than their local neighborhoods, for the purpose of selling the idea of pork to urban consumers. The National Pork Producers Association and state subsidiaries like the IPPA emerged in the early 1960s as a means to consolidate long-standing breeders' organizations and to bring newly specialized farmers together.[5]

For the Iowa Porkettes technological change and the growth of agribusiness provided new opportunities to challenge patriarchal hierarchies in agricultural organizations. Founding member Kathryn Louden explained that, as women became more involved in the bookkeeping and, often, the actual work of raising hogs, they "would accompany their men to meetings, and they wanted to be part of the action." She recalled that when the Porkettes came together in 1964, women were not satisfied to partake in leisure activities, like crafts and socializing, when their time was better spent promoting pork products to consumers. Realizing this ambitious objective took time because when the Porkettes first organized, there were few precedents for women's participation in commodity promotion or activist models that empowered women to work on an equal footing with men — or to even work in public spaces. It would be nearly a decade before female-led groups such as American Agri-Women and WIFE, formed in 1974 and 1976, demonstrated farm women's desire to organize separately, without male oversight. The Porkettes therefore drew from strategies employed by women in a variety of farm-focused groups, including the Farmers Union, state Farm Bureau federations, and extension service homemakers' clubs, that emphasized service and domesticity. It was only when women found these strategies to be ineffective that they sought alternatives.[6]

The Porkettes' evolution toward creating new spaces for women in agriculture was not unique to their organization. By the early 1970s a growing number of farm women across the country began to identify gender as an important and limiting factor in their lives. This seemed to be especially true of women in auxiliaries for commodity organizations committed to supporting the men who produced wheat, cattle, poultry, and dairy products, among others. In these groups women came together as a specialized group that grew out of new agricultural methods and attempted to connect with a modern, public, consumer culture. This fostered new conceptions of women's work once they participated in the public marketplace as agricultural producers. Sociologist Carolyn Sachs argues that the names of these organizations, like the Wheathearts, who were connected to the National Association of Wheat Producers, revealed a "lack of respect for women, not to mention minimal concern with feminist issues." Yet the Arizona Cowbelles, for example, adopted a feminist rhetoric even before notions of feminism were present in public discourse. Formed in 1939 to organize picnics, dances, and social activities for the Arizona Cattle Growers Association, members formed bonds shaped by their common labor as ranch women. Historian Michele K. Berry found that by the mid-1950s members of the Arizona Cowbelles increasingly viewed themselves as " 'professional' volunteers in charge of improving public relations between the cattle industry and the public at large, as well as bettering the economic viability of the industry as a whole." Like the Porkettes, they gained knowledge of marketing and advertising and launched statewide marketing campaigns. Berry asserts that the Cowbelles utilized language similar to that of Second Wave feminists and possessed a positive "gendered awareness" that women were "crucial to the operation of the industry as a whole."[7]

The Iowa Porkettes clearly had examples to follow, but the difficulties they encountered in their first decade suggest that developing a gendered awareness was not intuitive or even desired. The confidence to act as industry spokespersons required experience and perspective. Early members expressed a sense of subordination to the IPPA by organizing as an auxiliary, contriving a diminutive name, and setting dues at just $2 per year. With a limited budget they were unable to reimburse officers for their travel expenses or finance elaborate promotions. Nonetheless, members took pride in their work and considered their activities to be quite novel. Many reported feeling nervous as they approached strangers to talk about pork, and Kathryn Louden recalled that during her first few supermarket promotions she continually asked herself, "Am I supposed to be doing this?" In 1965 the Iowa Porkettes' second president, Myrtle Keppy, also expressed her apprehension at writing a regular column for the IPPA newsletter, *Pigtails*. She wrote that the job of president required her to perform new, unexpected, and awkward tasks. She wrote, "A person just doesn't know just what situations you can get yourself into when you accept a job. Little did I dream that I would be writing articles for publications such as this. But it is like the old saying goes—if you believe in something you will do it."[8]

Convincing women to join was problematic, and after gaining 240 members in 1964, membership declined steadily over the next three years, reaching a low of 133 in 1967. During these years a strong core of early leaders remained optimistic that they could build their numbers, given that by 1969 the IPPA enjoyed a membership of more than 13,000 men. They attributed the discrepancy to the fact that women did not believe they should belong to a commodity organization. When asked why women would hesitate to join the Porkettes, Louden said, "We had struggles because men being men, they were not always receptive to having a woman contribute, or question, or make any comments. It was just simply a men's organization." In October 1964 state officers set out to organize ten district Porkette organizations as local auxiliaries to existing IPPA district groups. Few women came forward, however, and as Louden recalled, Jan Jackson, the first state president, often "twisted a few arms" to find district leaders.[9]

Those who joined clearly saw value in their work, harbored greater ambitions for the organization, and were therefore more likely to develop a gendered awareness that they had been marginalized within the IPPA. Women who initially participated in the Iowa Porkettes at the state and district levels shared two important characteristics: access to disposable income and husbands who were members of the IPPA. Because the Porkettes did not receive reimbursements for their travel expenses, they required affordable and accessible transportation. In 1978, when the Porkettes began to reimburse officers for their travel expenses, they estimated that the state president traveled 4,200 miles annually. At the anticipated cost of fifteen cents per mile, this amounted to $630. District directors averaged 300 to 800 miles for travel to state meetings and 750 miles for activities within the district, amounting to $200 annually. During the organization's early years, these numbers may have been much lower because the Porkettes sponsored fewer events, but it indicates that in order for women to take on a leadership role, they needed to be able to cover these costs. In 1964 the national median farm income was $5,689, considerably less than the overall national average of $7,336. This left little room for extra expenses and clearly affected the geography of membership.[10]

In 1964 the sixth IPPA district, encompassing much of central Iowa, had the largest number of Porkettes, with forty-seven, or 19.5 percent of the 240 members, including the state president, Jan Jackson, and the state vice president, Mrs. Gerald Jackson. These women enjoyed easy access to the IPPA headquarters in Des Moines and could more easily participate in major events, such as annual IPPA meetings, the American Pork Congress and Trade Show, and the Iowa State Fair. The districts with the fewest members were situated in the outlying counties in the northwest and northeast corners of the state. The fourth district, for example, located in the northeast corner of the state had just eight members in 1964. In these districts a woman was often the only Porkette in her community, and such isolation played a significant role in the initial membership decline. Because the state organization was unable to provide financial assistance to local chapters, members in district and county Porkette groups had to either raise the money themselves through the sale of baked goods and pigskin crafts, find a local sponsor, such as a grocery store or a meat packer, or pay for supplies themselves. For women without other members in their communities, activities were difficult and expensive to organize.[11]

Karen McCreedy, who served as the state president in 1976 and 1977, recalled that during the early years the Porkettes relied heavily on one another and a strong sense of community based on their commitment to pork promotion. She wrote that before the Porkettes gained a professional staff in the late 1970s, "it was volunteerism all the way." The Porkettes not only planned all meetings and events but stuffed their own meeting packets, developed and printed brochures, and "even made table decorations and centerpieces." McCreedy found that the experience was valuable to many members, who gained skills that "could be used for 'paying' jobs later if necessary." Yet for those early members who lived in isolated communities, or found themselves belonging to an inactive local chapter, the amount of work was overwhelming.[12]

As women who needed to gain access to disposable income and to justify spending time away from the farm, the members of the Porkettes relied on supportive husbands who valued volunteer activities. This was not unique to the Porkettes but was a long-standing characteristic of women who participated in agricultural organizations. Historian Mary Neth found that even for

women who participated in farm bureau clubs, male approval was impera-
tive. In most households "men's labor was seen as crucial and women's as
peripheral." As a result a woman's ability to negotiate power within a family
depended not on the economic, social, or political value of her work but entirely on male cooperation and her husband's notion of proper gender roles.
In 1964 all of the 240 Porkettes had husbands in the IPPA. Only 37 of the
240 Porkettes, or 15 percent, were married to state, district, and county IPPA
officers, but most of the Porkettes had husbands who were highly involved
either in the IPPA or in groups devoted to specific breeds, further demonstrating that women shared the responsibilities and costs of membership
with husbands.[13]

The Porkettes' familiarity with the process of raising hogs and pigs also
suggests that the women shared an interest in the business and labor of farming, although working directly with livestock was not necessarily a prerequi-
site for membership. The women reported that they were highly involved
with daily farming operations in a variety of ways but not necessarily with
cultivating crops and raising livestock. Kathryn Louden cited her own experience with her husband, Warren, raising Duroc pigs. Because they had
three sons and a daughter who performed much of the labor, she rarely inter-
acted with the animals. Instead, she managed the financial aspects of their
business, especially at sales and auctions. Louden also asserted the importance of her domestic work when she said,

> Some people didn't want the women involved in the labor of the farm, but
> they wanted a good meal, they wanted to have a coffee break, they wanted
> someone to help promote their product, they wanted to be affirmed in what
> they were doing. And in that way, I don't think you had to leave the house to
> be a supportive person and be as interested as the women who actually got
> out and helped with the farrowing and helped mark the pigs.[14]

When she served as president in 1970, Louden encouraged women to
become "more aware of the in's and out's of this pig raising business," and
to "keep up with husbands in knowing what's what." By the early 1980s the
Iowa Porkettes' newsletter, the *Ladies' Pork Journal*, featured a column titled
"Hints from the Hog House." It assumed that women were "active in the
barn" and featured suggestions for farrowing techniques, instructions about
how to separate and care for sick pigs, and the newest medications and vac-
cines. Most of the hints emphasized the gendered work of farrowing and

caring for newborn pigs, but the women who wrote in appeared to have considerable experience. Still, the column was accessible and simple, often with encouraging words for women in the process of gaining new skills. It portrayed women's work with livestock in a positive and inclusive context but never as a requirement for membership.[15]

Throughout their history the Porkettes defined farm work broadly, reflecting the flexibility and diversity of women's labor. In 1978, for example, Iowa Porkette President Madeline Meyer reminded members about just what being a farm wife entailed. She wrote, "You handle the bookkeeping and you pay the bills. You prepare the meals, and you play midwife at farrowing time. You're responsible for watching the kids, you answer the telephone and you keep the house in order. You have all the responsibilities your husband doesn't, and then some. You're the wife of an Iowa Pork Producer." Such rhetoric was more direct in its assertions than that of the mid-1960s, as Meyer assumed that women had greater experience dealing directly with hogs and with the business of the farm, but she still assumed that women identified as "wives" who took responsibility for childrearing and household chores.[16]

Meyer's statement also illustrates that by the 1970s members of the Porkettes placed significant value on their work on the farm, in the home, and in the organization. Throughout the decade they progressively asserted their independence and took steps to operate as an independent organization. They found fault with their dependence on the IPPA for financial backing and approval, and they increasingly blamed men for limiting women's ability to conduct more extensive promotions. In 1975 membership topped 2,500 women, who worked primarily at the local level running Pork Queen contests, selling pig-related merchandise, handing out ribbons at hog shows, giving out samples at grocery store promotions, staging pigskin style shows, sponsoring bake-it-with-lard contests, and working with local schools and home economics teachers. For several years, however, many of these members active in local groups pushed themselves, and state leaders, to expand their marketing efforts. In July 1970 the Fayette County Porkettes hosted a luncheon for the Business and Professional Women (BPW) and other local dignitaries in Oelwein, Iowa, a community of approximately 6,000 residents and the largest town in Fayette County. They asked ten members of the BPW to fill out a survey on their use and knowledge of pork, which revealed that eight of the ten did not include pork products in their household budgets. None served pork to guests or used lard in their baking. Mrs. Howard

A cooking demonstration. Iowa Porkettes Records, Iowa Women's Archives, University of Iowa Libraries.

Fender, Fayette County Porkette president, sent the survey results to state leaders with a note that read, "This points up to the fact that we need to stop promoting pork to ourselves and really hit the markets!"[17]

State leaders shared Fender's opinion and sought to increase their visibility within the IPPA and with urban consumers by taking on greater responsibilities for large-scale marketing campaigns. By the 1970s they had provided volunteer labor for several promotions that they believed demonstrated their economic worth. In 1967, for example, the Iowa Porkettes assisted the National Pork Producers Committee (NPCC) by conducting a survey of consumers in Des Moines supermarkets. Myrtle Keppy, who was by then serving as a board member of the National Porkettes, chaired the consumer survey and estimated that by using the Porkettes' volunteer labor, the NPPC saved approximately $10,000. Such facts did not seem to sway members of the IPPA, however, who took the women's volunteer labor for granted and overlooked their activities entirely by sometimes neglecting to allocate money to women's activities.[18]

In 1973 and 1974 presidents Marie Brown and Donna Keppy asserted women's roles in the IPPA by using part of an already strained budget to hire Dan Murphy, an experienced farm journalist and freelance communications specialist, to review internal procedures. Murphy had served as editor of the *Iowa Farm Bureau Spokesman* throughout the 1950s and 1960s and was highly respected by agricultural leaders. In fact, in 1970 members made him an honorary Porkette in recognition of his service to the pork industry. As a consultant, he encouraged the Porkettes to reach wider audiences and tried to instill confidence when he wrote, "We ARE NEEDED by the pork industry. No one outside of the Porkettes can do certain kinds of pork promotion as well as this group." Murphy went beyond mere rhetoric, however, and encouraged the Porkettes to rethink women's roles. He took a professional risk by blaming the Porkettes' inability to move forward on a shaky relationship with the IPPA, poor communication with male leaders, and an inadequate budget. In a letter to president Donna Keppy, he noted that he could provide guidance, but that, given his working relationship with the IPPA, the Porkettes needed to handle negotiations with the men. In his trademark folksy style, he wrote, "I'd get in trouble if the men knew I was helping you raid their sacred treasury . . . but you gals do give the organization a huge lift and should receive consideration when funds and personnel assistance are being passed out."[19]

To overcome indifference from the IPPA, Murphy proposed a dual mem-

Kathryn Louden and Dan Murphy with an award. Iowa Porkettes Records, Iowa Women's Archives, University of Iowa Libraries.

bership plan that enabled husbands and wives to pay one membership fee to the IPPA, bringing in more women and garnering more funds for Porkette activities at the state, county, and local levels. The Porkettes praised Murphy for his work, but they did not share his enthusiasm for the dual membership plan. Instead, in 1976 they voted to incorporate as a not-for-profit organization, a move that would allow for higher levels of fundraising and greater control over their finances. Many expressed doubts that a dual membership structure would actually result in greater financial resources for women, given the men's resistance to funding Porkette activities. The men's attitudes did not change easily, even after incorporation. In 1978, for example, the new IPPA executive secretary, Russ Sanders, apologized to Porkettes treasurer, Sue Henrich, for his delay in sending the quarterly Porkette subsidy. He apologized "for the manner in which timeliness of this payment has been handled in the past. Hopefully we'll be able to start getting these checks to you on time." He then asked for advice on how he might improve the "financial relationship" between the Porkettes and the IPPA.[20]

Following incorporation, the Porkettes remained connected to the IPPA through a memorandum of understanding, by which the IPPA provided a subsidy and office space. Even with these formal connections in place, members of the Porkettes viewed incorporation as a promotion out of auxiliary status and an important step toward independent fund raising and decision making. All of this occurred within a changing national context and evolving farm women's movement. At the same time that Iowa women filed their incorporation papers, the National Porkettes chose to affiliate with the American Agri-Women, an entirely female-led coalition of farm women's organizations designed to address political and economic issues in agriculture. This seemingly small detail lends tremendous insight into the significance of the Iowa Porkettes' decision to incorporate and the Porkettes' translations of Second Wave agrarian feminisms.

By the mid-1970s growing numbers of farm women were compelled to act publicly and to speak about gender as a limiting factor in their lives. Women also regained a presence in the farm press that allowed for public expression of their personal experiences. Confident that farm women had little interest in the business of agriculture, most major farm periodicals had dropped women's sections by the end of the 1960s. Then, in 1970 publisher Roy Reiman of Greendale, Wisconsin, released the first issue of *Farm Wife News*, and within three weeks 38,000 women had subscribed. Within a decade circulation reached 2.3 million. *Farm Wife News* presented a wide variety of material, from recipes and sewing patterns to the latest news on agricultural policy from Capitol Hill and information on caring for livestock. The magazine was entirely free of ads, depending only on subscriptions for financing. Reader submissions constituted the bulk of the articles, fulfilling Reiman's vision of providing a "forum" for farm women. Content covered a broad range, detailing women's diverse views on agricultural policies, farming practices, consumer products, and current events. The success of this magazine led other major publications, including *Successful Farming*, to revive their own women's sections, with a specific focus on the business and professional sides of agriculture.[21]

One of the most frequently mentioned issues in *Farm Wife News* was inequitable inheritance tax policies. The gendered inequality of inheritance was central to women's realization that their work and economic contributions to the farm provided no legal protection or exemption from estate taxes on the death of their husbands. Federal estate tax law stipulated that, even if a husband and wife held property in joint tenancy, the entire value of the property would be included in the husband's estate. Unless a widow could prove her contribution to building the estate, she had to pay estate taxes on the entire value of the property. Because they rarely signed written partnership agreements, signed loan or mortgage papers, bought or sold equipment and produce, maintained separate bank accounts, or kept detailed work diaries that clearly documented their work on the farm, many widows were forced by rising land and equipment values throughout the 1960s and 1970s to sell off parcels of land—or even the entire farm—to pay estate taxes. Some women won refunds in court, but a growing awareness of the problem fueled calls for reform and required that women identify as producers and laborers, rather than mere "helpers." Women tended to frame the problem as an external threat by urban-policy makers with little understanding of women's work, and their demands focused almost entirely on changing federal policy. At a federal hearing in February 1981, Senator Nancy Landon Kassebaum of Kansas framed the issue as not simply a women's problem but as a crisis worthy of national attention. Federal policy that removed widows from their farms, she asserted, "strikes at the very heart of the American agricultural system."[22]

In 1979 economist Frances R. Hill identified the tax issue as the primary catalyst of women's activism because farm leaders eschewed women's demands for new tax laws and few of the major farm organizations acted on the issue. Women realized "they would have to organize on their own." These women did not identify as feminist because doing so would compromise their standing in close-knit agricultural communities and it would also give the appearance of hostility toward the family farm ideal. Hill asserted that the "non-threatening" tax issue that affected entire families was an advantageous way for farm women to express a covert feminist ideology. They could act publicly while asserting that they were not "libbers" or "man-hating, bra-burning feminists." Doing so assured them credibility in agricultural communities. Most amazing to Hill, however, was that the burgeoning women's groups were the first new general farm organizations "founded in a quarter century," thereby ushering in a new era in agricultural politics.[23]

The inheritance tax issue fueled calls to action in *Farm Wife News* and even in more general farm publications. Female-led agricultural organizations also appeared in response to inflation, unstable commodity prices, and consumer boycotts. In 1972, for example, a group of farm women in Michigan formed Women for the Survival of Agriculture in Michigan (WSAM) after picketing a local juice processor for underpaying apple growers. Their activities quickly expanded into direct political action, attempts to influence policy, and cooperative efforts with the USDA to recognize women's roles in agriculture. The following year a group of Missouri women formed the United Farm Wives to protest federal price controls and consumer beef boycotts. As the movement gained momentum, women from diverse economic and productive backgrounds called for greater cooperation and organization based on their identities as farm women. In November 1974, in response to reader demand, the editors of the *Farm Wife News* sponsored the first National Farm Women's Forum. The conference was a resounding success, with delegates voting to create a new coalition, American Agri-Women.[24]

By 1980 twenty-one women's organizations from the Midwest and the West had joined, including groups such as the American Hereford Auxiliary, the National Peach Partners, and the Associated Milk Producers. American Agri-Women did not limit its membership to producers and also welcomed agribusiness groups such as the Women of the National Agricultural Aviation Association and the Arizona Agri-Business Womens Association. Under this united banner members of the coalition lobbied at the local, state, and national levels, promoted consumer education, and most importantly used their growing social networks to develop a uniquely feminine approach to agricultural activism.[25]

For members of American Agri-Women, its affiliates, and the myriad of independent farm women's groups, breaking away from male-led organizations was an intentional choice intended to foster women's leadership. The members used gender-specific language in their official materials, referring to leaders as "spokeswomen," and they often discussed the advantages of organizing in an all-female group. Women in Farm Economics (WIFE), a farm women's political action group formed in Nebraska in 1976, promoted the development of female leadership as the cornerstone of its mission. A 1980 WIFE pamphlet explained that the group was "unique from most other farm women's organizations in that it is not an auxiliary to any other group. Therefore it is free to make its own policies, set its own priorities, and achieve its goals unhampered by precedence," with precedence referring to stifling male leadership.[26]

Organizing without men and with a clear purpose to work in public and political spaces represented a major shift in the way that many farm women conceptualized their work and voiced their concerns. For the first time individual activists expressed their personal satisfaction in seeking their independence. One member of WIFE best summed up this transformation when she wrote in 1983,

> *I spent more years and hours than I care to tabulate or remember working in a general agricultural organization. All that women are allowed to do in these groups are prepare coffee, bake cookies, make phone calls to remind members of the meeting, or at best educate younger members. No true leadership positions are available. . . . Any innovative ideas women have are frequently pirated away by the men and presented to the group as his idea. It happened to me frequently. WIFE gave me the opportunity to either be among the necessary and vital workers or take the initiative and step out into a leadership role.[27]*

As Frances Hill pointed out in 1979, women involved in new, female-led organizations reassured established male-led groups and members of the wider agricultural community that, even as separate organizations, their primary goal was the prosperity of American agriculture. This allowed women to co-opt aspects of Second Wave feminisms and transform them into unique agrarian feminisms that spoke to their interests. Central to that vision was preservation of the family farm operated by a heterosexual couple working for the collective good of the family. Even as they hailed women's separate organizing as a step in the right direction, members of WIFE were very careful to articulate their commitments to heterosexual marriage and to present themselves as professional, conservative, law-abiding citizens. At the 1977 national WIFE conference, for example, national president Betty Majors excited members with a speech detailing the ways in which they could get involved. Nonetheless, she still characterized farmers as male when she concluded, "We will be the silent majority no longer. Stand tall. When they ask what your husband does for a living, you can say, 'He feeds America.'"[28]

As an affiliate of American Agri-Women, members of the Iowa Porkettes would have been exposed to news of farm women's political activities and the rhetoric of separation and independence from male-led groups. These trends provided positive examples of how to apply agrarian feminisms to an organization, foster female leadership, and recognize gender as a limiting factor without generating an outwardly hostile response. The Porkettes publicly explained their break from the IPPA as a move based on financial considerations and perceived opportunities for leadership. They questioned patriarchy, but they did not entirely reject it. Their continued cooperation with the IPPA demonstrates that they believed it was best for men and women to work separately for the common good. This is a key component of the "politics of dependence." Farm women simultaneously expressed a desire for greater self-determination and equal access to the economic and political structures dominated by men, while also supporting the continuation of those structures. They stressed the economic value of their farm work while moving away from the maternal and domestic frameworks that had shaped farm women's activism for nearly a century.

The Porkettes' decision to incorporate had its desired effect, resulting in an immediate expansion and more business-like operation that allowed them to take on high-budget, public projects. Membership skyrocketed from 1,647 in 1974 to 5,671 in 1979. During the same period total state disbursements increased more than threefold, from $10,217 in 1974 to $35,806 in 1979, with membership dues accounting for most of this growth. Dues brought in $5,414 in 1975 but reached $22,000 by 1979. The IPPA also increased its general subsidy to the Porkettes, from $1,500 in 1975 to $3,000 in 1980. All of this enabled state Porkette leaders to reimburse state and district officers for travel, to purchase office supplies, and to hire a staff: a secretary and a part-time home economist responsible for creating original recipes and providing guidance for cooking demonstrations.[29]

The Porkettes essentially became the public-relations and marketing arm of the IPPA, with responsibility for major statewide marketing campaigns. In the summer of 1976, the Porkettes began working with Russ Sanders, then of the Iowa Development Commission, to promote the "Iowa Chop." Although it was little more than an ordinary pork chop, Sanders hoped that with proper marketing the term "Iowa Chop" would be for pork what the "New York Strip" had become for the beef industry—a representative, delicious, high-end meat that appealed to consumers for its freshness, flavor, tenderness, and culinary diversity. The Porkettes established the "Iowa Chop Committee" and set out to place the "Iowa Chop" on the menus of at least three hundred restaurants across the state. With a growing budget and a $3,000 grant from the IPPA, state leaders could assist the ninety county-level groups with their campaign by providing "promotional kits." These included professionally produced materials such as menu clip-ons, posters, cooking suggestions, recipe ideas, sample press releases, and advertising slicks for newspapers, as well as lists of meat distributors to ensure a steady supply to restaurants.[30]

Local members responded enthusiastically, although even by 1976 some still expressed anxiety about working in public, especially with male restaurant owners and meat processors. In her letter to county Porkette presidents, the head of the Iowa Chop Committee, Judy Scheffler acknowledged that approaching restaurant owners could be daunting, but she offered several suggestions to help Porkettes overcome any fears. She urged the women to "be prepared" and "know what you're talking about" by cooking the Iowa Chop themselves and offering samples. They could also team up with a male IPPA member. Scheffler believed this to be effective because restaurant managers, who did not always take women seriously, would see that "the Iowa Chop is of such importance that a busy Pork Producer will take time out at harvest to visit with him about the chop."[31]

Scheffler also encouraged women to overcome any doubts by taking ownership of the Iowa Chop campaign and to devise their own, unique marketing strategies. In November 1976 Scheffler reported that the Porkettes of Washington County had come up with a catchy slogan, "Hop to the top with the Iowa Chop," while several groups planned to give Iowa Chops to the family of the first baby born in 1977 in their county. The gift equaled the newborn's weight and was the ideal promotion because "usually the newspapers enjoy an interesting story of this sort and will often feature pictures with the article."[32]

Between March and December 1977 the Iowa Porkettes spent $3,199.30 on the Iowa Chop campaign, including advertising, buttons, recipe cards, labels, and telephone calls. This amount did not include expenses for local and county chapters or travel and personal expenses for the volunteers. Nonetheless, by the end of 1977, their efforts had resulted in 160 Iowa restaurants featuring the Iowa Chop on their menus. Meat counters across the state also reported increased consumer demand for that particular cut, even at a slightly higher price than those simply labeled as pork chops. More important than their ability to place the Iowa Chop on restaurant menus was the fact that the successful campaign demonstrated to both men and women the importance of women's work for the IPPA.

As a result of the Porkettes' incorporation, handling a growing budget, and managing large-scale campaigns, the IPPA welcomed women's involvement by forming joint committees with both men and women. In 1978 members of the IPPA joined the Porkettes' Pork in Education Committee, which was responsible for creating educational materials and marketing to schools. Initially, the Porkettes reported that working with men from the IPPA was "a totally new experience for us." But they also found that with access to IPPA resources, they gained new opportunities to expand their programs and include such materials as "radio tapes and crock pot cookbooks." They also developed a film titled "The Endless Varieties of Pork," which explained the various cuts and retail costs and could be distributed to home economics teachers, retailers, extension personnel, and marketers.[33]

By the early 1980s the Porkettes' successes had generated momentum that allowed women to claim legitimacy in the realm of pork promotion. In 1984, with the creation of a finance and revenue committee to solicit large donations from major agribusinesses, the Porkettes became entirely self-supporting on an annual budget of more than $32,000. Success brought new challenges, however, and many members questioned whether they should pursue closer working relationships with IPPA committees or continue to work as a separate, female-led commodity organization. This created considerable tension between younger, "business-oriented" members and older "traditional" members as to the direction of the organization.[34]

These tensions were best described in a 1983 external review that encouraged the Porkettes to become more "results oriented, rather than activity oriented" and implied that the primary focus of the group would no longer be creating a community, but running a business. The Porkettes had never truly been an activity-oriented organization, like an extension homemakers club, but this realization marked an important departure from strategies that had characterized rural women's organizations for generations. The Porkettes wanted to be considered equal partners on the farm and in the IPPA, but some feared that working with men would compromise their solidarity as women. Worse, it would hinder the development of women's leadership that only seemed possible in all-female organizations emphasizing collaboration and power sharing. Yet a growing and vocal group of younger women wanted to seek full equality with men and completely transform women's approach to activism by asserting authority in mixed groups.[35]

These conflicts played out in two debates: first, over the organization's name, then over the Porkettes' very existence. Beginning in the early 1980s state organizations across the country had abandoned the name "Porkettes" in favor of names that evoked fewer laughs from industry outsiders. The Michigan Porkettes, for example, became the Michigan Pork Partners. By the spring of 1985, one year after forming a task force to investigate the issue, the National Porkettes became the National Pork Council Women (NPCW). National president Carmen Jorgensen cited the fact that few government officials took her seriously. Likewise, the national vice president and former Iowa Porkette president, Karen McCreedy, believed that the new name was a step in the right direction. While the goals of the organization remained the same, McCreedy believed that the new name reflected a more professional image.[36]

Iowa women also debated the issue, and in January 1984 the name became a central issue at the Porkettes' annual meeting. Member Judy Antone of West Branch, Iowa, told the *Des Moines Register* that most people thought that the Porkettes was a club for dieters or even a cute name for a tenderloin sandwich. She preferred to identify herself as a "pork industry representative," which conveyed a "kind of image of professional farm women and of pork products." Ultimately, the Porkettes voted to retain the name because it was an important part of their history. Kathryn Louden explained, "People know who we are — people in the Legislature, in Des Moines, Washington. . . . We've been known for 20 years as Porkettes, and have that on our letterheads and all. It would cost a lot to change now." Likewise, the newly elected president, JoAnn Brincks of Carroll, Iowa, believed that the name Porkettes was distinct and memorable and implied that women were "pork partners" with their husbands on the farm.[37]

The Iowa Porkettes also began to acknowledge that tough economic times hampered their membership efforts and that market forces made their services obsolete. The poor economic conditions of the 1980s compelled many members to discontinue their association with the Porkettes, either because membership was too time consuming or expensive or because the members were leaving farming altogether. After nearly two decades of growth, membership began a steady decline from an all-time high of 8,366 in 1985 to 6,556 in 1989. At the same time the number of farms producing hogs and pigs in Iowa also fell from 49,012 in 1981 to 38,368 in 1987, a loss of more than 10,000 hog farms. Even if farm families managed to weather the economic crisis, many women took jobs off the farm in order to supplement the farm income and no longer had the time to participate in volunteer activities.[38]

As their numbers dwindled and advertising and consumer relations became even more sophisticated, the IPPA turned to professional advertising firms to manage the marketing and promotional campaigns that the women had once directed. On May 28, 1985, Iowa Governor Terry Branstad signed the state's first mandatory check-off law, which provided money for advertising and research by requiring farmers to deduct .0025 percent of the value of all hogs and pigs sold. The legislation divided the proceeds among various commodity organizations, with $716,478 going to the IPPA in 1985 alone, an amount that covered more than half of its annual operating budget. The new check-off legislation also created the Iowa Pork Producers Council (IPPC), whose membership mirrored that of the IPPA, to oversee another $1.6 million in check-off funds. This made it possible to utilize more expensive advertising in magazines and on television, reaching a much wider audience than the Porkettes could through their localized promotions.[39]

Even as their numbers declined, women continued as active members by serving on joint committees. These included the Pork in Education, planning, membership, promotions, and legislation committees. In 1986 seventeen of thirty-one IPPA committees included women, and in 1990 eighteen of thirty-two IPPA committees included women. Although they were in the minority, women still comprised 84 of the 274 total members serving on IPPA committees. As early as 1986, members of the Porkette Long Range Planning Committee viewed this as a positive development and encouraged more women to become part of joint committees, not only at the state level but also at the district and county levels.[40]

In February 1988 former president Margaret Ledger believed this trend to be a positive development. Joint committees, she wrote, were "an asset to both Pork Producers and Porkette organizations." Unlike her predecessors Ledger did not even refer to gender when she wrote, "This group [the Porkettes] has many well-qualified, forward thinking members who are working on a large variety of committees, all of which are working for the common goal." Yet the future of pork promotion did not appear to include the Porkettes as an independent organization. In January 1987 the IPPA and the Porkettes formed a joint Pork Producer/Porkette Planning Committee to determine whether it made sense to maintain separate organizations for men and women. They cited the declining number of families raising hogs and problems finding good leadership, and they concluded that merging the organizations would make it more economical to function as a group. A 1986 survey of the Iowa Porkettes revealed that many women favored this move, with more than two-thirds of respondents favoring a merger with the IPPA. But in August 1987, when one member of the committee moved that there be a vote to merge, that motion was defeated.[41]

The debate continued for four more years as many women feared losing their voice if they integrated with the IPPA. During the summer of 1987, a survey of eleven district IPPA officers and thirteen district Porkette officers revealed that more than half (fifteen of twenty-four respondents) favored a merger. When asked to list the disadvantages of joining the IPPA, however, several respondents indicated that women would be unable to convey their ideas in rooms full of dismissive men. One respondent wrote, "Women would be losing their identity as Porkettes." Another remarked, "Men aren't always interested in Porkette issues and vice versa—attitudes would have to change on both sides before it will work." Overall, many of the respondents believed that women represented a significant number of the "grassroots" members and that losing the Porkettes identity would alienate local organizations. Another respondent cited a case where a local group decided to merge and the board retained one woman as a "token" member. "The lone woman has lost much of her network," the respondent claimed. "She is trying to carry on Porkette programs—but is getting very discouraged." Several of the respondents also objected because they feared the men would not support the initiatives that women valued. One respondent wrote, "Men will be running everything just because they are men . . . and I can't see any board men from our county giving a home ec demo or assisting ladies clubs as some Porkettes do."[42]

Discouraging as such sexism could be, the Porkettes agreed that women needed to assert their presence simply for the sake of survival within the organization. The most vocal group of women came to believe that their fundraising and marketing activities with the Porkettes replicated those of the IPPA, a clear misuse of their already limited funds. In November 1989 Porkettes vice president Helen Pollock wrote an article in the *Iowa Pork Producer* in which she noted, "Many of the county groups are struggling to survive because not enough women are available to do the promotions. The women are employed or have too many other demands on their time and less time to commit to the Porkettes." Simply put, "there just are not enough people for all the slots." Furthermore, Pollock believed separate women's organizations to be outdated, as "the lines between the two groups' areas of responsibility are dimming . . . and there is no longer a need for two separate groups."[43]

Pollock proposed a unification plan that emphasized women's strengths.

She wrote, "Are women going to be lost in the shuffle? I think not! We are too strong for that. We have too many good ideas that are needed by our industry. We have women who will be involved." Citing the Porkettes' twenty-five-year history and the growth of the organization into a "proud, active group of farm women," she argued that the merger plan would allow the IPPA to survive the economic crisis and the uncertain decades ahead. At their annual meeting in January 1990, however, Pollock's merger plan failed to pass by just one vote.[44]

Over the following year membership fell by 22 percent, and without membership dues the women could not sustain their activities. Then, in October 1991, the NPCW merged with the NPCC, and national leaders asked state organizations to follow suit. A memorandum from the NPPC and the NPCW informed members that joint organizations would "facilitate greater involvement of more talented people in NPPC, effectively utilizing our resources in new ways. . . . We see this as a win-win situation." Ultimately, members of the NPCW recognized a particular brand of feminism when they asserted that basing organizational membership on one's gender was "inconsistent with long term trends in society." They believed that the merger would be a great advantage to women encountering "second class status in the pork industry." So in January 1992, at the Iowa Pork Congress, members of the IPPA officially adopted a resolution to merge with the Iowa Porkettes. The resolution guaranteed women full membership in the IPPA by allowing the "spouse of an Iowa Pork Producer" to be a voting member, as long as she sold at least two hogs in her name each year. The resolution also provided for committees that included women to oversee the mergers of the state, district, and county organizations, but it did not necessarily guarantee places on county and district boards for former Porkettes after a transition period of three years.[45]

Following the meeting in which the IPPA delegates accepted the resolution, the Porkettes sponsored a program titled "This is Your Life, Iowa Porkettes!" They honored all former state officers, then served cake and punch in order to allow "everyone time to visit with old friends and make new ones." As they looked back, few members participating in the celebration had any regrets, and most looked forward to new opportunities working with the IPPA. Karen McCreedy, who had served as state president in 1976 and 1977, then as national president from 1986 to 1988, believed that members of the Porkettes had learned much over their twenty-eight-year history and that their transformative leadership had united the various interests within the pork industry. Likewise, Kathryn Louden wrote,

Even as we have since closed the books on the Iowa Porkettes chapter, the fringe benefits persevere. I feel we did make a big impact on the history of Iowa Pork. And in the process we matured into women capable of accomplishing much in our own lives as well as to the point where we have grown more confident about meeting whatever challenges might come along in the future.

Although several members expressed concern for the future of women within the IPPA, many more worried for the future of the pork industry as a whole. Overall, they believed that women needed to work in tandem with men in their efforts to promote pork and educate consumers.[46]

Throughout the 1960s and 1970s farm women typically rejected the women's movement, labeling feminism as an ideology for middle-class urban women seeking to fulfill selfish ambitions. They asserted that feminism, with its challenges to patriarchy, had no place in rural communities characterized by male authority, gendered divisions of labor, and social relationships that provided support in times of need. Patriarchy remained firmly entrenched, so that by the early 1980s anthropologist Deborah Fink observed that rural Iowa women discounted the Equal Rights Amendment by placing "their faith—and fate—in the hope that family would provide what they needed, or that family would be friendlier to their interests than the legal system would be." As a result scholars searching for feminism in the countryside came up empty-handed and continued to look for the moment at which the women's movement made its appearance in farm organizations. In 1996 sociologist Carolyn Sachs noted that widespread mergers of women's auxiliaries with men's groups in commodity organizations suggested that "women on farms and in these organizations demand more respect for their participation in farm business and consider themselves partners rather than merely farm wives."[47]

The experiences of the Iowa Porkettes illustrates the challenges in detecting the agrarian feminisms that were influenced by but not necessarily directly related to the greater women's movement of the 1960s and 1970s. Furthermore, they demonstrate that by joining a men's organization in the 1990s, they did not entirely resolve the questions of gender and gendered divisions of labor. Women who joined the Porkettes valued their labor on the farm and, at least in the case of the founding members, enjoyed the support of their husbands and families. Throughout the 1960s and 1970s they developed and utilized agrarian feminisms to question patriarchal hierarchies and gain greater opportunities to act upon their interests in pork production.

Rather than merely rejecting or accepting urban-based, Second Wave feminisms, they invented new strategies based on established strategies, on their
collective identities as women and farm wives, and on their desire to assert
their roles as agricultural producers. They called attention to the value of
their volunteer labor and asked that they be recognized for their contributions, thereby setting important precedents for women in agricultural organizations who wanted to work on a more equal footing with men, rather than
in auxiliaries or in all-female groups. By the early 1980s, though, members of
the Porkettes found that even Second Wave agrarian feminisms could take
varied forms that challenged the membership and transformed women's
roles, especially as economic and social realities undermined their ability to
organize.

DID THE DEVELOPMENT OF AGRARIAN feminisms actually result in substantial changes for Iowa's farm women? In the early 1990s there were no definitive answers as the Porkettes hesitantly dissolved their organization and women's voices remained muted within the larger agricultural community. Certainly, a century of activism had awakened an empowering rhetoric that allowed women to claim an identity as advocates, but they were still generally excluded from larger debates in American agriculture. An uncertain future lay ahead, not just for Iowa's activist farm women but for feminist activists more broadly, who found themselves poised at another crossroads, asking: "What now?" Many Americans wondered whether feminism was in a state of decline. In 1990 *Newsweek* decried the "failure of feminism," and in her 1991 best seller, *Backlash: The Undeclared War Against American Women*, feminist author Susan Faludi, lamented that during the 1980s an "antifeminist culture daunted women more than it galvanized them." Others criticized younger women who took for granted the accomplishments of the Second Wave and declared feminism irrelevant to their daily lives.[1]

In the countryside women dealt with similar questions of decline and disappointment. Gone were the homemakers clubs that had defined rural women's activism. Once-active clubwomen, now in their golden years, disbanded their clubs and met only occasionally for coffee. Fred Stover, who passed away in 1990, spent the 1980s recruiting ambitious female community organizers like Carol Hodne to educate farmers about debt relief during the farm crisis. As he had during the 1950s, however, he still struggled to gain legitimacy and overcome his radical reputation. The NFO turned its sights to marketing and focused on offering services over ideology. The Porkettes became obsolete as the leadership gave preference to professional consultants over volunteer labor. For all of their forward momentum, women remained on the periphery of agricultural politics, often serving in token positions but never moving or acting together in large numbers. It could have been that there were simply fewer women to organize since the overall farm population had dwindled to just two percent of all Americans. More likely, however, was the fact that farm women remained a diverse group with specialized interests that made them notoriously difficult to organize, and the persistence of sexism kept them from acting effectively in even the most desperate situations. During the farm crisis of the 1980s, when female activism struck a cord in popular depictions such as the 1984 film *Country*, women continued to take on specific roles as caregivers and organizers of women.

On the other hand, the reality of the situation was not so grim for farm women and feminist activists more generally. Refusing to concede, Faludi urged women to resist the backlash while feminist scholars and activists declared the emergence of a Third Wave. They abandoned essentialist definitions of feminism in favor of discerning the intersections of race, class, and gender. Seeking to promote ideas of "female empowerment rather than male oppression," feminists of the 1990s made diversity, conflict, and difference the cornerstones of an intentionally splintered movement that allowed women and men to apply feminisms to their unique circumstances. Instead of defining absolute truths, they found new meaning in the contradictory notions of caring and earning, independence and interdependence, and equality and mutuality. As feminist scholar Whitney A. Peoples noted, ideological divisions became "the very sites of production of the issues at hand within pressing debates about the current and future directions of feminism." Exciting possibilities for coalitions and international movements materialized within this framework as understandings of race, social class, ethnicity, sexuality, and geography added depth and dimension to feminist debates.[2]

In Iowa farm women held fast to their tradition of joining organizations and supporting their local communities. A 1980 survey of American farm women confirmed the vitality of rural organizations when it found that 74 percent were involved in some sort of community activity, whether it was with a church, the PTA, a political party, or a service club. Approximately 40 percent of farm women were involved in a general farm organization, including the Grange, the farm bureau, or the National Farmers Union. Another 21 percent belonged to marketing or farm supply cooperatives, 14 percent belonged to a commodity producers' association, while just 2 percent reported membership in burgeoning farm organizations exclusively for women, such as the United Farm Wives, American Agri-Women, or Women in Farm Economics (WIFE). Yet, like everything else in the countryside, these organizations were in a constant state of transition as women began to recognize that they needed greater social, political, and legal rights in order to ensure greater prosperity for themselves and their families.[3]

By the early twenty-first century, revelations about land use and owner-ship became the critical juncture where farm women from varied back-grounds, age groups, and production methods quite literally found common ground. In 2002 the agricultural census revealed that women owned half of all the farmland in Iowa and the Midwest. Women were responsible for en-suring the region's productivity, but they still lacked access to vital resources and institutions. Whether these female landowners were inheriting widows who hired male tenants or were part of the small but growing minority who identified as principal farm operators, they were more likely to identify sex-ism as a problem because it directly affected their bottom line. Some women reported exploitation by tenants who rarely consulted them when making production decisions or who set the terms of the lease at rents well below the average. Similarly, farm service providers, including bankers, extension per-sonnel, and government agents, admitted in one survey to treating women differently because they perceived female landowners to be emotional, con-fused, and lacking in knowledge of agriculture. April Hemmes, who owned and operated a farm near Hampton, Iowa, stated in 2001 that even women who worked "thousands and thousands of acres" simply did not feel com-fortable going to organizational meetings with men. She believed women had to earn the respect of male farmers, bankers, and merchants, saying, "It seems like you have to keep proving yourself. I just take that for granted now."[4]

Modernization, landownership, and identities as producers did little to help women reconcile gendered expectations with identities deeply rooted in a masculine agricultural system. Even at the beginning of the twenty-first century, sexism clearly affected a woman's choices related to production. A 2001 survey revealed that farm women felt out of place when they visited tra-ditionally male meeting places, like feed mills, equipment dealerships, hay auctions, sale barns, and farm shows. Businessmen and government agents did not always take them seriously and assumed the women were just farm wives helping out their husbands. As a result these women were more likely to adopt organic agricultural practices because they could not, or would not, seek access to the financial, legal, and material resources necessary to run a modern, mechanized farm. The necessary skills and social networks needed to run an organic farm grew out of traditional women's farm work: raising small herds of livestock or flocks of chickens, growing fruits and vegetables, and selling the produce to local markets.[5]

Their chosen profession set them apart from urban women, who—they believed—enjoyed more fluid movement between their work lives and personal lives. When asked to define these differences, most of the women in the 2001 survey simply held out their hands to show their roughness and the dirt under their fingernails. One woman said, "It's obvious I work with my hands, and that sets me apart from most women I know." Many reported feeling "unfeminine" because of their work clothing and their inability to conform to popular fashions. Another informant said, "I don't feel very feminine. I don't have time to take baths and pamper myself. I don't have money to buy lingerie." These women equated femininity with urban notions of beauty and consumer culture, concluding that they operated on the periphery of "normal" feminine behavior. Their words demonstrate that sexism, as manifested by external actors and internalized by women in agriculture, resulted in an intense personal struggle that required women to manage a range of competing identities. This was especially true for women who depended on social networks for emotional, social, and financial support. Conformity to community standards secured economic and social security, while deviance carried severe penalties.[6]

Within these gendered locations women fostered unique, decidedly female identities and relationships with the land. In contrast to the story of decline and dispossession in the countryside, women expressed optimism and a real desire to contribute to the vitality of their local communities and to agriculture as a whole. The issue of landownership brought women together to talk because if they could take control of their assets, they realized, they could change the course of industrial agriculture. Interestingly, female landownership was not a new trend but one that had gone unrecognized for decades by federal agencies, farm service providers, and farm people themselves. Burgeoning women's organizations, like the Iowa-based Women, Food, and Agriculture Network, finally asked how women's choices could affect agricultural production and how farm service providers could better serve female landowners. More than any political ideology, commodity, or marketing practice, these questions brought women of varied ages and backgrounds together to discuss farming, production, and the idea that as women they had unique understandings of agriculture and the marketplace.[7]

When surveyed about land use, women favored sustainability over profitability, and they associated personal independence with community prosperity. They wanted freedom from outside control but characterized "outside control" as coming from corporate and political entities seeking to restrain production, land, and resources. Fully integrating family and traditional ideals into their perceptions of independence, women defined themselves not as producers of food and fiber but as the "locus of connections to family, community, and nature." By coming together and sharing their experiences, Iowa's farm women began to articulate a vision for American agriculture that eschewed intensive practices, rising land prices, corporate farming, and absentee landownership. Between 2006 and 2008 more than 800 Iowa farm women attended listening sessions and events sponsored by the Women, Land, and Legacy Project to assess women's attitudes. As they spoke and shared with one another at the listening sessions, women demonstrated how they tended to process information temporally, incorporating their present needs with their past experiences and their desires for the future. Integrating spirituality, natural beauty, and physical and emotional health with economic benefits and physical ownership of land, they tended to consider the needs of the wider community when planning for planting, harvesting, and marketing. Their main priority was creating sustainable operations for themselves and their neighbors that could support families over several generations. Gendered thinking and planning patterns proved to be highly complex and difficult to reconcile with government policies and programs, leading many of these women to seek out educational opportunities and organizations that better reflected their priorities.[8]

Rather than demand equal rights and privileges within well-established farm groups, Iowa's farm women in the first decade of the twenty-first century wanted entirely new models for organizing that empowered women to identify as farmers and producers using the time-honored strategies they had developed over the course of the twentieth century. The Women, Food, and Agriculture Network and Iowa Women in Agriculture, for example, created supportive, welcoming communities with an emphasis on cooperation, mentorship, friendship, and learning through storytelling and interactive educational opportunities. Women in agribusinesses and food industries were also welcomed as members to provide a more holistic understanding of production and marketing and to help create environments where women could learn from one another. Just as the members of women's clubs had done generations before, these organizations honored and celebrated women's ways of knowing. Yet with landownership, sustainability, and profits at stake, these groups also fostered women's economic power and asserted women's presence in public spaces as producers.

Members viewed themselves more as facilitators than as leaders. Their main priority became education through the organization of small-group discussions on a variety of issues ranging from tax codes, crop management, animal husbandry, leasing options for farmland, marketing, financial planning, conservation, health insurance, eminent domain, and technology. In order to accommodate personal and family responsibilities, they tended to meet in neutral settings where childcare could be provided and at times compatible with their work schedules. By organizing on their own terms and setting their own standards for success, these women finally asserted the value of female organizing strategies and agrarian feminisms as legitimate and powerful. They had taken the politics of dependence to a new level by not situating themselves within heterosexual marriages but within the agricultural community as a whole. The politics of dependence was still very much part of their strategy, but it had evolved into emphasizing the interdependence and cooperation of all people. That women could make these claims within organizations founded and financed by female farmers is indicative of substantial change, although as with all women's movements, it will surely continue to evolve.[9]

The development of agrarian feminisms provides an even clearer picture of the diversity, breadth, and pervasiveness of women's movements after 1945. This study joins much new scholarship on the expression of feminisms in specific localities that show how activists tended to place the needs of families and communities before feminist ideology. Furthermore, it demonstrates the importance of placing process and identity politics over the old metaphor of waves and self-identification in the history of American women and feminism. Farm women's movements are especially helpful in dealing with women who publicly rebuffed feminism as a political ideology and personal identity but who created their own strategies and harnessed elements of feminism suited to their daily lives. Just as women took up the cause of feminism for various reasons and in distinct ways, so too did they reject the feminist label.

Midwestern farm women were not merely conservatives or adherents to the traditionalism espoused by activists like Phyllis Schlafly. Their experience clearly shows the magnitude of the gray areas in feminist movements, and in the case of farm women's movements, they readily embraced feminist strategies of female cooperation, collaboration, and female empowerment and used these to build upon existing notions of mutuality and rural traditions that valued shared work. Their refusal to self-identify as feminist was a problem of association. Few farm women consulted theorists or scholars when formulating ideas about women's movements, and they defined feminism in terms of images on the evening news. The individualistic, combative, anti-male aspects of the women's liberation movement most often conveyed in the popular media were incompatible with the cohesive rural communities upon which these women relied.[10]

For Midwestern farm women, the second half of the twentieth century was about finding their voice and asserting their vital roles in a period of rapid and unsettling change. The development of agrarian feminisms was a response to modernization and the expectation that women, as producers, bookkeepers, and contributors to the farm, would come into contact with outside forces that rarely took them seriously. Their ongoing journey toward legitimacy has been slow and quiet, unfolding mostly at home between husbands and wives, fathers and daughters, brothers and sisters, who made careful decisions about who would inherit and operate the family farm. Women brought these private conversations to organizations, where they eventually came to understand that the strategies of mutuality that had defined women's work before 1945 implied nothing about legal ownership, access to profits, or entitlement to access distinctly male spaces. As industrialization transformed the landscape, depleted the population, and revolutionized production in the corn belt, women realized that claiming their social, economic, and legal equality was a vital part of realizing their vision for sustainability in agriculture.[11]

INTRODUCTION

1. Helen Karnes, "No Welcome Mat for Women," *Farm Journal* (April 1970), 72.

2. Benita Roth, *Separate Roads to Feminism: Black, Chicana, and White Feminist Movements in the Second Wave* (Cambridge: Cambridge University Press, 2004), 49, 50–67, 75, 80–93, 138–45. The concept of space was vital in the formation of Second Wave feminism in both urban and rural settings. Historian Anne Enke also recognized the importance of space, particularly in the built environment because "whenever women entered—much less sought to change—the public landscape, they encountered specters of sexual deviance." As a result, women often preferred to create new spaces, inhabited primarily by females, in which self-expression could take place without male judgment. Anne Enke, *Finding the Movement: Sexuality, Contested Space, and Feminist Activism* (Durham, NC: Duke University Press, 2007), 8.

3. J. L. Anderson, *Industrializing the Corn Belt: Agriculture, Technology, and the Environment, 1945–1972* (DeKalb: Northern Illinois University Press, 2009), 8.

4. Deborah Fink, *Agrarian Women: Wives and Mothers in Rural Nebraska, 1880–1940* (Chapel Hill: University of North Carolina Press, 1992), 21–29.

5. Andrew R. L. Cayton and Susan E. Gray, "The Story of the Midwest: An Introduction," in Andrew R. L. Cayton and Susan E. Gray, ed., *The Identity of the American Midwest: Essays on Regional History* (Bloomington: Indiana University Press, 2001), 23–25.

6. Deborah Fink, *Open Country, Iowa: Rural Women, Tradition, and Change* (Albany: State University of New York Press, 1986), 218.

7. Mary Neth, *Preserving the Family Farm: Women, Community, and the Foundations of Agribusiness in the Midwest, 1900–1940* (Baltimore, MD: Johns Hopkins University Press, 1995), 217; Mary Neth, "Building the Base: Farm Women, and the Rural Community and Farm Organizations in the Midwest, 1900–1940," in *Women and Farming: Changing Roles, Changing Structures*, ed. Jane B. Knowles and Wava G. Haney (Boulder, CO: Westview Press 1988), 351. For more on "mutuality," see Joan Jensen, *Loosening the Bonds: Mid-Atlantic Farm Women, 1750–1850* (New Haven, CT: Yale University Press, 1986); Nancy Grey Osterud, *Bonds of Community: The Lives of Women in Nineteenth-Century*

New York (Ithaca, NY: Cornell University Press, 1991); Donald B. Marti, *Women of the Grange: Mutuality and Sisterhood in Rural America, 1866–1920* (New York: Greenwood Press, 1991), 89–102.

8. Nancy K. Berlage, "Organizing the Farm Bureau: Family, Community, and Professionals, 1914–1928," *Agricultural History* 75, no. 4 (2001): 426–28; Dorothy Schwieder, *75 Years of Service: Cooperative Extension in Iowa* (Ames: Iowa State University Press, 1993), 20–22, 34–37; Jenny Barker Devine, "'Quite a Ripple but No Revolution': The Changing Roles of Women in the Iowa Farm Bureau Federation, 1921–1951," *Annals of Iowa* 64, no. 1 (Winter 2005): 1–3.

9. Jenny Barker Devine, "The Secret to a Successful Farm Organization": Township Farm Bureau Women's Clubs in Iowa, 1945–1970," *Annals of Iowa* 69, no. 4 (Fall 2010), 41–73; Louise I. Carbert, *Agrarian Feminism: The Politics of Ontario Farm Women* (Toronto: University of Toronto Press, 1995), 4, 29, 145–46.

10. Neth, *Preserving the Family Farm*, 26, 234–43; Katherine Jellison, *Entitled to Power: Farm Women and Technology, 1913–1963* (Chapel Hill: University of North Carolina, 1993), 178–80. See also Corlann Gee Bush, "'He Isn't Half So Cranky as He Used To Be': Agricultural Mechanization, Comparable Worth, and the Changing Farm Family," in *To Toil the Livelong Day: America's Women at Work*, ed. Carol Groneman and Mary Beth Norton (Ithaca, NY: Cornell University Press, 1987), 221; and Virginia S. Fink, "The Impact of Changing Technologies on the Roles of Farm and Ranch Wives in Southeastern Ohio," in *Women and Farming: Changing Roles, Changing Structures*, ed. Jane B. Knowles and Wava G. Haney (Boulder, CO: Westview Press 1988), 229–41.

11. Carbert, *Agrarian Feminism*, 146. Work by historian Alice Echols provides one example of what is implied here by "standard interpretations." In her work on urban feminist groups on the east coast, she asserts that while diverse approaches existed, feminist debates over "the left, class, race, elitism, and lesbianism," were consistent across varied regions. See Alice Echols, *Daring To Be Bad: Radical Feminism in America, 1967–1975* (Minneapolis: University of Minnesota Press, 1989), 21.

12. Lisa R. Pruitt, "Gender, Geography, and Rural Justice," UC Davis Legal Studies Research Paper Series, Research Paper No. 129 (August 2008): 25–29. See also Lisa R. Pruitt, "Toward a Feminist Theory of the Rural," UC Davis Legal Studies Research Paper Series, Research Paper No. 89 (October 2006): 426–441; Surveys from the 1990s also demonstrated the importance of wives' gaining the approval of their husbands before becoming active in organizations. See Julia Kleinschmit Rembert, "Factors Affecting Iowa and Nebraska Farm Women's Rural and Farm Advocacy Involvement" (master's thesis, University of Iowa, 1997).

13. Estelle B. Freedman, *No Turning Back: The History of Feminism and the Future of Women* (New York: Ballantine Books, 2002), 21–28, 124, 346. Some historians of feminism have generally equated the development of agriculture with the rise of patriarchal social systems. Historian Gerda Lerner, for example, asserts that patriarchy in Western cultures evolved from the need to control resources, surpluses, labor, production, and reproduction in agrarian societies. Such organization could only occur through men's subordination of women and children, whose labor was essential for

family survival. In this model feminism becomes a byproduct of capitalism, democracy, and urbanization that is entirely inconsistent with an agrarian way of life. Gerda Lerner, *The Creation of Patriarchy* (New York: Oxford University Press, 1986), 49–53.

Other historians have cautioned against using the term "feminism" too loosely because doing so negates its importance and specificity. See Nancy Cott, *The Grounding of Modern Feminism* (New Haven, CT: Yale University Press, 1987), 4–5, 40; Nancy Cott, "What's in a Name? The Limits of 'Social Feminism'; Or, Expanding the Vocabulary of Women's History," *Journal of American History* 76, no. 3 (December 1989): 820–21, 825.

14. Monda Halpern, *And on That Farm He Had a Wife: Ontario Farm Women and Feminism, 1900–1970* (Montreal: McGill-Queen's University Press, 2002), 6–9, 77–78.

15. Jellison, *Entitled to Power*, 180; Mark Friedberger, "Women Advocates in the Iowa Farm Crisis of the 1980s," in *American Rural and Farm Women in Historical Perspective*, ed. Joan M. Jensen and Nancy Grey Osterud (Washington, D.C.: Agricultural History Society, University of California Press, 1994), 224–34; William C. Pratt, "Using History to Make History? Progressive Farm Organizing during the Farm Revolt of the 1980s," *Annals of Iowa* 55 (Winter 1996): 40–42.

16. Berit Brandth, "On the Relationships between Feminism and Farm Women," Agriculture and Human Values 19 (2002): 108; Sara Elbert, "Women and Farming: Changing Structures, Changing Roles," in Women and Farming: Changing Roles, Changing Structures, ed. Wava G. Haney and Jane B. Knowles (Boulder, CO: Westview Press 1988), 262; Lorraine Garkovich and Janet Bokemeier, "Agricultural Mechanization and American Farm Women's Economic Roles," in Women and Farming: Changing Roles, Changing Structures, ed. Wava G. Haney and Jane B. Knowles (Boulder, CO: Westview Press, 1988), 223–24.

1. THIS RICH GIFT OF VOLUNTARY LEADERSHIP

1. Sarah Elizabeth Richardson, *Iowa Farm Bureau Messenger* (hereafter cited as IFBM) (September 1921): 1. Throughout this study the Iowa Farm Bureau women's committee will be referred to as the IFBFWC and the "women's committee." Use of the phrase "Farm Bureau women" will most often refer to all women participating in IFBF activities at the township, county, and state levels.

2. Richardson, "Women and the Farm Bureau," *Iowa Bureau Farmer* (hereafter cited as IBF) 1 (January 1937): 15. The IFBFWC operated as a functioning committee, not an auxiliary of the Iowa Farm Bureau Federation. Delegates from nine districts elected the nine members of the committee, and the chair served as a voting member of the IFBF executive committee. Women were also very active on the local level. The role of vice president of the county and township bureaus was usually reserved for women to ensure women's participation.

3. In 1921 the IFBF claimed 95,926 members, while in 1919 the IFU claimed just 10,625. Both groups experienced dramatic reductions in membership as the economy worsened throughout the 1920s and 1930s. Robert L. Tontz, "Memberships of Gen-

eral Farmers' Organizations, United States, 1874–1960," *Agricultural History* 38, no. 3 (1964): 155–56; Schwieder, *75 Years of Service*, 20–22, 34–37.

4. Louis Bernard Schmidt, "The Role and Techniques of Agrarian Pressure Groups," *Agricultural History* 30, no. 2 (April 1956): 53–54.

5. Donald B. Groves and Kenneth Thatcher, *The First Fifty: History of the Farm Bureau in Iowa* (Des Moines: Iowa Farm Bureau Federation, 1968), 51, 54.

6. Ibid.; Richardson, IFBM (September 1921): 1.

7. Annual Report of Home Economics Extension Work, 1923–1924, Cooperative Extension Service in Agricultural and Home Economics, Records, RS 16/3/0/1, University Archives, Special Collections, Parks Library, Iowa State University, Ames, Iowa (hereafter cited as Cooperative Extension Service records).

8. "Women's Part in Bureau Growing," IFBM 4, no. 6 (February 1923); "The Women's Side of the Farm Bureau Convention," *Iowa Homestead* (January 21, 1926).

9. R. K. Bliss, "Farm Bureau Educational Program, an Address." Iowa Farm Bureau Federation at Des Moines, January 16, 1924, Iowa Farm Bureau Federation Records, MS 105, Special Collections, Parks Library, Iowa State University, Ames, Iowa. (Hereafter referred to as IFBF records). Local male leaders often made similar positive comments regarding women's work. See W. H. Stacy and H. J. Metcalf, "Farm People Testify to Farm Bureau Work," *Burlington Hawkeye* (February 13, 1926); H. J. Metcalf, "Farm Bureau Leaders Here," *Estherville Enterprise* (December 30, 1925); Mrs. A. A. Graham, "Women Are Busy in Farm Bureau Work," *Kossuth County Advance* (January 1923), IFBF records. In spite of all the praise for farm women involved in community activities, news reporters and members of organizations still found it necessary to check that women still fulfilled their primary roles as wives and mothers. For example, in 1929 the *Des Moines Register* awarded free subscriptions to eleven farm women who exemplified community activists. Rather than report on their activities, however, the headline announcing their awards read, "Eleven Do Not Neglect Homes: Community Boosters Are Homemakers, Too." The article reported that nine of the eleven rated as "far above average" homemakers, one rated as "above average," and one rated as "average." Furthermore, all of the women's families had radios, telephones, and automobiles, while nine of the eleven lived in homes with electric lights, running water, and furnace heat. This indicates that the women recognized for activities in their community were from extremely prosperous farms, since most Iowa farm families still did not enjoy these modern conveniences. All of the women were also avid readers, and two of the women reported reading six or eight different farm journals, though not necessarily for intellectual or professional development. Their reading and efforts to be good homemakers, the women reported, were part of a greater goal to "obtain for their children a better education than they themselves have received." See "Eleven Do Not Neglect Homes," *Des Moines Register* (August 18, 1929).

10. "Clay County," *Annual Narrative Report* (1922): 31.

11. Historian Mary Neth observed that within the Wisconsin Farm Bureau women discussed agricultural issues but were primarily relegated to an auxiliary organization devoted to issues of the community, home, and family. She found that Wisconsin

women valued the importance of their work but often struggled to gain recognition for their efforts within the organization. Neth, "Building the Base," 339–56; Memorandum, "Farm Bureau Women Adopt Unified State Plan," IFBF records, 1923; "Township Organization for Home Project Work," IFBF records, 1923.

12. The IFBFWC sought to consolidate state programs by creating uniform county organizations, with a woman serving as vice president, and a five-woman committee in charge of selecting projects. The objectives of the women's committee also included provisions to work with men whenever possible in order to strengthen the organization. "Women Took Active Part in Convention," "Special Appropriation for Women's Work," and "Women Plan Work for the Year," IFBM 5, no. 6–7, (February–March 1924).

13. Schwieder, *75 Years of Service*, 36–37.

14. "Women of Iowa Farms Have Shown Great Enthusiasm in Furthering Interests of Better Agriculture," Cooperative Extension Service records, 1922; "Statistical Report of Project Work Done by Specialists and Home Demonstration Agents, 1922–1923," Cooperative Extension Service records; Knowles, "Annual Report of Work Done by Neale S. Knowles, State Leader of Home Demonstration Agents, 1922–1923," Cooperative Extension Service records.

15. Dorothy Schwieder, "Changing Times: Iowa Farm Women and Home Economics Cooperative Extension in the 1920s and 1950s," in *Midwestern Women: Work, Community, and Leadership at the Crossroads*, eds. Lucy Eldersveld Murphy and Wendy Hamand Venet (Bloomington: Indiana University Press, 1997), 207; Mrs. A. A. Graham, "Women Are Busy in Farm Bureau Work," *Kossuth County Advance* (June 1922): 23.

16. "Mrs. Richardson's Report" and "The Women's Side of the Farm Bureau Convention," *Iowa Homestead* (January 21, 1926); Mrs. Walter (Josephine) Van Zomeren, "Mahaska County Farm Bureau Women's Club," Mahaska County Farm Bureau Women's Clubs Records, Iowa Women's Archives, University of Iowa Libraries (December 1971).

17. "Citizenship Course for Rural Women Planned by Bureau," IFBM 6 (July 1925), 3.

18. Julie McDonald, *Ruth Buxton Sayre: First Lady of the Farm* (Ames: Iowa State University Press, 1980), 39–42; *Iowa Farm Bureau Messenger* 7, no. 4 (December 1925); Dorothy Schwieder, *Iowa: The Middle Land* (Ames: Iowa State University Press, 1996), 148–50.

19. "Says American Farm Housewife Has Many New Responsibilities," IFBM 7 (February 1926), 3; "Scrapbook, 1923–1926," Freedom Township Women's Club Records, Iowa Women's Archives, University of Iowa Libraries.

20. The seventeen counties included Hancock, Muscatine, Howard, Chicksaw, Floyd, Greene, Boone, Ida, Sioux, Shelby, Buchanan, Story, Wayne, Davis, Monroe, Carroll, Sac, and Calhoon. Women outnumbered the men at eight of the meetings; an equal number attended at two meetings; and men outnumbered women at seven meetings. The largest margin was in Sioux County, with twenty-one women and ten

men attending. Photographs and County Leadership Training School Rosters, 1922–1933, IFBF records.

21. "Union News Letter," *Iowa Union Farmer* 9, no. 20 (October 27, 1926), 4.

22. "First Policy Holder," and "Farmers Have a Jolly Time," *Iowa Union Farmer* 6, no. 5 (April 4, 1923): 1, 3.

23. Mary H. Dunn, "The Woman's Auxiliary Letter Box," *Iowa Union Farmer* 8, no. 7 (April 29, 1925): 3; Mrs. Glen Bowles, "A Brief History of the Iowa Farmers Union Auxiliary," in the *Official Yearbook of the Iowa Farmers Union Ladies Auxiliary*, 1942, MS 92, Iowa Farmers Union Records, Special Collections, Parks Library, Iowa State University, Ames (hereafter cited as IFU records); "The Woman's Auxiliary Letter Box," *Iowa Union Farmer* (April 29, 1925): 3; "The Woman's Auxiliary Letter Box," *Iowa Union Farmer* 9, no. 12 (October 27, 1926), 3.

24. Dunn, "Woman's Auxiliary Letter Box," *Iowa Union Farmer* 8, no. 7 (April 29, 1925), 3; Bowles, "Brief History of the Iowa Farmers Union Auxiliary"; "Woman's Auxiliary Letter Box," *Iowa Union Farmer* 9, no. 12 (October 27, 1926), 3; *Iowa Union Farmer* 8, no. 14 (May 20, 1931); Hattie VerSteegh, *Iowa Union Farmer* 17, no. 6 (May 23, 1934).

25. Deborah Fink and Dorothy Schwieder. "Iowa Farm Women in the 1930s: A Reassessment," *Annals of Iowa* 49, no. 7 (Winter 1989), 577, 579–80.

26. According to historian Lowell K. Dyson, the National Farmers Union became an influential voice in the Roosevelt administration because its leaders were primarily interested in curbing inflation, securing prices, and limiting production. In Iowa, however, membership wavered, primarily due to the controversial leadership of Milo Reno. As a fiery orator and advocate of holding actions, Reno's involvement in the Farm Holiday Movement repelled many of Iowa's liberal farm families that continued to favor legislative action. Lowell K. Dyson, *Red Harvest: The Communist Party and American Farmers* (Lincoln: University of Nebraska Press, 1982), 190, 192.

27. Specific developments, especially for women's activities, are difficult to track because between 1926 and 1936 the IFBF's official publication covering statewide news was relegated to just a few pages in the American Farm Bureau Federation newsletter. Low membership numbers probably made it difficult to finance an official statewide publication, while most county farm bureaus relied on local newspapers to advertise their activities. Although they lost a significant number of members, Cherokee County continued to publish a monthly four-page newspaper and kept regular meeting minutes, and the county extension reports are generally complete. For these reasons the section of this book dealing with the years between 1926 and 1936 will rely primarily on events in Cherokee County. "Cherokee County," *Annual Narrative Report* (1929): 32; Fink and Schwieder, *Iowa Farm Women*, 583.

28. Groves and Thatcher, *First Fifty*, 187, 195, 197.

29. McDonald, *Ruth Buxton Sayre*, 53.

30. IFBM 5, no. 3 (November 1923); IFBM 6, no. 6 (February 1925); Peter Hoehnle, "Iowa Clubwomen Rise to World Stage: Dorothy Houghton and Ruth Sayre," *Iowa Heritage Illustrated* (Spring 2002): 44; Ruth Buxton Sayre, "Partners in Progress," Iowa

Farm Bureau Federation Administrative Report, IFBF records (1937): 23, 24; McDonald, *Ruth Buxton Sayre*, 6, 57, 61.

31. McDonald, *Ruth Buxton Sayre*, 58; "Report of the State Chairman," Iowa Farm Bureau Federation Women's Committee, IFBF records (1939).

32. "Iowa Bureau Farmer and Publicity," Iowa Farm Bureau Federation Administrative Reports 1940, 1942, 1943, IFBF records.

33. "Prospectus" for *My 70-Year Affair with the Wabash*, Bess Short Newcomer Papers, Iowa Women's Archives, University of Iowa, Iowa City. In her article on Wisconsin farm bureau women, historian Mary Neth emphasized the importance of early life experiences in shaping farm women as leaders and the factors that influenced their perceptions of work, gender, and organization. In her analysis of farm bureau leader Isabel Baumann, Neth found that, because she participated in farm labor as a child and worked in the fields alongside her mother, Baumann had an all-encompassing sense of women's work on the farm. She did not believe that women's work was limited to the home, garden, and chicken house. Likewise, in Newcomer's writing it is clear that she understood her unique circumstances and how her mother's work and sacrifice shaped her perceptions as an adult. Newcomer dedicated her second column in the *Iowa Bureau Farmer*, in July 1938, to her mother for instilling in her children appreciation for work and nature and a sensible "philosophy of life." Newcomer wrote, "She was short on money, so she gave us work; she was long on sense, so she gave us leisure. We were poor but never knew it." If she and her brother complained about the difficult farm labor, "[Mother] pointed out how spindly was the corn growing in the shade of orchard trees." Neth, "Building the Base," 342–45; Newcomer, "Hobby or Heritage: A Tribute to my Country Mother," IBF 2, no. 7 (July 1938): 9.

34. Newcomer, "Hobby or Heritage." The editor's surveys are no longer available to confirm her statements, but in the 1943 IFBF Administration Report, the information department included a statement specifically thanking Newcomer, "whose monthly features have been outstanding." No other writer or contributor received such recognition, either in 1943 or other years. IFBF Administration Report, Annual Conference, Des Moines, Iowa, November 1943; Bess Newcomer, "Farm Women Put 2 and 2 Together and Get Answer, First State Camp for Farm Women Proves Big Success," IBF 5, no. 8 (August 1941): 6.

35. Newcomer, "2 and 2 Together." No other state farm bureaus at this time held such meetings for their women's committees or auxiliaries; Iowa was the first to do so.

36. Newcomer, "We Marshall Our Reserves," IBF 6, no. 8 (August 1942): 5.

37. "VICTORY in the Hands of Farm Women," Iowa Farm Bureau Federation Women's Committee Records, Iowa Farm Bureau Federation Records, MS 189, Special Collections, Parks Library, Iowa State University, Ames, Iowa (hereafter referred to as IFBFWC records); Newcomer, "Please Pass the Ammunition!" IBF 7, no. 3 (March 1943): 7; Newcomer, "Country Culture Clinic," IBF 8, no. 8 (August 1944): 5.

38. Newcomer, "Marble and Mud," IBF 6, no. 1 (January 1942): 6; Newcomer, "Caught Off Guard!" IBF 6, no. 2 (February 1942): 7; Newcomer, "Seasoned Timber," IBF 8, no. 5 (May 1944): 5.

39. Schwieder, *Iowa*, 276–79; Bess Newcomer, "Scars and Stars of Agriculture," *IBF* 7 (January 1943): 9, 17; Newcomer, "Please Pass the Ammunition!" 7; Newcomer, "Caught Off Guard!" 7.

40. Bess Newcomer, "I Am a Farmer," *IBF* 8 (July 1944): 3; Newcomer, "Practical Patriotism in War or Peace," *IBF* 7 (October 1944): 4.

41. Bess Newcomer, "Brain Derbies for Farm Women," *IBF* 9, no. 8 (August 1945): 6. In 1945 wartime shortages also affected the *Iowa Bureau Farmer*. The magazine had to use smaller paper and discontinue using a glossy paper for the cover. "Bureau Farmer Goes to War," *IBF* 8, no. 4 (April 1944): 5.

42. Bess Newcomer, "Parable of the Apple Peddlers," *IBF* 9, no. 11 (November 1945): 4; Gladys Skelley, "Farm Homemakers Meet," *IBF* 9 (December 1945): 10.

43. Pearl Green to the *Iowa Union Farmer* 29, no. 5 (April 27, 1946): 3; *Official Yearbook of the Iowa Farmers Union Ladies Auxiliary*, 1942, IFU records.

44. Tontz, "General Farmers' Organizations, 156; *Official Bulletin of the Iowa Farm Bureau Federation* (October 1945): 1; (May 1946): 1; (April 1947): 1.

45. Bess Newcomer, "The Leaven and the Lump," *IBF* 9, no. 4 (April 1946): 14; Newcomer, "New Blood in Our Veins," *IBF* 9, no. 11 (November 1946): 9; Newcomer, "She Married a Farmer," *IBF* 9, no. 8 (August 1946): 8; McDonald, *Ruth Buxton Sayre*, 59.

46. Susan Lynn, "Gender and Progressive Politics: A Bridge to the Social Activism of the 1960s," in *Not June Cleaver: Women and Gender in Postwar America, 1945–1960*, ed. Joanne Meyerowitz (Philadelphia: Temple University Press, 1994).

47. Vera McCrea, "Ladies Make the Wheel Go Round," *Iowa Union Farmer* 16, no. 3 (March 22, 1941): 3.

2. AS NATURAL A PROCESS

1. Nell M. Forsyth, "Cedar Valley Club History" (June 1945), Cedar Valley Community Club records, Iowa Women's Archives, University of Iowa, Iowa City.

2. Schmidt, "Agrarian Pressure Groups," 52.

3. "No Problem Too Big for Women in the IFBF," *Iowa Farm Bureau Spokesman* (hereafter *Spokesman*) 24, no. 19 (January 4, 1958): 2A.

4. Carbert, *Agrarian Feminism*, 27–28; Lynn, "Gender and Progressive Politics," 104; Catherine E. Rymph, *Republican Women: Feminism and Conservatism from Suffrage through the Rise of the New Right* (Chapel Hill: University of North Carolina Press, 2006), 133, 137–38; Olga Rouse, "Contact Meeting Held by Farm Bureau Women," undated news clipping in "Scrapbook, 1954," in Freedom Township Women's Club records.

5. Halpern, *On that Farm*, 76–78; Laura Schroeder, "A History of the Swastika Club," in "Scrapbook, 1948," Freedom Township Women's Club Records; Christine Inman, "Strength of Structure Depends on Foundation," *Spokesman* 22, no. 40 (May 29, 1954): 12. Regarding the title of the second source: in 1923, when the women of Freedom Township formed their organization, they selected the name "Swastika Club." The Swastika, an ancient emblem, was comprised of 4 "L's" and represented "luck, light, love, and light." In 1942, following the entry of the United States into the

Second World War, members voted to change the name of their club to the Freedom Township Women's Club.

6. United States Department of Agriculture, *Agricultural Statistics: 1967* (Washington, D.C.: Government Printing Office, 1967): 443, 573; Willis Goudy et al., *Rural/Urban Transitions in Iowa* (Ames: Census Services, Department of Sociology, Iowa State University, 1996), 59, 82; Margaret Hanson, Willis Goudy, Renea Miller, and Sharon Whetstone, *Agriculture in Iowa: Trends from 1935 to 1997* (Ames: Census Services, Department of Sociology, Iowa State University, 1999), 29.

7. United States Bureau of the Census, *1960 Census of Housing* (Washington, D.C.: Government Printing Office, 1963); Jellison, *Entitled to Power*, 155, 174; Jewell G. Fessenden, "These Are the Women Who Are Members of Home Demonstration Organizations in the United States: A Report from a National Study of Home Demonstration Members," Extension Circular 528 (Washington, D.C.: United States Department of Agriculture, 1958): 2–5.

8. Neth, *Preserving the Family Farm*, 134–35; Deborah Fink, *Open Country*, 217; Berlage, "Organizing the Farm Bureau," 408; Fessenden, "These Are the Women," 2–3; "Scrapbooks" (1923–1967), Freedom Township Women's Club.

9. Dorothy Schwieder, "Cooperative Extension and Rural Iowa: Agricultural Adjustment in the 1950s," *Annals of Iowa* 51 (Fall 1992): 610–13; Summer Conference booklet, Iowa Farm Bureau Women's Committee summer conference (1970) IFBFWC records; "Young People Farm Because They Like It; Join Farm Groups to Have Stronger Voice," *Spokesman* 36, no. 8 (October 18, 1969): 13.

10. Memorandum, "Funds Expended in 1951 for County Extension Program," IFBF records; Memorandum, "State Farm Bureau-Extension Relationships," (1950), IFBF records; E. Howard Hill to County Farm Bureau Presidents (November 29, 1954), IFBF records; Schwieder, "Cooperative Extension," 606; Schwieder, *75 Years of Service*, 196; "Scrapbooks" (1954–1955), Freedom Township Women's Club; Mrs. I. J. Bulyer, Cherokee County, "Looking Both Ways," in "The Summer Echo," published during the IFBFWC summer conference (June 27, 1955), Irene Hoover Papers, Iowa Women's Archives, University of Iowa Libraries.

11. "Buchanan County Farm Bureau Women Have Lively Program," *Spokesman* 23, no. 32 (April 6, 1957): 13; "Linn County," *Annual Narrative Reports of County Extension Agents* (State of Iowa, 1959): 26.

12. Jellison, *Entitled to Power*, 170–175; Fessenden, "These Are the Women," 2–5; "Farm Bureau's 10-Point Program for Agricultural Prosperity," (Des Moines: Iowa Farm Bureau Federation, 1953), IFBF records; "The Summer Echo," published during the IFBFWC summer conference (June 10, 1952), Irene Hoover Papers.

13. Christine Inman, "How Do You Decide Whether Money Goes into Farm Machinery or Home?" *Spokesman* 21 (April 30, 1955): 12; "Secretary's Book, 1956–1957," Franklin Township Women's Club Records; Fink, *Open Country*, 217; Laura Schroeder, "A History of the Swastika Club," in "Scrapbook, 1948," Freedom Township Women's Club Records.

14. "Score Sheet for Rural Women's Clubs" for Freedom Township, in Freedom Township Women's Club Records (1954); "Farm Bureau Women's Township Re-

port and Score Sheet" for Westburg Township (September 29, 1971), Anita Crawford Papers.

15. "Women's Point of View," *Spokesman* 24, no. 37 (May 3, 1958): 2.

16. "The Summer Echo," published during the IFBFWC summer conference (June 10, 1952), Irene Hoover Papers.

17. McDonald, *Ruth Buxton Sayre*, 59; "Farm Wives Chic-to-Chic . . ." *Spokesman* 27, no. 29 (March 18, 1961): 4.

18. Letters from Iowa farm women appeared regularly in the *Iowa Farm Bureau Spokesman* and most often offered responses to articles regarding agricultural production and politics. For examples, see Mrs. L. Gustafson to Dan Murphy, *Spokesman* 22, no. 30 (March 24, 1956): 4; Mrs. Horace Thee to Dan Murphy, *Spokesman* 23, no. 6 (October 13, 1956): 4; *Spokesman* 36, no. 39 (May 30, 1970): 4. Unattributed news clippings dated September 1958 and September 22, 1959 in "Scrapbooks, 1958–1959," Freedom Township Women's Club Records; meeting minutes, March 7, 1960, Highland Do-Better Club Records.

19. Meeting minutes, October 1952–June 1953, Freedom Township Women's Club records.

20. Neth, *Preserving the Family Farm*, 134–35; membership roll, October 1959 to June 1960, Franklin Township Women's Club Records; see also secretary's books and membership rolls, 1959–1970, Franklin Township Women's Club records; membership roll, December 1959–December 1960, Highland Do-Better Club records; membership roll, December 1960–December 1961, Sharon Township Women's Club records.

21. *Iowa Farm Bureau Women's Program* (Des Moines: Iowa Farm Bureau Federation, 1959), 1, in "Scrapbook, 1959," Freedom Township Women's Club records; "Palo Alto County Farm Bureau Women's Club Handbook," 1959, in "Scrapbooks, 1959," Freedom Township Women's Club records.

22. "Palo Alto County Farm Bureau Women's Club Handbook," in "Scrapbook, 1960," Freedom Township Women's Club records.

23. "1960 Annual Program," in "Scrapbook, 1960–1974," Cleona Township Women's Club records, Iowa Women's Archives, University of Iowa Libraries.

24. "Large Crowd of Palo Alto Farm Women at Annual Program Here," and "Freedom Wins Despite 'Atomic Bombs,'" unattributed news clippings, in "Scrapbook, 1948," Freedom Township Women's Club records; "127 at County Rural Women's Day," "Mrs. Mavis is Speaking at Rural Women's Meeting," and "Large Group Attends F. B. Women's Workshop," unattributed news clippings in "Scrapbooks, 1954–1956," Freedom Township Women's Club records.

25. Nell M. Forsyth, "Cedar Valley Club History," June 1954, Cedar Valley Community Club records; meeting minutes, 1942–1947, 1948–1959, Cedar Valley Community Club records; "History of the Cedar Valley Community Club, 75th Anniversary," May 1995, Cedar Valley Community Club records.

26. Meeting minutes, 1952–1953, in the Friendly Neighbors Club, Deep River, Iowa, records; "Scrapbook, 1952–1963," Friendly Neighbors Club, Deep River, Iowa, records, Iowa Women's Archives, University of Iowa Libraries.

27. Carbert, *Agrarian Feminism*, 29; Josephine Van Zomeren, "Mahaska County

Farm Bureau Women: A History" (December 1971), 112–17, Mahaska County Farm Bureau Women's Clubs records.

28. Wayne L. Natvig to Crawford, December 3, 1970, and Art Kitner to Anita Crawford, February 6, 1967, Anita Crawford Papers; IFBFWC Annual Conference programs, 1969–1974, Anita Crawford Papers; meeting notes, 1969–1971, Anita Crawford Papers.

29. Membership rolls, Highland Do-Better Club, 1960–1984, Highland Do-Better Club records; Membership rolls, 1961, 1970, 1980, 1983–1984, Sharon Township Women's Club Records; Jenny Barker Devine, "'Our Cherished Ideals': Rural Women, Activism, and Identity in the Midwest, 1950–1990," (PhD diss, Iowa State University, 2008), 186–90; Rachel Ann Rosenfeld, *Farm Women: Work, Farm, and Family in the United States* (Chapel Hill: University of North Carolina Press, 1985), 198–215.

30. Carbert, *Agrarian Feminism*, 17; Barker Devine, "Our Cherished Ideals," 186–88; Richard L. Forstall, ed., "Iowa," in *Population of Counties by Decennial Census: 1900 to 1990* (Washington, D.C.: Bureau of the Census, 1995), http://www.census.gov/population/cencounts/ia190090.txt; *51st Annual Iowa Year Book of Agriculture* (Des Moines: Iowa Department of Agriculture, 1950), 549; *Iowa Book of Agriculture*, Fifth Biennial Report (Des Moines: State of Iowa, 1961), 330; *Iowa Book of Agriculture*, Tenth Biennial Report (Des Moines: State of Iowa, 1971), 345; "Scrapbooks, 1969–1970," Freedom Township Women's Club.

3. DOES YOUR MAN BELONG TO THE FARMERS UNION?

1. Edna Untiedt to Fred Stover, March 28, 1950, Fred Stover Papers, MS 92, Special Collections, University of Iowa; Gladys Talbott Edwards, *This is the Farmers Union* (Denver: National Farmers Union, 1951), 13; *Iowa Union Farmer*, November 20, 1948.

2. Roy Wortman, "Gender Issues in the National Farmers' Union in the 1930s," *Midwest Review* 15 (1993): 74.

3. Edna Untiedt to Fred Stover, March 28, 1950, Stover Papers.

4. Bruce E. Field, *Harvest of Dissent: The National Farmers Union and the Early Cold War* (Lawrence: University Press of Kansas, 1998), 56; Jacqueline McGlade, "More a Plowshare than a Sword: The Legacy of US Cold War Agricultural Diplomacy," *Agricultural History* (Winter 2009), 79–102; "Drew Pearson on the Washington Merry-Go-Round," *Washington Post*, May 13, 1948, quoted in Virgil Dean, *An Opportunity Lost: The Truman Administration and the Farm Policy Debate* (Columbia: University of Missouri Press, 2006), 56; House Committee on Agriculture, *General Farm Program, including Joint Hearings with the Senate Committee on Agriculture and Forestry*, 81st Congress, 1st Session, pt.2 (1949), 140–43.

5. William C. Pratt, "The Farmers Union and the 1948 Henry Wallace Campaign," *Annals of Iowa* 49, no. 5 (Summer 1988): 358; Field, *Harvest of Dissent*, 157.

6. Schmidt, "Agrarian Pressure Groups," 50–51; William P. Tucker, "Populism Up-to-Date: The Story of the Farmers Union," *Agricultural History* 21, no. 4 (October 1947), 207–8.

7. Tontz, "General Farmers' Organizations," *Agricultural History* 38, no. 3 (Summer 1964), 155. The NFU membership was more common on the Great Plains. In 1953 North Dakota counted 41,415 members; South Dakota had 15,963; Nebraska had 15,963; and Kansas counted 7,651. This is compared to just 1,311 in Iowa.

8. Field, *Harvest of Dissent*, 81–82; Fred Stover to Ed Andregg, January 6, 1950, Fred Stover Papers; "Come Let Us Reason Together," *Iowa Union Farmer* (February 1952): 5.

9. Fred Stover, "Farmers Also Victims of Operations Killer: To Draft More Farm Boys Than in World War II," *Iowa Union Farmer* (April 1951); Joseph Alsop and Stewart Alsop, "What is Liberalism?" *Life* (January 7, 1946): 26; "Tragedy of Liberalism," *Life* (May 20, 1946): 69–70.

10. Field, *Harvest of Dissent*, 24; Susan Hartman, "Women's Employment and the Domestic Ideal in the Early Cold War Years," in *Not June Cleaver: Women and Gender in Postwar America, 1945–1960*, ed. by Joanne Meyerowitz (Philadelphia, PA: Temple University Press, 1994) and Dorothy Sue Cobble, "Recapturing Working Class Feminism: Union Women in the Postwar Era," in *Not June Cleaver: Women and Gender in Postwar America, 1945–1960*, ed. Joanne Meyerowitz (Philadelphia, PA: Temple University Press, 1994), 72–75, 85; Landon R. Y. Storrs, "Attacking the Washington 'Femmocracy': Antifeminism in the Cold War Campaign against 'Communists in Government,'" *Feminist Studies* 33, no. 1 (Spring 2007), 118–52; *Iowa Union Farmer*, August 20, 1951. Historian William Pratt has also argued that the ideological battle was part of a more complicated move to promote NFU businesses and adopt a friendly attitude toward free enterprise. NFU businesses such as cooperatives, fertilizer manufacturers, and insurance companies continually sought new clients, who might steer clear of a controversial organization. See Pratt, "The Farmers Union, McCarthyism, and the Demise of the Agrarian Left," *Historian* 58, no. 2 (Winter 1996): 337. See also Michael W. Flamm, "The National Farmers' Union and the Evolution of Agrarian Liberalism, 1936–1946," *Agricultural History* 68, no. 3 (1994), 54–80.

11. Edwards, *Farmers Union*, 13; Mary Neth, *Preserving the Family Farm*, 141–42; John A. Crampton, *The National Farmers Union: Ideology of a Pressure Group* (Lincoln: University of Nebraska Press, 1965), 148–49.

12. *Iowa Union Farmer*, November 20, 1947.

13. Betty Lownes to Mary Nicoletto, November 18, 1948, Fred Stover Papers; "Club History, 1926–1972," Ever Ready Club records, Iowa Women's Archives.

14. Edna Untiedt to Members and State Board of Iowa Farmers Union, January 17, 1949, Fred Stover Papers.

15. *Iowa Union Farmer*, May 14, 1946; *Iowa Union Farmer*, October 13, 1949; Mary Nicoletto, "Three Buses, Three Days in Washington, and Three Pigs in Quest of Parity," *Iowa Union Farmer*, March 18, 1950.

16. Wortman, "Gender Issues," 73, Crampton, *National Farmers Union*, 102–3.

17. Edwards, *Farmers Union*, 39–40, 80–82.

18. Harold V. Knight, "Advice to the Young Lady Considering Marriage," n.d., IFU records; *Handbook for Farmers Union Locals and Counties*, n.d., IFU records, 7. This

publication was produced under the auspices of the NFU Education Service in Denver, which would have been under the direction of Gladys Talbott Edwards.

19. Shirley E. Greene, *This Earth, This Land* (Denver: National Farmers Union, 1955), 3, 118–19; *Handbook for Farmers Union Locals and* Counties, 7.

20. *A Guide for Farmers Union Action Officials* (Denver: National Farmers Union, n.d.), 3–4, 9–20.

21. Mary Nicoletto to Pearl Green, January 30, 1948, Fred Stover Papers; *Iowa Union Farmer* (August 20, 1951), 3; *Handbook for Farmers Union Locals and* Counties, 8; Mrs. Clifford Nelson to Mary Nicoletto, January 5, 1949, Fred Stover Papers; Richard Ronfeldt to Mary Nicoletto, May 16, 1950, Fred Stover papers; Mary Nicoletto to Richard Ronfeldt, May 18, 1950, Fred Stover Papers. Pearl Green had played a key role in the development of the Federation of Clinton County, mentioned in chapter 1, which brought together several diverse groups to work on joint projects in the county. Her leadership experience was not limited to the IFU ladies auxiliary.

22. Edna Untiedt to Fred Stover, undated, Fred Stover Papers.

23. Eleanor Biederman to Fred Stover, February 13, 1949, Fred Stover Papers; Fred Stover to Eleanor Biederman, February 23, 1949, Fred Stover Papers.

24. Alice Sponheim to Fred Stover, November 30, 1951, Fred Stover Papers.

25. Betty Lownes to Mary Nicoletto, January 30, 1948, and December 24, 1948, Fred Stover Papers.

26. Field, *Harvest of Dissent*, 89–91, 136–42; William C. Pratt, "Farmers, Communists, and the FBI in the Upper Midwest," *Agricultural History* 63, no. 3 (Summer 1989): 63, 72–73; *Des Moines Register*, September 22, 1950.

27. Fred Stover to M. Ida Rink, August 30, 1950, Fred Stover Papers; Fred Stover, *Atomic Blessing or Atomic Blasting?* (Hampton, IA: U.S. Farmers Association, 1950), 13–16. Stover later had his convention speech printed as a twenty-eight-page pamphlet that remained in high demand throughout the 1950s.

28. Ida Guernsey to Fred Stover, August 23, 1950, Fred Stover Papers.

29. Pratt, "Farmers, Communists," 74; *Des Moines Register*, September 22 and 25, 1950; Oral history interview with Lois Linse Gleiter, with Dale Treleven, August 19, 1974, Wisconsin Agriculturalists Oral History Project, Wisconsin Historical Society Archives.

30. Fred Stover to Elmer Gustafson, October 30, 1950, Fred Stover Papers; Fred Stover to Arthur Gerlach, October 27, 1950, Fred Stover Papers; Fred Stover to Carl Ketcham, October 30, 1950, Fred Stover Papers; Field, *Harvest of Dissent*, 147–49. Hoffman challenged Stover's presidency by claiming he had engaged in partisan activities while serving as chairman of the Progressive Party in 1948. The constitution of the NFU required that all leaders remain nonpartisan while serving the organization. Despite a lawsuit over the matter, in April 1951 the Iowa courts sided with Stover and declared him the legitimate president of the IFU. See Bruce Field, "The Price of Dissent: The Iowa Farmers Union and the Early Cold War," *Annals of Iowa* 55 (Winter 1996), 10–11.

31. Ida Guernsey to Fred Stover, August 23, 1950, Fred Stover Papers; Fred Stover to Ida Guernsey, September 12, 1950, Fred Stover Papers.

32. In Leonard Hoffman's testimony it became clear that Untiedt had been intentionally excluded from any discussions among state board members related to ousting Stover. Transcript of *Mathwig v. Holden*, Eq. No. 60745, Dist. Court of Iowa, March 1951, Fred Stover Papers; "What Farmers Should Know About the Farmers Union: The Inside Story of the Outside Interference in the Iowa Farmers Union" (Des Moines: Iowa Farmers Union, 1956), 19–20, IFU records; Field, *Harvest of Dissent*, 150, 157. The Farmers Union Grain Terminal Association was one of many cooperatives that contributed a significant amount of money to the social and educational activities of the Farmers Union. Between 1943 and 1950 the FUGTA provided $1.5 million to state affiliates in North Dakota, South Dakota, Montana, Minnesota, and Wisconsin. According to political scientist John A. Crampton, the commercial activities of the NFU were vital to building and sustaining membership. He notes, "When the Union's commercial activities failed . . . the membership decline was as drastic as the growth had been." On the other hand, building membership was not always the most lucrative venture. In the postwar period, as the NFU established a fertilizer co-op and developed more insurance and investment businesses, it actually spent less on social and educational organizing. By 1960 nearly half of the NFU's income came from selling insurance, quickly outpacing the amount generated by dues from ordinary members. See Crampton, *National Farmers Union*, 149–50.

33. Betty Lownes, "Peace Needed Most," *Iowa Union Farmer* (April 1951): 4; Edna Untiedt to Fred Stover, October 13, 1950, Fred Stover Papers; Myrtle Locken to Fred Stover, August 1, 1950, Fred Stover Papers.

34. Myrtle Locken to James Patton, September 30, 1950, in Ida M. Rink, ed., *Which Shall It Be for the Farmers Union? Democracy from the Rank and File or Dictatorship from the Top Down*, Farmers Union Defense Committee, n.d., IFU records.

35. Merle Hansen to Mrs. Carl Benna, November 11, 1951, Fred Stover Papers; Lucille Olson to Fred Stover, November 26, 1951, Fred Stover Papers (italics in original); Susie Stageberg to Richard E. Fallow, editor, *Iowa Union Farmer*, April 30, 1952; Fred Stover to Susie Stageberg, May 16, 1952, Fred Stover Papers.

36. Pratt, "The Farmers Union, McCarthyism, and the Demise of the Agrarian Left," *Historian* 58, no. 2 (1996): 330–33; Dyson, *Red Harvest*, 198.

37. Field, *Harvest of Dissent*, 155–57; Field, "Price of Dissent," 13; "A Report of the Executive Committee of the Board of Directors of Farmers and Educational and Cooperative Union of America to the Full Board Regarding the Future Status of Those State Organizations of the Farmers Union Which Had Failed to Reach a Membership of 3500 by the end of the 1953 Fiscal Year," quoted in Field, "Price of Dissent," 21; Scott Nearing to Fred Stover, June 13, 1952, Fred Stover Papers.

38. "Farmers Union Defeats Issue on Cease Fire," *Dallas Morning News* (March 15, 1952); "Patton Elected Union President," *Dallas Morning News* (March 13, 1952). It seems that, in preserving his own leadership, Patton was moving in the right direction. According to one newspaper report, many members grumbled that Patton's ideas were "too far off to the left" in the context of a conference where the NFU adopted resolutions that encouraged private enterprise, limited government sponsorship of coopera-

tives, and increased defense spending. For the first time the NFU was silent on members' calls for immediate parity in agriculture. See "Farmers Union Attack Loosed on Rival Group," (March 11, 1952) and Field, "Price of Dissent," 18.

39. "Whither the National Farmers Union?" Rank and File Committee of Farmers Union Members, n.d., IFU records.

40. Fred Stover to Elmer and Pauline Gustafson, May 15, 1952, Fred Stover Papers; Horton Gilbert to Fred Stover, June 12, 1952, Fred Stover Papers; Earl Ronfeldt to Fred Stover, November 24, 1952, Fred Stover Papers; Edna Untiedt to Fred Stover, May 27, 1953, Fred Stover Papers.

41. Fred Stover to George H. Wharam, Mrs. Vincent E. Hendricks, Mrs. Clifford Struble, and John Bedner, January 24, 1953, Fred Stover Papers; Edna Untiedt to Fred Stover, March 2, 1954; transcript of *Mathwig v. Holden*, Fred Stover Papers.

42. Edna Untiedt to Fred Stover, July 14, 1956, Fred Stover Papers; "What Farmers Should Know About the Farmers Union," 1955, IFU records.

43. Fred Stover to Edna Untiedt, Martha Joens, Karl Krell, and Charles Dengler, December 21, 1955, Fred Stover Papers; *Farmers Educational and Co-operative Union of America v. Iowa Farmers Union*, 150 F. 2 (S.D. Iowa, 1957); *Iowa Farmers Union and Iowa Union Farmers Association v. Farmers Educational and Cooperative Union of America*, 247 F. 2d 809 (8th Cir. 1957).

44. Edna Untiedt to Fred Stover, April 9, 1959, Fred Stover Papers. Betty Lownes also continued to work closely with Stover in the USFA.

45. "Breakdown of 1957 and 1958 Iowa Membership by County," IFU records; County meeting reports, 1958–1959, IFU records. The nine counties were Allamakee, Chickasaw, Clay, Dallas, Hardin, Jackson, Jones, Linn, and Scott; "The Woman's Touch," *Iowa Farmers Union Spotlight* 4, no. 6 (November 1964): 8; "Woman Leader Elected," *Iowa Farmers Union Spotlight* 4, no. 13 (December 1965): 3.

4. BECAUSE SOMEBODY HAD TO DO IT

1. Interview of Luella Zmolek by Doris Malkmus, September 10, 2001, Voices from the Land, Oral History Collection, Iowa Women's Archives, University of Iowa Libraries; Seth S. King, "Drop in Farm Income Worries Grain Belt," *New York Times* (May 8, 1955): E8; William M. Blairs, "Slump Continues for Farm Prices," *New York Times* (December 31, 1955): 19.

2. For more on the rise of the "rural decline" narrative, see Robert Wuthnow, *Remaking the Heartland: Middle American since the 1950s* (Princeton, NJ: Princeton University Press, 2011), 58–59.

3. Sara Evans, *Personal Politics: The Roots of Women's Liberation in the Civil Rights Movement and the New Left* (New York: Vintage Books, 1979), 72, 82, 86–87.

4. Betty Friedan, *The Feminine Mystique* (New York: W.W. Norton, 1963), 338–78; Halpern, *On That Farm*, 113–14. Historian Elizabeth Fox-Genovese proposed that feminist scholars rethink the nature of community as a locus of empowerment and attempt to reconcile the "uneasy coexistence of communitarian and individualistic

commitments." Elizabeth Fox-Genovese, *Feminism without Illusions: A Critique of Individualism* (Chapel Hill: University of North Carolina Press, 1991), 38–42. The importance of women's relationships with their husbands cannot be overstated. The nature of agricultural production made demands on families that were unique to their occupation. Longitudinal studies that traced women throughout their married lives from the 1940s into the 1970s found that only twenty-eight percent of those married to men with careers in business, academics, science, the trades, or the law reported having directly contributed to their husbands' careers through unpaid labor. Those who remained distant from their husbands' work more often reported feelings of isolation, a desire for greater personal autonomy, a wish that they had pursued careers themselves, the very ideas typically associated with the rise of Second Wave feminisms and demands for equal rights. The wives of clergy or small business owners, on the other hand, reported very high levels of involvement with their husbands' work because, like farm women, they and their husbands had subjugated individual aspirations for a larger good. Those women also reported a high level of professional satisfaction because they found appropriate outlets for their skills and interests, making them more likely to act publicly as members of distinct occupational groups. Most important is a strong class consciousness and a perception of shared oppression with their husbands. During the 1960s and 1970s women married to Appalachian coal miners joined their husbands on strike because, even though they did not share work spaces, they shared a clear identity shaped by work in the coal mines. Eliza K. Pavalko and Glen H. Elder, Jr., "Women Behind the Men: Variations in Wives' Support of Husbands' Careers," *Gender and Society* 7, no. 4 (December 1993): 555; Nancy J. Davis and Robert V. Robinson. "Do Wives Matter? Class Identities of Wives and Husbands in the United States, 1974–1994." *Social Forces* 98, no. 3 (March 1998): 1074–75; Sally Ward Maggard, "Women's Participation in the Bookside Coal Strike: Millitance, Class, and Gender in Appalachia," *Frontiers: A Journal of Women's History* 9, no. 3 (1987): 20. Women working within politically active religious organizations often had similar transformative experiences when acting publicly on their religious beliefs, again because of shared beliefs with a wider community. See Rona Sheramy, "'There Are Times When Silence Is A Sin': The Women's Division of the American Jewish Congress and the Anti-Nazi Boycott Movement," *American Jewish History* 89, no. 1 (March 2001): 105–21.

5. Don Muhm, *The NFO: A Farm Belt Rebel: A History of the National Farmers Organization* (Rochester, MN: Lone Oak Press, 2000), 21–23.

6. According to historian Robert L. Tontz, in the mid-1950s the NFO reported a membership of 40,000 families. By the mid-1960s Tontz calculated NFO membership to be approximately 180,000 farm families. See Tontz, "General Farmers' Organizations," 145–46.

7. Muhm, NFO, 23–36; Linda A. Tvrdy, "The Free Market Revolt of the National Farmers Organization," paper presented at the Agricultural History Society Conference, Cambridge, MA (June 2006): 1; "Nemaha County at 231 Members," *NFO Reporter* 5, no. 2 (March 1961): 6.

8. Jane Adams, "The *Farm Journal's* Discourse of Farm Women's Femininity,"

Anthropology and Humanism 29, no. 1 (2004): 49, 56; "Women Who Work in the Field," *Wallace's Farmer* (December 3, 1960): 28–29; "Decisions, Decisions, Decisions," *Wallace's Farmer* (August 18, 1962): 44; Rex Gogerty, "How To Stay on Speaking Terms . . . Though Married," *Farm Journal* (November 1962): 38–39; "Things a Man Should Never Tell His Wife . . . Or Should He?" *Farm Journal* (November 1962): 62D-62F; "Who Babysits When You Are in the Field?" *Wallace's Farmer* (April 18, 1959): 52; Joan McCloskey, "Should A Farm Wife Work Outside the Home?" *Successful Farming* (September 1968): 57; Ruth Hanna, "How Young Wives Help Their Husbands," *Successful Farming* (September 1965): 113; for more on rural women and portrayals of domesticity, see Janet Galligani Casey, " 'This is YOUR Magazine': Domesticity, Agrarianism, and *The Farmer's Wife*," *American Periodicals* 14, no. 2 (2004): 179–211.

9. R. Douglas Hurt, *Problems of Plenty: The American Farmer in the Twentieth Century* (Chicago: Ivan R. Dee), 119, 143–44. Typical scholarly studies of the NFO include J. Ronnie Davis and Neil A. Palomba, "The National Farmers Organization and the Prisoner's Dilemma: A Game Theory Prediction," *Social Science Quarterly* 50, no. 3 (1969), 742–48. The number of master's theses and doctoral dissertations to emerge in the 1960s and 1970s is particularly telling of the perceived novelty of the NFO. Coming from a variety of disciplines, these include Truman David Wood, "The National Farmers' Organization in Transition," PhD dissertation, University of Iowa, 1961; and James Riddle Hundley, "A Test of Theories in Collective Behavior: The National Farmers Organization," (PhD diss., Ohio State University, 1965). Other scholars have performed rhetoric analyses of NFO leaders and published materials, but again, these emphasize male leaders and typically male concerns, such as marketing. For examples, see David Allen Carter, "The National Farmers' Organization and the Rhetoric of Institutionalization," (PhD dissertation, University of Iowa, 1976); Darrell Arden Disrud, "President Oren Lee Staley, 1958–1978: A Rhetorical Analysis of the National Farmer's Organization," (master's thesis, University of New Mexico, 1983); and Celia E. Shapland, "Protest in the Newspaper: A Case Study of the National Farmers Organization," (master's thesis, Iowa State University, 1986). For inside perspectives, see works by members and supporters, including: Charles Walters, *The Biggest Farm Story of the Decade: A Searching Look at Farm Trouble and the Search for an Equitable Answer* (Kansas City, MO: Halcyon House, 1968); Charles Walters, *Angry Testament* (Kansas City, MO: Halcyon House, 1969); Charles Walters, *Holding Action* (Kansas City, MO: Halcyon House, 1968); Willis Rowell, *Mad As Hell* (Corning, IA: Gauthier Publishing, 1984); and Willis Rowell, *The National Farmers Organization: A Complete History* (Ames, IA: Sigler Printing, 1993).

10. Interview of Martha Linn by Doris Malkmus, September 10, 2001, Voices from the Land.

11. Tvrdy, "Free Market Revolt," 2–4.

12. NFO *Reporter* 4, no. 5 (September 1960): 3; NFO *Reporter* 2, no. 4 (May 1957): 5; "NFO Ladies on Bus Tour," NFO *Reporter* 6, no. 5 (June 1962): 3; "Auxiliary Is Formed," NFO *Reporter* 6, no. 11 (January 1963): 3.

13. Monica Tvrdy, interview by author, August 16, 2007, National Farmers Organization records, MS 481, Special Collections, Parks Library, Iowa State University (hereafter NFO records); Mabel Schweers interview, Voices from the Land. Tvrdy also compared the NFO with other commodity-specific organizations, such as the Porkettes or the Cowbelles, in which women were typically responsible for building relationships with urban consumers. While she appreciated the efforts of commodity-specific organizations in promoting agriculture to the general public, she did not believe that promoting specific cuts of meat or certain products would result in higher commodity prices. Tvrdy stated that farmers did not "have to promote food, really, because people are going to eat." Organizations can emphasize the healthful benefits of milk or a specific cut of meat, but unless farmers demand a fair price, "it won't make a whole lot of difference." She believed that the NFO offered a more practical solution to the problem of unstable commodity prices by allowing farmers to set their own standards, as opposed to asking that processors and consumers establish acceptable prices.

14. Interview of Ilo Rhines by Doris Malkmus, October 26, 2001, Voices from the Land.

15. Ibid.; Zmolek interview, Voices from the Land.

16. Evans, *Personal Politics*, 93; Linn interview, Voices from the Land.

17. Rowell, *Mad as Hell*, 78–79.

18. Oren Lee Staley, "The President's Message . . ." NFO Reporter 1, no. 1 (September 1956): 1; Rowell, *Mad as Hell*, 78–79.

19. "We Salute Our Wives," NFO Reporter 6, no. 2 (March 1962): 3.

20. NFO Reporter 6, no. 1 (February 1962): 4.

21. *Adams County Free Press*, December 8, 1960; *Sioux County Capital*, February 2, 1961; *Alton Democrat*, February 2, 1961.

22. "Letters to the NFO," NFO Reporter 5, no. 2 (March 1961): 2, 3, 6.

23. Film: *The U.S. Farm Report: Iowa Farm Women* (1965), NFO records.

24. Film: *The U.S. Farm Report: Farm Wives' View of Farming* (July 27, 1966), NFO records; film: *The U.S. Farm Report: Ladies Talk NFO* (November 10, 1966), NFO records.

25. Zmolek interview, Voices from the Land; Linn interview, Voices from the Land.

26. Schweers interview, Voices from the Land.

27. Embree interview, Voices from the Land; Rhines interview, Voices from the Land. Though the NFO expected women to play a role in the organization, the exact role of children was less clear. During the 1950s and 1960s photographs of children regularly appeared in the NFO Reporter as they participated in parades and family events, such as ice-cream socials and sausage feeds. Occasionally, photographs of children appeared as human-interest features, with quips about the future of the organization. For example, in November 1967 the NFO Reporter featured a portrait of Jerome Humliech, the one-year-old son of Bernard A. Humliech of Prague, Nebraska, wearing a tiny NFO T-shirt. Overall, though, it appears that children were to be under the watchful guise of mothers or babysitters. In their oral histories women often stated

that in order to attend meetings they needed a babysitter because children were too distracting. Others mentioned that when they sold hogs their children would often go to the checkpoints to socialize and eat doughnuts. See NFO *Reporter* 11, no. 11 (November 1967):16; Zmolek interview, Voices from the Land; Linn interview, Voices from the Land; Tvrdy interview, NFO records; Arlene Fricke interview by author, August 16, 2007, NFO records; Marcia Fick interview by author, August 16, 2007, NFO records.

28. Embree interview, Voices from the Land. In the early 1980s Monica Tvrdy's husband, Edwin, told her she needed to work at the NFO office in David City, Nebraska. They were short staffed and needed part-time help. Although she saw several benefits to working at the office, it was not an ideal situation, and it required that she learn difficult skills, such as working with office equipment and computers. Tvrdy still had two children at home and "resented it a lot," but she found some benefit in that it enabled her to learn more about the NFO. She said, "That was one good thing about coming to work at the office because I was more in tune with what was going on." Tvrdy interview, NFO records.

29. Tensions among the NFO, the IFBF, and the IFU were more than obvious by the end of the 1950s. In January 1956 Hillis R. Wilson, a farmer from Iowa Falls, Iowa, informed Iowa Farm Bureau Federation President E. Howard Hill that he had been a loyal Farm Bureau member for several decades but was increasingly disappointed with IFBF policies on price supports. A founding member of the Benton County NFO, Wilson estimated that the NFO would have 1,100 to 1,200 members in the county, fifty percent of whom also held Farm Bureau memberships, and he offered to take Hill on a tour of the county to talk with farmers if he should "doubt the information in this letter."

Similarly, in 1964 Alfred Smith, a farmer from Cascade, Iowa, wrote a letter to the *Iowa Farm Bureau Spokesman*, the Iowa Farm Bureau's official magazine, in which he described NFO holding actions in the "northern tier of townships in Dubuque county." A Farm Bureau member for ten years and an NFO member for three, Smith found "over 2,000 head of hogs being held by Farm Bureau members as well as others." He called on the Farm Bureau membership to join in the holding and cooperate for the good of all farmers. In his reply to Smith's letter, however, *Spokesman* editor Dan Murphy expressed typical Farm Bureau sentiments that only strained relations between the two organizations. Murphy called the holding action a "flop" and wrote, "I know of no other incident in agricultural history which has made genuine cooperation and trust more difficult to reach. Farm Bureau people do believe in working together. But not with a fence-cutting tool." This was in reference to NFO members who intimidated nonparticipating farmers by cutting fences and turning their livestock loose. Hillis R. Wilson to E. Howard Hill, January 31, 1956, E. Howard Hill Papers, Special Collections, Parks Library, Iowa State University; *Iowa Farm Bureau Spokesman* 31, no. 8 (October 24, 1964): 4; Harvey Rickert to Kenneth Schumann, October 11, 1959, IFU records; *Chickasaw County Union Farmer* (October 10, 1959), IFU records.

30. Wilma Zubrod to Kenneth Schumann, October 20, 1960, IFU records.

31. Zmolek interview, Voices from the Land; Schweers interview, Voices from the

Land. Stories of personal conflicts with friends and family were common throughout oral histories. Ilo Rhines explained that after her sister-in-law sold calves during one holding action, the two families ended their tradition of collaborating on holiday celebrations. Likewise, Martha Linn stated that she and her neighbors did not talk for more than four years because the neighboring farmer refused to go to an NFO meeting with her husband, Darwin. Rhines interview, Voices from the Land: Linn interview, Voices from the Land; Jean Wardman interview by author, August 16, 2007, NFO records; Tvrdy interview, NFO records.

32. Muhm, *NFO*, 50, 113–14.

33. *NFO Reporter* 6, no. 8 (October 1962): 1; "Auxiliary Is Formed," *NFO Reporter* 6, no. 11 (January 1963): 3; *NFO Reporter* 11, no. 5 (May 1967): 16.

34. Rowell, *Mad as Hell*, 79; *NFO Reporter* 11, no. 6 (June 1967): 15.

35. Zmolek interview, Voices from the Land; Embree interview, Voices from the Land; Schweers interview, Voices from the Land.

36. Muhm, *NFO*, 175.

37. Schweers interview, Voices from the Land; Zmolek interview, Voices from the Land; Tvrdy interview, NFO records.

38. "Letters to the NFO," "Nemaha County at 231 Members," and "NFO Rolling in Nebraska," *NFO Reporter* 5, no. 2 (March 1961): 2, 3, 6; Muhm, *NFO*, 56–57; Rowell, *Mad As Hell*, 78–79.

39. Zmolek interview, Voices from the Land.

40. Ibid.; minutes, NFO board of directors, January 9, 1956, NFO records.

41. Zmolek interview, Voices from the Land.

42. Linn interview, Voices from the Land.

43. Ibid.

44. Zmolek interview, Voices from the Land.

45. Ibid.

46. Linn interview, Voices from the Land.

5. HOP TO THE TOP WITH THE IOWA CHOP

1. Mrs. Wayne (Jan) Jackson, "Iowa Pork-ettes Newsletter" (1964), 1971 Iowa Porkette Project Book, Iowa Porkettes Records, 1964–1996, Iowa Women's Archives, University of Iowa Libraries (hereafter IPR).

2. Halpern, *On That Farm*, 136; interview of Kathryn Louden by Doris Malkmus (April 18, 2001), IPR.

3. Carbert, *Agrarian Feminism*, 4.

4. *The Iowa Porkettes Twenty-Eight Year History: January 1964–January 1992* (1992), 2, 11, IPR; National Porkettes, *Porkette Handbook* (Des Moines, IA: January 1979), 5, IPR; Myrtle Keppy, "Greetings to All Porkettes" (1964), in the 1971 Iowa Porkette Project Book, IPR. Keppy, who became the second president of the Iowa Porkettes, oversaw a statewide contest to name "Lady Loinette." Other names under serious consideration included "Lady Leantreat, Miss Tenderatta, Lean Baconette, Reddi Pork, Porkaleana, Dandyloin, Madame Sizzler, Lady Utterworth, and Mrs. Hampion."

5. Hanson et al., *Agriculture in Iowa*, 143; Herrell Degraff, "Introduction: At the Crossroad," in David G. Topel, ed., *The Pork Industry: Problems and Progress* (Ames: Iowa State University Press, 1968), xi–xiv; J. L. Anderson, "Lard to Lean, 30–32; Mark R. Finlay, "Hogs, Antibiotics, and the Industrial Environments of Postwar Agriculture," in *Industrializing Organisms: Introducing Evolutionary History*, ed. Susan R. Schrepfer and Philip Scranton (New York: Routledge, 2004), 239, 248; Roger Horowitz, *Putting Meat on the American Table: Taste, Technology, Transformation* (Baltimore: Johns Hopkins University Press, 2006), 2.

6. Louden interview (2001), IPR; Lorna Clancy Miller and Mary Neth, "Farm Women in the Political Arena," in *Women and Farming: Changing Roles, Changing Structures*, ed. Wava G. Haney and Jane B. Knowles (Boulder, CO: Westview Press 1988), 370, 360.

7. Carolyn Sachs, *Gendered Fields: Rural Women, Agriculture, and the Environment* (Boulder, CO: Westview Press, 1996), 137; Michelle K. Berry, "'Be Sure to Fix the Fence': The Arizona Cowbelles' Public Persona, 1950–1960," *Frontiers: A Journal of Women's Studies* 25, no. 2 (2004): 157, 172.

8. Louden interview (2001), IPR; Myrtle Keppy, "Greetings to All Porkettes," undated news clipping, 1971 Iowa Porkette Project Book, IPR.

9. "Iowa Porkette Newsletter" (October 1969), 1971 Iowa Porkette Project Book, IPR; Louden interview (2001), IPR.

10. Memorandum: "Mileage Estimates for Porkettes" (1978), IPR; United States Department of Agriculture, Economic Research Service, "Farm Structure: Farm Operator Household Income Data," http://www.ers.usda.gov/Briefing/FarmStructure /Data/historic.htm.

11. *Iowa Porkettes History*, 8–10, IPR.

12. Karen McCreedy, "None of Us Live on an Island," in Muhm, *Iowa Pork and People: A History of Iowa's Pork Producers* (Clive, IA: Iowa Pork Foundation, 1995), 88–89.

13. Neth, *Preserving the Family Farm*, 26; *Iowa Porkettes History*, 8–10, IPR; *Iowa Swine Producers Directory, 1964–1965* (Des Moines: Iowa Swine Producers Association, 1964).

14. Louden interview (2001), IPR.

15. "Komments from Kathryn," *Iowa Porkette Newsletter* (January 1970), IPR; *Ladies' Pork Journal* 1, no. 1 (Fall 1983), IPR.

16. Madeline Meyer, "Porkettes," *Iowa Pork Producer* (August 1978): 23.

17. Mrs. Howard Fender to Oelwein Housewives, n.d.; Oelwein Chamber of Commerce to guests, n.d.; Survey of Housewives at event, 1971 Iowa Porkette Project Book, n.d., IPR.

18. "Porkettes to Survey Consumers in 5 Major Cities This Fall," undated news clipping, and "Porkette President's Annual Report" (1967), 1971 Iowa Porkette Project Book, IPR; "Komments from Kathryn," *Iowa Porkette Newsletter* (September 1970), IPR.

19. Dan Murphy to Donna Keppy, n.d., IPR; Dan Murphy to Marie Brown, n.d., IPR. The Porkettes paid Murphy for consultations, speeches, press releases, and other

communication needs, although the budget for such items remained modest. In 1975 the Porkettes paid Murphy $514 out of an annual budget of approximately $8,500.

20. "Memorandum of Understanding between the Iowa Pork Producers Association and the Iowa Porkettes," December 15, 1982, IPR; Russ Sanders to Sue Henrich, May 18, 1978, IPR.

21. "Sugar and Spice," *Farm Wife News* 5, no. 11 (November 1975): 3; "Sugar and Spice," *Farm Wife News* 6, no. 11 (November 1976): 2; Cheryl Tevis, "Woman Interest," *Successful Farming* (August 1979): 14; Cheryl Tevis, "How Does Estate Tax Law Cut the Cake — Equal Partner or Marital Helpmate?" *Successful Farming* (September 1979): 30–31; Cheryl Tevis, "Woman Interest," *Successful Farming* (November 1979): 18.

22. "Widow's Tax Assailed in Capital," *New York Times* (February 5, 1981): D19. See also Eileen Shannon, "Plan For Revising Estate Tax Given," *New York Times* (May 23, 1976): 27.

23. Frances Hill, "Women and Farm Politics — National Level," *Nebraska's New Land Review* (Summer 1979): 10.

24. "The Voice of the American Agri-Woman," American Agri-Women Annual Report and Directory, 1980, Women in Farm Economics (WIFE) records, University of Nebraska–Lincoln.

25. Ibid.

26. The members of WIFE debated affiliating with American Agri-Women but ultimately opted not to join. "Background Information on WIFE," pamphlet, 1980, WIFE records.

27. Ann Perry-Barnes, "An Exchange Theory Analysis of Satisfaction with Membership in an American Voluntary Organization," (master's thesis, Colorado State University 1985), 98; Pratt, "Using History," 25.

28. Neth, *Preserving the Family Farm*, 26; Jellison, *Entitled to Power*, 178–80; "Hey, President Carter! These Women Are M.A.D.!" *Rural Electric Nebraskan* (January 1978): 14–15, WIFE records.

29. Miller and Neth, "Farm Women," 361; "Budget" (December 31, 1974), IPR; "Iowa Porkettes Financial Statement" (December 31, 1975), IPR; "Iowa Porkettes Financial Statement" (December 31, 1976), IPR; "Iowa Porkettes Financial Statement" (December 31, 1977), IPR; "Iowa Porkettes Financial Statement" (December 31, 1978), IPR; "Iowa Porkettes Revised Budget, 1979" (n.d.), IPR; "Iowa Porkettes Proposed and Revised Budget, 1980" (n.d.), IPR.

30. Judy Scheffler, Chairman of the Porkette Iowa Chop Committee to County Porkette Presidents (September 1976), IPR; "Iowa Chop Test Restaurant Program: A Summary" (September 23, 1976), IPR; Steve Weinberg, "Pork Purists Arise: Hail the Iowa Chop," *Des Moines Register* (March 6, 1977).

31. Scheffler, to County Porkette Presidents (September 1976), IPR.

32. Scheffler to County Porkette Presidents (November 1977), IPR.

33. *Iowa Porkettes History*, 4, IPR; "Pork Education Committee Report," *Iowa Pork Producer* (August 1978): 23; Joyce Hoppes, "Pork and the Consumer," in *Iowa Pork and*

People, ed. Muhm, 159–61; "Iowa Check-off Success Stories," http://www.iowapork. org/pork_checkoff/consumer/iowachop.html; Scheffler to County Porkette Presidents (October 1978), IPR.

34. Keith Heffernan, Lois Kiester, and Russ Sanders, "Iowa Porkette Organizational Review" (1983), IPR.

35. Ibid.

36. Madeline Meyer, "Building Our Organizational Skills in 1979," *Iowa Pork Producer* (June 1979):10; "The Iowa Porkettes," *Iowa Pork Producer* (April 1982): 24; "New Pork Cook-off Announced for 1985; Iowa Porkettes Involved in APC Activities," *Iowa Pork Producer* (May 1984): 18; "Iowans Attend National Meeting; Name Change, APC Plans Discussed," *Iowa Pork Producer* (November 1984); *Ladies Pork Journal* 5, no. 1 (Spring 1985), IPR.

37. Don Muhm, "'Porkette' Critics Lose Fight for New Name," *Des Moines Register* (January 27, 1984), IPR.

38. Ibid.; it is important to note that, while the number of farms producing hogs and pigs declined, the number of hogs and pigs produced did not. In fact, the number of hogs and pigs produced in Iowa increased significantly, from 23.8 million in 1981, to 26.8 million in 1992. See Margaret Ledger, ". . . When You're Having Fun," *Iowa Pork Producer* (February 1988): 6; *Iowa Porkettes History,* 7, IPR; Hanson et al., *Agriculture in Iowa,* 143.

39. Although the IPPA ultimately reaped the benefit of the money, the legislation stipulated that a new Iowa Pork Producers Council (IPPC) be formed to oversee and administer the check-off funds. The IPPC worked closely with the IPPA, however, and often utilized IPPA staff. "Mandatory Checkoff Set," *Iowa Pork Producer* (June 1985): 5; "Governor Signs History-Making Checkoff Law," *Iowa Pork Producer* (July 1985): 6–7; "Finance Committee Meeting Minutes," IPPA (September 20, 1985), IPR.

40. "1986 IPPA Committees," IPR; "Pork Committee Structure, 1990–1991," IPR; "Iowa Porkettes Long Range Planning Suggestions For 1986" (1986), IPR; "Mandatory Checkoff Set," *Iowa Pork Producer* (June 1985): 5; "Governor Signs History-Making Checkoff Law," *Iowa Pork Producer* (July 1985): 6–7; "Finance Committee Meeting Minutes," IPPA (September 20, 1985), IPR.

41. "Pork Producer/Porkette Planning Committee" IPPA office, Clive, Iowa (January 13, 1987), IPR; "Pork Producer/Porkette Planning Committee" IPPA office (August 14, 1987), IPR; "Pork Producer/Porkette Planning Committee" IPPA office (November 5, 1987), IPR.

42. "Board of Directors Survey," Porkette/Pork Producers Planning Committee (1989), IPR.

43. Ibid.; "Iowa Porkette Special Delegate Session, Starlite Village, Ames, Iowa, Tentative Agenda," September 25, 1991, IPR; Helen Pollock, "Facing up to Change," *Iowa Pork Producer* (November 1989): 4.

44. Pollock, "Facing up to Change," 4.

45. "Meeting Minutes," Iowa Porkette Board, Ames, Iowa (September 25, 1991), IPR; "Merger Resolution" (January 1992), IPR; "Memorandum from John Hardin and

Lorraine Harness to NPPC Board of Directors, NPPC State Presidents, National Pork Board, State Executive and Contacts, and NPCW State Presidents," October 18, 1991, IPR; *Iowa Porkettes History*, 7, IPR.

46. "Meeting Minutes," Iowa Porkette Board (September 25, 1991), IPR; "Merger Resolution" (January 1992), IPR; *Iowa Porkettes History*, 7; "The Final Hours of the Iowa Porkettes," *Iowa Pork Producer* (January 1992): 12; Karen McCreedy, "None of Us Live on an Island," in *Iowa Pork and People*, ed. Muhm, 88–89; Kathryn Louden, "Porkettes . . . and Opportunity to Serve," in *Iowa Pork and People*, ed., Muhm, 86–88.

47. Brandth, "Feminism and Farm Women," 108; Deborah Fink, *Open Country*, 196; Friedberger, "Women Advocates," 224–34; Pratt, "Using History," 40–42; Sachs, *Gendered Fields*, 137.

CONCLUSION

1. Kay Ebeling, "The Failure of Feminism," *Newsweek* (November 18, 1990): 9; Susan Faludi, *Backlash: The Undeclared War against American Women* (New York: Anchor Books, 1991), 458.

2. Freedman, *No Turning Back*, 6; Whitney A. Peoples, "'Under Construction': Identifying Foundations of Hip-Hop Feminism and Exploring Bridges Between Black Second Wave and Hip-Hop Feminisms," in *No Permanent Waves: Recasting Histories of U.S. Feminism*, ed. Nancy A. Hewett (New Brunswick, NJ: Rutgers University Press, 2010), 414.

3. Rosenfeld, *Farm Women*, 193, 196–98.

4. Bill Hord, "'Love for the Land' Has Women Running Farms," *Omaha World Herald* (July 8, 2001); Heidi Marttila-Losure, "Farmwork Network: Farm Women Help Each Other Learn and Succeed," *Facets*, published by the *Ames Tribune* (August 2006): 12–19; Anne Fitzgerald, "In Large Part, the Land's Future Is Up to Women," *Des Moines Register* (July 17, 2005); Bregendahl et al., "Women, Land, and Legacy: Results from the Listening Sessions" (Ames, IA: North Central Regional Center for Rural Development, 2007), 3, 9, 30–31.

5. Amy Trauger, "'Getting Back to Our Roots': Women Farmers in Sustainable Agriculture: Work, Space, and Representation," (master's thesis, Pennsylvania State University, 2001), 55–69.

6. Ibid. Historian Nancy Grey Osterud has also written extensively on the importance of women's perceptions of and relationships to the land and the ways in which women have internalized sexism in the countryside. See Nancy Grey Osterud, "Land, Identity, and Agency in the Oral Autobiographies of Farm Women," in *Women and Farming: Changing Roles, Changing Structures*, ed. Jane B. Knowles and Wava G. Haney (Boulder, CO: Westview Press 1988), 76–86.

7. Michael Duffy and Darnell Smith, *Farmland Ownership and Tenure in Iowa, 1982–2002: A Twenty-Year Perspective* (Ames: Iowa State University Extension, 2008), 14; Bregendahl et al., "Women, Land, and Legacy," 11.

8. Bregendahl et al., "Women, Land, and Legacy," 32.

9. Ibid., 40–41. See also Corry Bregendahl and Matthew Hoffman, "Women, Land, and Legacy: Change Agents and Agency Change in Iowa, Evaluation Results" (Ames, IA: Leopold Center for Sustainable Agriculture, 2011). By 2011 it appeared as though the listening sessions had resulted in a high degree of women's empowerment and evidence that applying women's ways of understanding had, in fact, been quite successful in helping female landowners gain awareness.

10. A growing number of historians are taking note of the faulty historiographic emphasis on the urban feminist experience. In her history of feminist organizations in Dayton, Ohio, for example, historian Judith Ezekiel contests the idea that "heartland feminism" was a "toned down" version of radical action taking place in major cities like Chicago, New York, and Washington, D.C. Judith Ezekiel, *Feminism in the Heartland* (Columbus: Ohio State University Press, 2007), viii–x; See also Melissa Estes Blair, "'A Dynamic Force in Our Community': Women's Clubs and Second-Wave Feminism at the Grassroots," *Frontiers: A Journal of Women's Studies* 30, no. 3 (Fall 2009): 45; Stephanie Gilmore, ed., *Feminist Coalitions: Historical Perspectives on Second-Wave Feminism in the United States* (Urbana: University of Illinois Press, 2008); Carbert, *Agrarian Feminism*, 4. Several essays challenged the entire notion of "waves" and the emphasis on major movements toward political change in Nancy A. Hewitt, *No Permanent Waves: Recasting Histories of U.S. Feminism* (New Brunswick, NJ: Rutgers University Press, 2010).

11. Sandra K. Schackel, *Working the Land: The Stories of Ranch and Farm Women in the Modern American West* (Lawrence: University Press of Kansas, 2011), 97.

ARCHIVAL COLLECTIONS

Iowa Women's Archives, University of Iowa Libraries

Anita Crawford Papers.
Bess Short Newcomer Papers.
Cedar Valley Community Club Records.
Cleona Township Women's Club Records.
Ever Ready Club Records.
Franklin Township Women's Club Records.
Freedom Township Women's Club Records.
Friendly Neighbors Club, Deep River, Iowa, Records.
Highland Do-Better Club Records.
Iowa Porkettes Records.
Irene Hoover Papers.
Mahaska County Farm Bureau Women's Club Records.
Sharon Township Women's Club, Records.
Voices from the Land, Oral History Collection, Records.

Special Collections, Parks Library, Iowa State University

Cherokee County Farm Bureau Records, MS-92.
Cooperative Extension Service in Agricultural and Home Economics
    Records, RS 16/3/0/1.
E. Howard Hill Papers, RS 21/7/4.
James R. Howard Papers, MS-157.
Iowa Farm Bureau Federation Records, MS 105.
Iowa Farm Bureau Federation Women's Committee Records, MS 189.
Iowa Farmers Union Records, MS 92.
National Farmers Organization Records, MS 481.
Ruth Buxton Sayre Papers, MS 109.
Voices from the Land, Oral History Collection, Records, MS 638.

Special Collections, University of Iowa Libraries

Fred Stover Papers, MsC 165.

Special Collections, University of Nebraska–Lincoln

Women in Farm Economics (WIFE) Records, MS 32.

State Historical Society of Iowa, Iowa City

Ruth Buxton Sayre Papers.

Women's History Resource Center, Washington, D.C.

General Federation of Women's Clubs, Conference Records.

GOVERNMENT DOCUMENTS

Coughlin, Kenneth M., ed. Perspectives on the Structure of American Agriculture: Vol. 1, The View from the Farm — Special Problems of Minority and Low-Income Farmers. United States Department of Agriculture, 1980.

Fessenden, Jewell G. "These Are the Women Who Are Members of Home Demonstration Organizations in the United States: A Report from a National Study of Home Demonstration Members." Extension Circular 528. Washington, D.C.: United States Department of Agriculture, 1958.

Forstall, Richard L., ed. "Iowa," in *Population of Counties by Decennial Census: 1900 to 1990*. Washington, D.C.: Bureau of the Census, 1995. http://www.census.gov/population/cencounts/ia190090.txt.

Historical Population Reports. Nebraska State Data Center, Center for Public Affairs Research. Omaha: University of Nebraska, 2005.

House Committee on Agriculture. *General Farm Program, including Joint Hearings with the Senate Committee on Agriculture and Forestry*. 81st Congress, 1st Session, pt.2, 1949.

United States Bureau of the Census. *1960 Census of Housing*. Washington, D.C.: Government Printing Office, 1963.

United States Census of Agriculture 1969, Vol. 1, Part 20: Nebraska. Washington, D.C.: U.S. Government Printing Office, 1972.

United States Census of Agriculture 1974, Vol. 1, Part 27: Nebraska. Washington, D.C.: U.S. Government Printing Office, 1977.

United States Census of Agriculture 1982, Vol. 1, Part 27: Nebraska. Washington, D.C.: U.S. Government Printing Office, 1984.

United States Department of Agriculture. *Agricultural Statistics*. Washington, D.C.: Government Printing Office, 1967.

United States Department of Agriculture, Economic Research Service. "Farm Structure: Farm Operator Household Income Data." http://www.ers.usda.gov/Briefing/FarmStructure/Data/historic.htm.

BOOKS, PERIODICALS, AND DISSERTATIONS

Adams, Jane. "The *Farm Journal's* Discourse of Farm Women's Femininity." *Anthropology and Humanism* 29, no. 1 (2004): 45–62.

Anderson, J. L. *Industrializing the Corn Belt: Agriculture, Technology, and the Government, 1945–1972.* DeKalb: Northern Illinois University Press, 2009.

———. "Lard to Lean: Making the Meat-Type Hog in Post–World War II America." In *Food Chains: From Farm Yard to Shopping Cart,* edited by Warren Belasco and Roger Horowitz, 29–46. University of Pennsylvania Press, 2009.

Barker Devine, Jenny. "'Quite a Ripple but No Revolution': The Changing Roles of Women in the Iowa Farm Bureau Federation, 1921–1951," *Annals of Iowa* 64, no. 1 (Winter 2005), 1–36.

———. "The Secret to a Successful Farm Organization": Township Farm Bureau Women's Clubs in Iowa, 1945–1970," *Annals of Iowa* 69, no. 4 (Fall 2010), 41–73.

Berlage, Nancy K. "Organizing the Farm Bureau: Family, Community, and Professionals, 1914–1928." *Agricultural History* 75, no. 4 (2001): 406–37.

Berry, Michelle K. "'Be Sure to Fix the Fence': The Arizona Cowbelles' Public Persona, 1950–1960." *Frontiers: A Journal of Women's Studies* 25, no. 2 (2004): 151–75.

Blair, Melissa Estes. "'A Dynamic Force in Our Community': Women's Clubs and Second-Wave Feminism at the Grassroots." *Frontiers: A Journal of Women's Studies* 30, no. 3 (Fall 2009): 30–51.

Brandth, Berit. "On the Relationships between Feminism and Farm Women." *Agriculture and Human Values* 19 (2002): 107–17.

Bregendahl, Corry, and Matthew Hoffman. "Women, Land, and Legacy: Change Agents and Agency Change in Iowa, Evaluation Results." Ames, IA: Leopold Center for Sustainable Agriculture, 2011.

Bregendahl, Corry, Carol R. Smith, Tanya Meyer-Dideriksen, Beth Grabau, and Cornelia Flora. "Women, Land, and Legacy: Results from the Listening Sessions." Ames, IA: North Central Regional Center for Rural Development, 2007.

Bush, Corlann Gee. "'He Isn't Half So Cranky as He Used To Be': Agricultural Mechanization, Comparable Worth, and the Changing Farm Family." In *To Toil the Livelong Day: America's Women at Work,* edited by Carol Groneman and Mary Beth Norton, 213–29. Ithaca, NY: Cornell University Press, 1987.

Carbert, Louise I. *Agrarian Feminism: The Politics of Ontario Farm Women.* Toronto: University of Toronto Press, 1995.

Carter, David Allen. "The National Farmers' Organization and the Rhetoric of Institutionalization." PhD diss., University of Iowa, 1976.

Casey, Janet Galligani. "'This is YOUR Magazine': Domesticity, Agrarianism, and *The Farmer's Wife.*" *American Periodicals* 14, no. 2 (2004): 179–211.

Cayton, Andrew R. L., and Susan E. Gray. "The Story of the Midwest: An Introduction." In *The Identity of the American Midwest: Essays on Regional History,* edited by Andrew R. L. Cayton and Susan E. Gray, 1–26. Bloomington: Indiana University Press, 2001.

Cobble, Dorothy Sue. "Recapturing Working Class Feminism: Union Women in the Postwar Era." In *Not June Cleaver: Women and Gender in Postwar America, 1945–1960*, edited by Joanne Meyerowitz, 57–83. Philadelphia: Temple University Press, 1994.

Cott, Nancy F. *The Grounding of Modern Feminism*. New Haven, CT: Yale University Press, 1987.

———. "What's in a Name? The Limits of 'Social Feminism'; Or Expanding the Vocabulary of Women's History," *Journal of American History* 76, no. 3 (December 1989): 808–29.

Crampton, John A. *The National Farmers Union: Ideology of a Pressure Group*. Lincoln: University of Nebraska Press, 1965.

Davis, J. Ronnie, and Neil A. Palomba. "The National Farmers Organization and the Prisoner's Dilemma: A Game Theory Prediction." *Social Science Quarterly* 50, no. 3 (1969): 742–48.

Davis, Nancy J., and Robert V. Robinson. "Do Wives Matter? Class Identities of Wives and Husbands in the United States, 1974–1994." *Social Forces* 98, no. 3 (March 1998): 1063–86.

Dean, Virgil W. *An Opportunity Lost: The Truman Administration and the Farm Policy Debate*. Columbia: University of Missouri Press, 2006.

Degraff, Herrell. "Introduction: At the Crossroad." In *The Pork Industry: Problems and Progress*, edited by David G. Topel, xi–xiv. Ames: Iowa State University Press, 1968.

Disrud, Darrell Arden. "President Oren Lee Staley, 1958–1978: A Rhetorical Analysis of the National Farmer's Organization." Master's thesis, University of New Mexico, 1983.

Duffy, Michael, and Darnell Smith. *Farmland Ownership and Tenure in Iowa, 1982–2002: A Twenty-Year Perspective*. Ames: Iowa State University Extension, 2008.

Dyson, Lowell K. *Red Harvest: The Communist Party and American Farmers*. Lincoln: University of Nebraska Press, 1982.

Echols, Alice. *Daring To Be Bad: Radical Feminism in America, 1967–1975*. Minneapolis: University of Minnesota Press, 1982.

Edwards, Gladys Talbott. *This Is the Farmers Union*. Denver: National Farmers Union, 1951.

Elbert, Sarah. "Women and Farming: Changing Structures, Changing Roles." In *Women and Farming: Changing Roles, Changing Structures*, edited by Wava G. Haney and Jane B. Knowles, 245–64. Boulder, CO: Westview Press, 1988.

Enke, Ann. *Finding the Movement: Sexuality, Contested Space, and Feminist Activism*. Durham, NC: Duke University Press, 2007.

Evans, Sara. *Personal Politics: The Roots of Women's Liberation in the Civil Rights Movement and the New Left*. New York: Vintage Books, 1979.

Ezekiel, Judith. *Feminism in the Heartland*. Columbus: Ohio State University Press, 2007.

Faludi, Susan. *Backlash: The Undeclared War against American Women.* New York: Anchor Books, 1991.

Field, Bruce. *Harvest of Dissent: The National Farmers Union and the Early Cold War.* Lawrence: University Press of Kansas, 1998.

———. "The Price of Dissent: The Iowa Farmers Union and the Early Cold War, 1945–1954." *Annals of Iowa* 55 (Winter 1996): 1–23.

Fink, Deborah. *Agrarian Women: Wives and Mothers in Rural Nebraska, 1880–1940.* Chapel Hill: University of North Carolina Press, 1992.

———. *Open Country, Iowa: Rural Women, Tradition, and Change.* Albany: State University of New York Press, 1986.

Fink, Deborah, and Dorothy Schwieder. "Iowa Farm Women in the 1930s: A Reassessment." *Annals of Iowa* 49, no. 7 (Winter 1989): 570–89.

Fink, Virginia S. "The Impact of Changing Technologies on the Roles of Farm and Ranch Wives in Southeastern Ohio." In *Women and Farming: Changing Roles, Changing Structures,* edited by Jane B. Knowles and Wava G. Haney, 229–41. Boulder, CO: Westview Press, 1988.

Finlay, Mark R. "Hogs, Antibiotics, and the Industrial Environments of Postwar Agriculture." In *Industrializing Organisms: Introducing Evolutionary History,* edited by Susan R. Schrepfer and Philip Scranton, 237–60. New York: Routledge, 2004.

Flamm, Michael W. "The National Farmers Union and the Evolution of Agrarian Liberalism, 1936–1946." *Agricultural History* 68, no. 3 (1994): 54–80.

Flora, Cornelia Butler. "Farm Women, Farming Systems, and Agricultural Structure: Suggestions for Scholarship," *Rural Sociology* 1, no. 6 (1981): 383–86.

Fox-Genovese, Elizabeth. *Feminism without Illusions: A Critique of Individualism.* Chapel Hill: University of North Carolina Press, 1991.

Freedman, Estelle B. *No Turning Back: The History of Feminism and the Future of Women.* New York: Ballantine Books, 2002.

Friedan, Betty. *The Feminine Mystique.* New York: W. W. Norton, 1963.

Friedberger, Mark. "Women Advocates in the Iowa Farm Crisis of the 1980s." In *American Rural and Farm Women in Historical Perspective,* edited by Joan M. Jensen and Nancy Grey Osterud, 224–34. Washington, D.C.: Agricultural History Society, University of California Press, 1994.

Garkovich, Lorraine, and Janet Bokemeier. "Agricultural Mechanization and American Farm Women's Economic Roles." In *Women and Farming: Changing Roles, Changing Structures,* edited by Jane B. Knowles and Wava G. Haney, 211–28. Boulder, CO: Westview Press, 1988.

Gilmore, Stephanie, ed. *Feminist Coalitions: Historical Perspectives on Second-Wave Feminism in the United States.* Urbana: University of Illinois Press, 2008.

Goudy, Willis, Sandra Charvat Burke, Seung-pyo Hong, Liu Dong Wang, Liu Qiang, and John Wallize. *Rural/Urban Transitions in Iowa.* Ames: Census Services, Department of Sociology, Iowa State University, 1996.

Greene, Shirley E. *This Earth, This Land.* Denver, CO: National Farmers Union, 1955.

Groves, Donald B., and Kenneth Thatcher. *The First Fifty: History of the Farm Bureau in Iowa*. Des Moines: Iowa Farm Bureau Federation, 1968.

———. *The First Five of the Second Fifty*. Lake Mills, IA: Graphic Publishing, 1974.

A Guide for Farmers Union Action Officials. Denver, CO: National Farmers Union, n.d.

Halpern, Monda. *And on That Farm He Had a Wife: Ontario Farm Women and Feminism, 1900–1970*. Montreal: McGill-Queen's University Press, 2002.

Hanson, Margaret, Willis Goudy, Renea Miller, and Sharon Whetstone. *Agriculture in Iowa: Trends from 1935 to 1997*. Ames: Census Services, Department of Sociology, Iowa State University, 1999.

Hartman, Susan M. "Women's Employment and the Domestic Ideal in the Early Cold War Years." In *Not June Cleaver: Women and Gender in Postwar America, 1945–1960*, edited by Joanne Meyerowitz, 84–100. Philadelphia, PA: Temple University Press, 1994.

Hewitt, Nancy A. *No Permanent Waves: Recasting Histories of U.S. Feminism*. New Brunswick, NJ: Rutgers University Press, 2010.

Hoehnle, Peter. "Iowa Clubwomen Rise to World Stage: Dorothy Houghton and Ruth Sayre." *Iowa Heritage Illustrated* (Spring 2002): 30–46.

Horowitz, Roger. *Putting Meat on the American Table: Taste, Technology, Transformation*. Baltimore, MD: Johns Hopkins University Press, 2006.

Hundley, James Riddle. "A Test of Theories in Collective Behavior: The National Farmers Organization." PhD diss., Ohio State University, 1965.

Hurt, R. Douglas. *Problems of Plenty: The American Farmer in the Twentieth Century*. Chicago: Ivan R. Dee, 2002.

Iowa Swine Producers Directory, 1964–1965. Des Moines: Iowa Swine Producers Association, 1964.

Jellison, Katherine. *Entitled to Power: Farm Women and Technology, 1913–1963*. Chapel Hill: University of North Carolina Press, 1993.

Jensen, Joan. *Loosening the Bonds: Mid-Atlantic Farm Women, 1750–1850*. New Haven, CT: Yale University Press, 1986.

LaBerge, Marie Anne. "'Seeking a Place to Stand': Political Power and Activism among Wisconsin Women, 1945–1963." PhD diss., University of Wisconsin–Madison, 1995.

Lerner, Gerda. *The Creation of Patriarchy*. New York: Oxford University Press, 1986.

Lynn, Susan. "Gender and Progressive Politics: A Bridge to Social Activism of the 1960s." In *Not June Cleaver: Women and Gender in Postwar America, 1945–1960*, edited by Joanne Meyerowitz, 103–27. Philadelphia: Temple University Press, 1994.

Maggard, Sally Ward. "Women's Participation in the Bookside Coal Strike: Militance, Class, and Gender in Appalachia." *Frontiers: A Journal of Women's History* 9, no. 3 (1987): 16–21.

Marti, Donald B. *Women of the Grange: Mutuality and Sisterhood in Rural America, 1866–1920*. New York: Greenwood Press, 1991.

McCreedy, Karen. "None of Us Live on an Island." In *Iowa Pork and People: A History of Iowa's Pork Producers*, edited by Don Muhm, 88–89. Clive, IA: Iowa Pork Foundation, 1995.

McDonald, Julie. *Ruth Buxton Sayre: First Lady of the Farm*. Ames: Iowa State University Press, 1980.

McGlade, Jacqueline. "More a Plowshare Than a Sword: The Legacy of US Cold War Agricultural Diplomacy." *Agricultural History* (Winter 2009), 79–102.

Miller, Lorna Clancy, and Mary Neth. "Farm Women in the Political Arena." In *Women and Farming: Changing Roles, Changing Structures*, edited by Wava G. Haney and Jane B. Knowles, 357–80. Boulder, CO: Westview Press, 1988.

Muhm, Don, ed. *Iowa Pork and People: A History of Iowa's Pork Producers*. Clive, IA: Iowa Pork Foundation, 1995.

———. *The NFO: A Farm Belt Rebel: A History of the National Farmers Organization*. Rochester, MN: Lone Oak Press, 2000.

Neth, Mary. "Building the Base: Farm Women and the Rural Community and Farm Organizations in the Midwest, 1900–1940." In *Women and Farming: Changing Roles, Changing Structures*, edited by Wava G. Haney and Jane B. Knowles, 339–55. Boulder, CO: Westview Press, 1988.

———. *Preserving the Family Farm: Women, Community, and the Foundations of Agribusiness in the Midwest, 1900–1940*. Baltimore, MD: Johns Hopkins University Press, 1995.

Osterud, Nancy Grey. *Bonds of Community: The Lives of Women in Nineteenth-Century New York*. Ithaca, NY: Cornell University Press, 1991.

———. "Land, Identity, and Agency in the Oral Autobiographies of Farm Women." In *Women and Farming: Changing Roles, Changing Structures*, edited by Jane B. Knowles and Wava G. Haney, 76–86. Boulder, CO: Westview Press, 1988.

Pavalko, Eliza K., and Glen H. Elder, Jr., "Women Behind the Men: Variations in Wives' Support of Husbands' Careers." *Gender and Society* 7, no. 4 (December 1993): 548–67.

Peoples, Whitney A. "'Under Construction': Identifying Foundations of Hip-Hop Feminism and Exploring Bridges Between Black Second Wave and Hip-Hop Feminisms." In *No Permanent Waves: Recasting Histories of U.S. Feminism*, edited by Nancy A. Hewett, 403–30. New Brunswick, NJ: Rutgers University Press, 2010.

Perry-Barnes, Ann. "An Exchange Theory Analysis of Satisfaction with Membership in an American Voluntary Organization." Master's thesis, Colorado State University, 1985.

Pratt, William C. "Farmers, Communists, and the FBI in the Upper Midwest," *Agricultural History* 63, no. 3 (Summer 1989), 61–80.

———. "The Farmers Union and the 1948 Henry Wallace Campaign," *Annals of Iowa* 49, no. 5 (Summer 1988): 356–61.

———. "The Farmer's Union, McCarthyism, and the Demise of the Agrarian Left." *Historian* 58, no. 2 (1996): 329–42.

————. "Using History to Make History? Progressive Farm Organizing during the Farm Revolt of the 1980s." *Annals of Iowa* 55 (Winter 1996): 24–45.

Pruitt, Lisa R. "Gender, Geography, and Rural Justice." UC Davis Legal Studies Research Paper Series, Research Paper No. 129 (August 2008).

————. "Toward a Feminist Theory of the Rural." UC Davis Legal Studies Research Paper Series, Research Paper No. 89 (October 2006).

Rembert, Julia Kleinschmit. "Factors Affecting Iowa and Nebraska Farm Women's Rural and Farm Advocacy Involvement." Master's thesis, University of Iowa, 1997.

Rosenfeld, Rachel Ann. *Farm Women: Work, Farm, and Family in the United States.* Chapel Hill: University of North Carolina Press, 1985.

Roth, Benita. *Separate Roads to Feminism: Black, Chicana, and White Feminist Movements in the Second Wave.* Cambridge: Cambridge University Press, 2004.

Rowell, Willis. *Mad As Hell.* Corning, IA: Gauthier Publishing, 1984.

————. *The National Farmers Organization: A Complete History.* Ames, IA: Sigler Printing, 1993.

Rymph, Catherine E. *Republican Women: Feminism and Conservatism from Suffrage through the Rise of the New Right* (Chapel Hill: University of North Carolina Press, 2006).

Sachs, Carolyn. *Gendered Fields: Rural Women, Agriculture, and the Environment.* Boulder, CO: Westview Press, 1996.

Schackel, Sandra K. *Working the Land: The Stories of Ranch and Farm Women in the Modern American West.* Lawrence: University Press of Kansas, 2011.

Schmidt, Louis Bernard. "The Role and Techniques of Agrarian Pressure Groups." *Agricultural History* 30, no. 2 (April 1956): 49–58.

Schwieder, Dorothy. "Changing Times: Iowa Farm Women and Home Economics Cooperative Extension in the 1920s and 1950s." In *Midwestern Women: Work, Community, and Leadership at the Crossroads,* edited by Lucy Eldersveld Murphy and Wendy Hamand Venet, 204–22. Bloomington: Indiana University Press, 1997.

————. "Cooperative Extension and Rural Iowa: Agricultural Adjustment in the 1950s." *Annals of Iowa* 51 (Fall 1992): 606–7.

————. *Iowa: The Middle Land.* Ames: Iowa State University Press, 1996.

————. *75 Years of Service: Cooperative Extension in Iowa.* Ames: Iowa State University Press, 1993.

Seibert, Robert Franklin. "The Development of Agrarian Interest Articulation: The Case of the National Farmers Organization." Master's thesis, Tulane University, 1966.

Shapland, Celia E. "Protest in the Newspaper: A Case Study of the National Farmers Organization." Master's thesis, Iowa State University, 1986.

Sheramy, Rona. "'There Are Times When Silence Is A Sin': The Women's Division of the American Jewish Congress and the Anti-Nazi Boycott Movement." *American Jewish History* 89, no. 1 (March 2001): 105–21.

Storrs, Landon R. Y. "Attacking the Washington 'Femmocracy': Antifeminism in the Cold War Campaign against 'Communists in Government,'" *Feminist Studies* 33, no. 1 (Spring 2007), 118–52.

Tontz, Robert L. "Memberships of General Farmers' Organizations, United States, 1874–1960," *Agricultural History* 38, no. 3 (1964): 143–56.

Trauger, Amy. "Getting Back to Our Roots: Women Farmers in Sustainable Agriculture: Work, Space, and Representation." Master's thesis, Pennsylvania State University, 2001.

Tucker, William P. "Populism Up-to-Date: The Story of the Farmers Union." *Agricultural History* 21, no. 4 (October 1947): 198–208.

Tvrdy, Linda A. "The Free Market Revolt of the National Farmers Organization." Paper presented at the Agricultural History Society Conference, Cambridge, MA, June 2006.

Walters, Charles. *Angry Testament.* Kansas City, MO: Halcyon House, 1969.

——. *The Biggest Farm Story of the Decade: A Searching Look at Farm Trouble and the Search for an Equitable Answer.* Kansas City, MO: Halcyon House, 1968.

——. *Holding Action.* Kansas City, MO: Halcyon House, 1968.

Wood, Truman David. "The National Farmers' Organization in Transition." PhD diss., University of Iowa, 1961.

Wortman, Roy. "Gender Issues in the National Farmers' Union in the 1930s." *Midwest Review* 15 (1993): 71–83.

Wuthnow, Robert. *Remaking the Heartland: Middle America since the 1950s.* Princeton, NJ: Princeton University Press, 2011.